On Judicial and Quasi-Judicial Independence

On Judicial and Quasi-Judicial Independence

Editors

Prof. Suzanne Comtois
Dr. Kars de Graaf

eleven
international publishing

Published, sold and distributed by Eleven International Publishing
P.O. Box 85576
2508 CG The Hague
The Netherlands
Tel.: +31 70 33 070 33
Fax: +31 70 33 070 30
Website: www.elevenpub.com

Sold and distributed in USA and Canada
International Specialized Book Services
920 NE 58th Avenue, Suite 300
Portland, OR 97213-3786, USA
Tel: 1-800-944-6190 (toll-free)
Fax: +1 503 280-8832
orders@isbs.com
www.isbs.com

Eleven International Publishing is an imprint of Boom uitgevers Den Haag.

ISBN 978-94-6236-094-5
ISBN 978-94-6094-862-6 (e-book)
NUR 822

Printed in The Netherlands.

Preface

This issue of the *Netherlands Institute for Law and Governance Series* is the result of an international conference on the theme 'Judicial and Quasi-Judicial Independence' held on 25 May 2012 in Groningen, the Netherlands.

We are grateful to the speakers from France, the United Kingdom, Sweden and Canada, as well as from the Dutch universities of Amsterdam, Utrecht, Tilburg and Groningen, who accepted to take part in this conference and generously accepted to make their essays available to a wider audience by contributing to this publication.

In addition to the debt we owe to our contributors, we wish to express our gratitude to the *Groningen Centre for Law and Governance* and the Department of Administrative Law and Public Administration of the University of Groningen for financing this project. Finally, we would like to thank Jasper Wesselman, graduate student at the University of Groningen, for his assistance with the logistics of the conference as well as the members of the peer review committee for their meticulous work, which resulted in numerous constructive comments for the authors.

It has been a pleasure to edit these essays and we trust that this new issue of the Netherlands Institute for Law and Governance Series on judicial and quasi-judicial independence will contribute to a better understanding of the competing values, complexities and contemporary challenges pertaining to these concepts.

July 2013

Suzanne Comtois
Kars de Graaf

Table of Contents

Detailed Table of Contents

Contributors

Biezeveld, Gustaaf
Professor of environmental law at the Faculty of Law, University of Groningen, the Netherlands and environmental public prosecutor in the Netherlands until 2012. He is still involved in activities designed to improve co-operation between administrative and criminal environmental law enforcement.

Canivet, Guy
Member of the Constitutional Council, Paris, France, and First Honorary President of the Court of Cassation in France. He was Associate Professor at the University of Paris V-René Descartes and later at the Institut d'Etudes Politiques de Paris. He is commander of the Legion of Honor, Commander of the Academic Palms and Commander of Arts and Letters.

Comtois, Suzanne
Visiting Professor at the Faculty of Law, University of Groningen, the Netherlands, and Professor at the Faculty of Law, Université de Sherbrooke, Québec, Canada. She is an Associate-member of the International Academy of Comparative Law and member of the Quebec Bar. Her current research focuses on the changing nature of the relationship between courts and administrative decision makers.

de Graaf, Kars
Associate Professor of administrative and environmental law at the University of Groningen, the Netherlands. He is the managing editor of the *Review of European Administrative Law* (REALaw) and honorary judge of the district court in the North of the Netherlands.

Evans, John
Judge in the Federal Court of Appeal of Canada since 1999. He was a Professor at Osgoode Hall Law School from 1975- 1998 and also thought at the University of Oxford, the University of Chicago, the London School of Economics and Monash University in Melbourne, Australia.

Hazell, Robert
Professor of Government and the Constitution, School of Public Policy, University College London, England and Director of the Constitution Unit in the School of Public Policy. He founded the Constitution Unit in 1995 as an independent think-tank specializing in constitutional reform. He is currently leading a three year research project into the Politics of Judicial Independence.

Jans, Jan
Professor of Administrative Law at the University of Groningen, the Netherlands, and Vice Chair of the Advisory Commission on Competition Act Objections (*Adviescommissie bezwaarschriften Mededingingswet*). He is a member of the Dutch Commission on Environmental Impact Assessment, honorary judge and member of the editorial boards of the *Journal of Environmental Law, SEW* (Dutch Journal on European and Economic Law), *Legal Issues of Economic Integration, Journal for European Environmental & Planning Law* (JEEPL), *Review of European Administrative Law* (REALaw) and *The Columbia Journal of European Law*. He is member of the Commission on Environmental law of the IUCN and the Avosetta Group of European Environmental Lawyers.

Konijnenbelt, Willem
Emeritus Professor at the University of Amsterdam. Lecturer in Constitutional and Administrative Law at the Free University of Amsterdam. He has worked as a personal assistant to the Lord Mayor of Amsterdam, constitutional and legislative drafter at the Ministry of the Interior. Professor of Constitutional and Administrative Law and Legislative Drafting in Tilburg (1976-1985) and Amsterdam (University of Amsterdam, 1985-2011).

Lubach, Dick
Professor of construction law at the University of Groningen, the Netherlands, and Of Counsel for Damsté Advocaten en Notarissen in Enschede. He is chairman of several municipal advisory committees on damage compensation. He is also member of the Decision-making committee (DMC) of the Schadeschap Schiphol.

Marseille, Bert
Professor in Empirical Studies of Administrative Law at Tilburg University, the Netherlands and senior lecturer at the Department of Administrative Law and Public Administration at the University of Groningen. His research focuses on the functioning of dispute settlement procedures in administrative law. He is a member of the board of the Dutch Association of Administrative Law (VAR) and an honorary judge in the district court in the North of the Netherlands.

Ottow, Annetje
Professor Public Economic Law at the European Institute, Utrecht University, the Netherlands and member of the board of the telecommunications authority in the Netherlands (OPTA) the Dutch independent post and telecommunications authority, until 1 April 2013. She is one of the governors of Utrecht University's Europa Institute, President of the Dutch Association of European law (*Nederlandse Vereniging voor Europees Recht*), editor of the Dutch competition law review (*Markt & Mededinging*) and is founder of the new Dutch multi-disciplinary journal on (market) supervision (*Tijdschrift voor Toezicht*). Her current research relates to independent regulators, with special focus on the supervisory and enforcement instruments, within the context of Dutch administrative and European law.

Outhuijse, Annalies
Student at the Law Faculty of the University of Groningen. The article has been written within the context of the faculty research programme *Public Trust & Public Law*.

Valois, Martine
Assistant Professor of law at the Université de Montreal, Canada and a member of the Quebec Bar. She practiced law in a private firm and in government until 2011 where she joined the Faculty of Law of the University of Montreal. She received her doctoral degree from the University of Montreal in 2009. Her current research focuses on the workings of the institutions of the modern state.

Winter, Heinrich
Professor of Regulatory Compliance at the Department of Administrative Law and Public Administration of the Faculty of Law, University of Groningen, the Netherlands. He is also director of Pro Facto, a research and consultancy firm, active in the fields of public law and public administration.

Zamboni, Mauro
Professor in Legal Theory at the Stockholm Centre for Commercial Law, Faculty of Law, Stockholm University (Sweden) and Visiting Professor at the Faculty of Law, University of Groningen, the Netherlands. He was Guest Scholar at Stanford University (2003-2004), Harvard Law School (2008-2009) and at the Collaborative Research Center 597 'Transformations of the State', Bremen (2009-2011). His current research topics focus on the relations between law and politics.

Introduction

On Judicial and Quasi-Judicial Independence: Introductory Remarks

*Suzanne Comtois**

Principles of Judicial and Quasi-Judicial Independence are fundamental to all democracies. Yet, despite the acknowledged importance of these principles, the notion of independence in the judicial and quasi-judicial contexts is still elusive. What is judicial or quasi-judicial independence and why is it important? Who and what are the judiciary and quasi-judicial bodies to be independent from? What legal safeguards are appropriate or necessary for the protection judicial or quasi-judicial independence? Are there, and if so, what are the sociological pre-conditions needed to allow courts or quasi-judicial bodies to be shielded from inappropriate pressures or influences? How do we define what is inappropriate in that respect? How do we measure or compare the sufficiency of the independence guarantees granted to individual judges, higher courts, constitutional courts, quasi-judicial bodies and administrative decision-makers? To what extent can courts, especially constitutional courts, make law without crossing the separation divide between law and politics? If they do cross that threshold, can judges – who are independent – also be held accountable? If so, what are judges to be accountable for? Is the expansion of the judiciary's power a threat to judicial independence?

Quasi-judicial and administrative decision-makers' independence is also the source of an important debate. To what extent should principles of independence apply to quasi-judicial bodies such as tribunals (the so called 'adjudicative branch of government'[1]), regulatory and policy-making authorities, advisory committees, enforcement bodies and other administrative decision-makers? What is meant by independent regulatory and enforcement bodies? How much independence should they have? To what extent should agencies, tribunals and other administrative bodies be independent from the branches of government that have created them or the industry they are charged to regulate? How should their degree of independence be determined?

It is the objective of this book, as of the conference that preceded it, to bring eminent judges and scholars, from various jurisdictions to reflect on the fundamental principles of judicial and quasi-judicial independence, to help clarify the concepts and to discuss the threats and challenges that perhaps call for different safeguards

* Prof. S. Comtois is Visiting Professor at the Faculty of Law, University of Groningen, the Netherlands, and Professor at the Faculty of Law, Université de Sherbrooke, Québec, Canada.

1 This is the term used by the Supreme Court of Canada in *Ocean Port Hotel Ltd. v. Colombie-Britannique*, [2001] 2 R.C.S. 781.

or solutions. Within those parameters, the essays in this collection have been grouped into four sections:

- Independence and the Rule of Law;
- Independence and Accountability of Judges and Adjudicators;
- Independence of Regulatory Agencies, Supervisory and Enforcement Authorities and
- Independence of Advisory and Complaint Committees and Final Dispute Resolution by the Administrative Courts.

1. Independence and the Rule of Law

The essays included in this section explore the historical, cultural, sociological and legal-theoretical dimensions of judicial independence. Guy Canivet's historical perspective in *Effective Protection of the Independence of the Judiciary in France* provides valuable insight on the specifically French conception of the principle of judicial independence and the transformation of French law in that respect. As he points out, the notion of an autonomous Judicial Power does not exist in the French constitution. The text refers instead to the Judicial Authority of which the President of the Republic, assisted by the High Council of the Judiciary, shall be the guarantor of the independence.[2] However, the lack of an explicit judicial independence norm has not prevented the recognition of a strong principle of judicial independence. Guy Canivet's essay shows how, in the specific historical and cultural context of France's legal structure not specifically conductive to the development of a strict and absolute conception of judicial independence,[3] substantial guarantees giving effective protection have nonetheless been set up. He shows how the Constitutional Council has built an efficient apparatus for protecting the independence of the judiciary by reconciling the special treatment of the power to judge in the French political tradition with the fundamental guarantees set forth in the preamble and body of the Constitution in order to establish a requirement of judicial independence consistent with international standards. He notes, as examples, the convergence of the decisions of the French constitutional judge with, on the one hand, those of the European Court of Human Rights based on Article 6 of the European Convention on Human Rights and, on the other hand, those of the Court of Justice of the European Union based on fundamental principles of European law. And he concludes that such a convergence is indispensable in a European framework which requires that justice be rendered in all European Union member States according to identical standards of quality in order to be mutually recognized and executed throughout the European territory.

2 Article 64 of the French Constitution

3 Namely, the absence of an autonomous Judicial Power, the division of the jurisdictional function into three distinct orders (judicial, administrative and constitutional) and the place of the public prosecutor in the courts.

In *The Coming of Age of Review of Administrative Action in the Netherlands: A Battle of Effectiveness and the Rule of Law*, Willem Konijnenbelt traces the evolution of the system of review of administrative action in the Netherlands. In the first part of his essay, he analyses the slow evolution from a long-standing approach where control over administrative action was exercised mostly by the Crown towards an independent and impartial process of review by an administrative court. He notes that this shift was necessary to comply with the rule of law and the requirements of Article 6 of the European Convention for the Protection of Human Rights and Fundamental Freedoms, following the 1985 European Court of Human Rights decision in the *Benthem* case.

In the second part of his essay, Willem Konijnenbelt, discusses the impact of replacing administrative review by judicial review. He submits that the administrative courts might be ill suited to tackle the non-legal, policy aspects of administrative decisions, given the broad remedial power conferred upon them in the *General Administrative Law Act*, and he questions whether, or to what extent, the requirements of review by an independent court and the search for effective review are compatible.

Martine Valois' article on *The Function of Judicial Independence in Modern Legal Systems: Preserving the Boundaries of Law* focuses on the sociological conditions required for securing judicial independence in a modern legal system where the court's 'law making' role over social and moral issues is increasingly important. The main purpose of her essay is to explore the consequences of the transformation of the judiciary's role in the light of the theoretical framework of Niklas Luhmann's systems theory. In the first part of her essay she explains the conceptual underpinnings of systems theory and how it can be used to elucidate the legal system's functioning. In the second part, she concentrates on the role of the courts in modern legal systems and, in the last part, she explains how judicial independence contributes to law's organizational closure as one of the essential conditions for the preservation of the rule of law.

Acknowledging the threats to judicial independence even in legal systems where both principles are constitutionally guaranteed, she concludes that certain sociological conditions are required for judicial independence to be really effective. These sociological requisites are: 'the preservation of the conditional programmes of law and the limitation of the judges' responsibility for the consequences of their decisions in the social system.'

Following on a similar theme, Mauro Zamboni's article on *'Markers' vs. 'Makers': Are Constitutional Courts Legal or Political Actors?* explores further the relation between law and politics in the light of the debate on judicial activism taking place in constitutional courts and highest courts in western democracies. He addresses the concerns often voiced about the extent to which constitutional courts' activism is compatible with the very idea of democracy. To this end, he proceeds to evaluate whether these courts should be considered as legal actors simply enforcing the statutes and constitutions written by political actors or as 'makers' of the constitution, i.e. institutional actors whose predominant role is political: determining what the law should say.

After having stressed the importance of constitutional court 'activism' inside the general issue of judicial activism and the reasons why constitutional courts in established Western democracies can be seen as occupying an 'in-the-middle' position between the legal arena and the political arena, he explains why, from a legal theoretical perspective, constitutional courts and higher courts are primarily legal actors from an institutional, structural and functional perspective. Using a distinction between 'outcome' and 'output', he notes that while 'these Courts play without any doubt a role in the political game; their location as an institutional actor should be based upon the direct effects of their decisions ('outputs') within the legal arena rather than on the indirect consequences ('outcomes') on the political arena'. Thus, courts being understood as legal, not political ac tors, he concludes that judicial review of the constitutionality of legislation is compatible with democracy. Finally, to help preserve the legal nature of the constitutional courts and make them more 'compatible' with Habermas's ideal of a democratic form of political organization, Mauro Zamboni suggests a shift of focus from 'democratic' constitutional court decisions to 'democratic' constitutional courts procedures.

2. Independence and Accountability of Judges and Adjudicators

This section offers a structural analysis of the constitutional framework within which judicial independence is secured in Canada and the United Kingdom, two countries with a long tradition of judicial independence. The essays by John Evans and Robert Hazell enclosed in that section describe how these two systems are structured internally, then they examine current issues involving tensions between judicial independence and accountability.

John Evans's essay on *Adjudicative independence in Canada* addresses both judicial and quasi-judicial independence. In the first part, he gives a brief account of the Canadian constitutional arrangements for protecting the independence of the judiciary and he compares, in that respect, the situation of judges and members of administrative tribunals. He notes some of the complications that arise in a federal constitutional structure and certain decisions of the Supreme Court of Canada that have extended the scope of judicial independence beyond the express provisions of the Constitution by drawing on underlying constitutional values. In contrast, he observes that the Court has so far declined to draw on these same values to find, in the constitution, similar guarantees of independence for administrative decision-makers, even those performing jurisdictional functions analogous to those of courts. However, in the absence of constitutional protection, he notes that some legislatures have addressed the issues and statutorily reinforced the independence of some of their administrative tribunals.

In the second part of his essay, he identifies three current issues involving tension between judicial independence and notions of accountability: the judicial appointment process, judicial compensation, and the discipline of judges. He notes that these three examples show that judicial independence is not an absolute value and that it must be balanced against other constitutional principles. To achieve an appropriate balance, he suggests that regular review and recalibration might be required.

Robert Hazell's essay on *Judges and the Executive in Britain: an Unequal Partnership?* examines the impact of the United Kingdom's *Constitutional Reform Act of 2005* on the division of powers between the executive and the judiciary. He first notes that the adoption of this important reform has led to a greater separation of powers between the judiciary and the executive in England and Wales: "The Lord Chief Justice became head of the Judiciary, in place of the Lord Chancellor, the Justice Minister; an independent Judicial Appointments Commission was established; and the Courts Service has become an independent Agency, run as a partnership between the Lord Chancellor and Lord Chief Justice". After a brief description of those changes, he explores the consequences of this new constitutional order for the relationship between the executive and judiciary, namely its impact on their respective responsibilities for upholding judicial independence and ensuring proper judicial accountability. He asks questions such as: might judges have become more powerful? If so, in what ways? Are they sufficiently accountable in the exercise of their new powers? He applies a Rhodes resource-dependency model of power, in which power is a function of the resources available to the different actors, in this case, the judiciary or/and the executive. He uses 'resources' in a wide sense to include not only financial resources and staff but also elements such as autonomy, authority, information, and influence. His analysis strives to deduce the balance between judicial independence and accountability that might be achieved as a result of the 2005 Constitutional Reform.

His findings lead him to the conclusion that despite greater formal separation, the partnership still relies on the executive and judiciary working closely together. In that respect, he notes that in several areas (the Courts Service, judicial appointments, complaints and discipline) they have a mutual veto. The judiciary has become more powerful, especially with regard to appointments. Judges have more resources under their control and the executive struggles to be an intelligent partner, because it has lost so much of its staff to the judiciary. Thus, judicial independence has been strengthened but the accountability of the judiciary to the executive (i.e. the Lord Chancellor) and to Parliament remains strong.

3. Independence of Regulatory Agencies, Supervisory and Enforcement Authorities

Section III and IV focus on the independence of administrative and quasi-judicial authorities, including those performing functions such as provision of expert advice, enforcement, surveillance, control and regulation. These organizations are variously called regulatory agencies, enforcement bodies, advisory committees, etc.

How much independence should these administrative bodies enjoy? To what extent should agencies, administrative law enforcers, tribunals and other administrative bodies be independent from the branches of government who have created them and from the parties (market or industries) they regulate? Moreover, how should that degree of independence be determined?

Given the diversity of mandates and functions performed by these administrative authorities, no single model of independence, not even a model designed for the judiciary, is likely to be always appropriate.[4] For instance, in policy-making cases where some form of workable 'general'[5] interactions between political and administrative accountability mechanisms are called for, complete independence might even conflict with democratic principles.[6]

However, even if one does not aim for uniformity nor for the highest degree of judicial independence standards, in some cases (perhaps most) a minimum of independence may be required, to allow for legal, impartial and autonomous decisions in individual cases and to help preserve the public's and the parties' confidence in administrative justice. It is the purpose of section III to give an account of the legal framework under which specific administrative bodies operate and to show the extent to which guarantees of independence conferred upon them meet the threshold of independence called for in theses specific contexts.

In her essay on *The Different Levels of Protection of National Supervisors' Independence in the European Landscape*, Annetje Ottow focuses on the independence of national supervisory authorities engaged in various regulated sectors, such as market supervisory authorities. She first discusses the legal requirements, foundations and importance of safeguarding the independence of these national supervisory authorities at a European level. Then, using five published cases related to regulated sectors drawn from the *Netherlands, Germany, France and Hungary*, she assesses the practical impact that various European independence requirements might have on the independence of national supervisory authorities. These examples, as Professor Ottow explains, show that the independence of national supervisors is fragile. However, she notes that the European Commission's proposals on independence requirements have since been incorporated into various directives and that their importance has been acknowledged in the jurisprudence of the European Court of Justice. In her conclusion, she acknowledges that in defining

4 Laverne Jacobs, Caught between Judicial Paradigms and the Administrative State's Pastiche: 'Tribunal' Independence, Impartiality, and Bias, *in* Colleen M. Flood & Lorne Sossin (eds.), *Administrative Law in Context* (2nd edition), Emond Montgomery, Toronto, 2012, p. 233-278.

5 In the form of abstract guidelines, as opposed to direct interference in a specific record.

6 On this point see Jerry L. Mashaw, Judicial Review of Administrative Action: Reflections on Balancing Political, Managerial and Legal Accountability, *Revista Direito GV* 2005/1 (*special issue*), p. 153.

the appropriate level of independence, a distinction between government involvement in individual cases and government involvement in general instructions may be relevant (even essential in some cases) for democratic reasons, but she notes that the line between the two is not always easy to draw. She therefore suggests that policy considerations emanating from the legislator must be balanced against independence, to make sure that the national independent supervisors have sufficient discretion within this framework to be able to take autonomous decisions in individual cases, in conformity with the provisions of European law.

Heinrich Winter's essay *Regulatory Enforcement in The Netherlands: Struggling with Independence* focuses on the independence of regulatory enforcement authorities. After discussing the three main causes underlying the current debate over the independence of these authorities the public demand for more effective, less burdensome law enforcement; the reaction to inappropriate political and administrative interferences in the enforcement process; and the incentive to comply with European law – Heinrich Winter gives a brief account of the framework, threats and constraints within which inspectorates and authorities operate in the Netherlands. Among the constraints and threats facing the inspectorates and authorities' independence, he notes the risk of capture, the status and close relationship of the inspectorates and authorities with the minister (considered under the umbrella of ministerial responsibility), the overlapping functions of the inspectorate as both law enforcer and expert advisor on policy-making and the minister's concerns with the indirect consequences of its decisions (political, economic or social).

He notes that in some cases the legislation provides for administrative forms of organization and legislative safeguards that reinforce inspectorates and authorities' independence throughout the process, from information gathering to the final decision. But he concludes that these organizational forms and safeguards cannot simply be transposed to all such inspectorates and authorities. Acknowledging the constraints that are inherent in regulatory enforcement, such as the need for information and cooperation between the regulator and the regulated party and, to a certain extent, between the regulator and the minister, he concludes that the standards of independence of inspectorates and authorities should be viewed on a continuum, where the appropriate level of independence fluctuates according to the characteristics of the function and the context.

In *A Call for Independent Environmental Law Enforcement*, Gustaaf Biezeveld focuses on the status of environmental supervisory authorities in the Netherlands. The first part of his paper provides an overview of environmental supervision in the Netherlands. The second part discusses what he considers to be the major cause of the shortcomings of environmental law enforcement in the Netherlands: the political stance of supervisory authorities. His central point is that a level of independence analogous to those enjoyed by economic supervisory authorities under European Law is a prerequisite to effective environmental enforcement.

In his reasoning, he acknowledges that following serious cases of non-compliance, such as the 1982 *Uniser* case, considerable efforts and money have been expended in the Netherlands over the last 30 years to strengthen environmental law enforcement capacity and expertise in both, the administrative and the criminal sectors. However, he questions the effectiveness of those reforms. Reading from those non-compliance cases and the reports of the independent commissions that followed, he suggests that there is a direct link between the structural inadequacies of enforcement supervision in the Netherlands and the political position of the supervisory authorities. He therefore concludes that so long as the environmental supervisory authorities lack independence, the reforms in question offer only a partial solution.

4. Independence of Advisory and Complaint Committees and Final Dispute Resolution by Administrative Courts

Section IV addresses issues of independence at the pre- and post-decisional stages of the administrative decision-making process. The first essay, by Jan Jans and Annalies Outhuijse, examines the involvement of an external expert advisory committee in internal review by an administrative authority of its own decisions (the objections procedure). The second essay, by Dick Lubach, deals with interventions by external advisory committees in cases involving claims for damage compensation resulting from legal decisions pertinent to zoning law. The third essay, by Kars de Graaf and Bert Marseille, concentrates on external review by administrative courts over administrative decisions, more precisely on the courts' role in final dispute resolution under the Dutch General Administrative Law Act (GALA).

Following the restructuring of various Dutch administrative authorities into a new organization to be known as the Consumer and Market Authority (*ACM*) and the proposed abolition of the objection procedure, Jan Jans and Annalies Outhuijse's paper on *Advisory Objection Procedures in the Netherlands: A Case Study on their Usefulness in Dutch Competition Law* explores the relative merit of GALA's objection procedure in the enforcement context of the Dutch Competition Act. The first part of the paper describes the objection procedure and the role of the Advisory Commission on Competition in that procedure. The second part analyses the reasons and potential consequences of the proposed abolition of the objection procedure in relation to ACM decisions imposing fines. From a functional perspective, the authors note that the objection procedure is very similar to the procedure before a first-instance administrative court, both in terms of procedure and grounds for review. Although the statute allows for a full review, they note that for various reasons such as complexity, delays, and the highly factual or discretionary nature of the issues, the Advisory Committee tends not to get involved in the merit of the decision nor reassess the severity of the sanction. They also note that the procedure may add significant costs and delays. Nonetheless, they observe that in the context of the ACM's decisions imposing fines, a multi-level decisional structure presents advantages that should not be overlooked. Among others, they note that an external expert and independent Advisory Commission plays a major role in structuring the debate. Thus, the objection procedure enhances the capacity of the Competition Authority to make legitimate, coherent and effective decisions. And they worry that the abolition of the objection procedure might prove burdensome on the administrative courts, given the large caseload.

In *Advisory Committees on Damage Compensation in Zoning and Infrastructural Planning: A Quest for Independence,* Dick Lubach discusses the extent to which external advisory committees have to function independently from the political authorities to whom they give advice. Using the example of Dutch advisory committees on damage compensation in zoning and infrastructural planning, he notes that neither the legislation nor the jurisprudence make clear whether, and if so why, these advisory committees ought to be independent. Based on his experience with several external damage compensation committees, he suggests that the need and the level of independence that should be required from such external advisory committees depend on a wide variety of factors such as the context, the nature of the enabling statute, the reasons for which the committee was created in the first place, the way it is structured, the extent to which the authority is bound by the committee's advice and whether the decisional authority may be held accountable for its decisions.

Following this approach, he makes some observations on the context and legal framework within which external advisory committees on damage compensation in zoning and infrastructural planning operate. Among other relevant characteristics, he notes that in disputes about damage compensation taken under article 6.1 of the *Wet ruimtelijke ordening* the lawfulness of the initial decision alleged to have caused the damage is not at stake. The committee is asked to give advice for damage compensation claims resulting from a *per se* lawful decision. Therefore, the issue before the committee is beyond the strict question of conformity to the law. Then, distinguishing his views from those expressed by his colleagues De Graaf and Marseille in a previous article, he discusses the reasons why such external advisory committees are important and why they should be independent from the public authority to whom they give advice.

Kars de Graaf and Bert Marseille's essay on *Final Dispute Resolution by Dutch Administrative Courts: Slippery Slope and Efficient Remedy,* discusses the role of Administrative Courts in final dispute resolution under the Dutch General Administrative Law Act (GALA). In the first part of their paper, the authors give a brief account of the evolution of the Dutch Administrative Courts' statutory powers to bring about final dispute resolution. Then, using empirical data derived from case law, they examine the extent to which those powers have been used and, in such cases, the criteria applied by courts in deciding whether to make the final resolution or return the case to the public authority for decision. They note that for various reasons – such as GALA's recent amendment providing administrative courts with broader powers for bringing about final dispute resolution, complaints about the functioning of the administrative jurisdictions in the Netherlands and the Higher Administrative Court's emphasis on securing effective final dispute resolution – there has been a significant increase in the percentage of cases in which the administrative courts, at all levels, have tried to bring about final dispute resolution. They fear that increased pressure on the courts to decide issues that were previously left to the administrative authorities might open the door to undue infringement on administrative power, especially in cases involving administrative discretion, and that it might even threaten the independence of the administrative Court from the executive.

In conclusion, this book, like the conference on which it is based, is an opportunity to revisit the concepts and safeguards of judicial and quasi-judicial independence and to thereby reflect on our commitment to the independence of courts and administrative decision-makers and the need to reconcile it with other core values. We are pleased to present this collection of essays and we trust that you will find it useful and stimulating.

I – Independence and the Rule of Law

Effective Protection of the Independence of the Judiciary in France

*Guy Canivet**

1. Introduction

1 – The issue of the independence of the judiciary is raised from time to time in France. Whether it be alleged government interference in the hearing and judgement of cases involving political figures, the procedure for appointing and transferring judges and prosecutors or more generally government influence on the operation of justice, the media reports on suspected interference periodically, giving the public a biased and distorted view of the requirement of good legal governance. The result is a great disparity between the principle of judicial independence as proclaimed by the Constitution and reality as perceived by public opinion.

2 – The principle of judicial independence is nonetheless inherent in any democracy. It appears in all charters of rights and freedoms in one form or another and is reproduced in all international, regional and, of special interest to us, European human rights conventions. It is a central aspect of the right to a fair trial stemming from Article 6 of the European Convention on Human Rights reiterated in Article 47 of the Charter of Fundamental Rights of the European Union under the guarantees of the proper administration of justice. The words are very familiar: *"In the determination of his civil rights and obligations or of any criminal charge against him, everyone is entitled to a fair and public hearing within a reasonable time by an independent and impartial tribunal established by law"*.

3 – Deeply rooted in the various legal traditions, judicial independence is nonetheless diversely regulated by member States. As a result, it is a recurring theme in comparative judicial law and the subject of many international meetings of judges. In both the civil law and common law traditions, although the ideological, political and institutional foundations of judicial independence may vary, it is nonetheless an essential component of the Rule of Law. From this comparative perspective, it can be shown that, although the organisation of the French legal system is unique, it comprises the international doctrine of the protection of the independence of the judiciary.

* G. Canivet is a Member of the Constitutional Council, Paris, France, and First Honorary President of the Court of Cassation in France.

4 – This will be the focus of the following brief review which will endeavour to show how, in the specific historical and cultural context of France's legal structure, which was not conducive to the development of a strict and absolute conception of judicial independence, substantial guarantees giving effective protection have nonetheless been set up. This analysis will show that there is a specifically French conception of the principle which is the subject of this international symposium, which I would like to thank the organizers for having invited me to attend.

2. The French Context of Judicial Independence

5 – French law has traditionally been subject to two types of constraints — those relating to the specificities of our legal structure and those relating to the place of judges in the national institutional environment.[1]

A. *Judicial Independence and the Specificities of the French Legal Structure*

6 – The two essential characteristics of the French legal structure are the separation of powers and the place of the public prosecutor in courts of law.

1. *The Separation of Powers*

7 – Prevalent throughout the complex legal structure of the Former Regime, the separation of powers was systematized by the Revolution.[2] As a reaction against the resistance of high-level bodies (the Parliaments) to orders from the royal authority, the 1791 Constitution considerably curtailed judges' authority and prohibited them from interfering in affairs of the State. This political principle at first reduced contentious dealings between citizens and the State to a recourse to hierarchical authority. However, over two centuries it has allowed the progressive building of an administrative justice protective of public freedoms which has resulted in the setting up of a complete set of courts totally separate from the judicial branch that is made up of administrative courts, administrative courts of appeal and the *Conseil d'État* (Council of State). This pyramidal structure was completed with the overhaul of administrative justice in 1987.[3]

8 – Constitutional justice came about much later. For a long time, the dogma of the Rule of Law, the expression of the general will, which also stems from the political principles of 1789, prevented a constitutional review of the law from being set up. It was finally introduced half-heartedly during the 1958 constitutional reform which instituted the review of a statute's constitutional compliance before its enactment. After a long maturation, the 2008 constitutional reform completed

1 Serge Guinchard *et al.*, *Institutions juridictionnelles* (10th Ed.), Dalloz, Paris, 2009.

2 Jean-Pierre Royer, Jean-Paul Jean & Bernard Durand, *Histoire de la justice en France*, PUF, Paris, 2009.

3 Act No. 87-1127 of 31 December 1987 governing reform of administrative litigation (1).

this process by setting up a true forum for challenging the constitutionality of statutes promulgated by referral from the judicial or administrative branches. Constitutional justice was henceforth entrenched.[4]

9 – For these historical reasons, in each of these branches, the protection of the independence of judges is treated differently, which prevents a clear, unambiguous and unconditional view of a notion which is nonetheless the existential guarantee of justice.

2. *The Place of the Government in the Judicial Branch*

10 – The combining of judges and prosecutors into a single body should be added to this separation of the judicial branch.[5] The existence of an attorney representing the executive branch before the courts is a French tradition that dates back to feudal times,[6] but it was the Napoleonic reforms that turned it into a means of the government controlling the courts. This control was carried out in three ways.

11 – First, a public prosecutor was set up for each court of law:[7] a prosecutor of the Republic for the lower level courts [and] a Chief Public Prosecutor for each second-level court and the appeal courts. These prosecutors and their substitutes are organized hierarchically and are subject to the central authority of the executive branch — the Minister of Justice. The *Cour de Cassation* [Supreme Court] also has a public prosecutor, assisted by advocates general, so there is a public prosecutor for each court who is based within the court. Public prosecutors are specific to courts of law, as they are not found in either the administrative courts or the Constitutional Council.

12 – Like judges, prosecutors are members of the judiciary. The Constitutional Council has entrenched this principle of unity within a single body while noting that judges and prosecutors perform different roles:[8] the first are responsible for prosecuting offenders while the second judge them. With only a few exceptions, notably that of the guaranteed irremovability of judges, they have the same status. They are hired and trained the same way, they follow the same career path, and they can shift back and forth from being a judge to being a prosecutor without restriction. The result of this interchangeability is a unique *esprit de corps* among members of the judiciary who are sometimes subject to the authority of the executive branch and sometimes not. The statutory lack of differentiation applied to different functions, which is harmful to the professionalization of both these legal

---

4 Pierre Pactet & Ferdinand Mélin-Soucramanien, *Droit Constitutionnel*, Sirey, Paris, 2012.

5 Roger Perrot, *Institutions judiciaires* (13e ed.), Montchrestien, Paris, 2008.

6 Jean-Marie Carbasse, *Histoire du parquet*, PUF, Paris, 2000.

7 Guinchard *et al.* (2009) *supra* footnote 1.

8 Constitutional Council, Decision No. 92-395 DC of 21 February 1992; Decision No. 93-926 DC of 11 August 1993.

vocations, hinders the building of a culture of independence of judges that is as solidly established as in common law.

13 – Lastly, the intervention of these prosecutors is indispensable in all penal matters. They refer matters before the courts, even when public action is initiated by the victims. This is one of the essential features of an inquisitional system. In certain civil matters, such as those involving civil status, they also act as parties. They also intervene as joined parties in certain matters of public order, such as corporate bankruptcy, and they submit conclusions in all matters where they deem it necessary. They have a right of appeal, the right to have the legitimacy of *Cour de Cassation* judgements reviewed and the right to submit the constitutionality of a statute to the Constitutional Council.

14 – In trials, especially in penal matters, prosecutors have special prerogatives. In penal investigations, they can have people suspected of breaching a penal statute arrested and held in police custody. It is therefore not surprising that their position in the courts and the powers they are given in terms of infringing on fundamental freedoms raise certain problems in terms of the fair trial standards stemming from the jurisprudence of the Constitutional Council or imposed by that of the European Court of Human Rights, based on Article 6 of the European Convention on Human Rights. With respect to Article 5 of the Convention, there is also the question of the prosecutor's ability to deprive a person suspected of committing a crime of his freedom. Several decisions of the national constitutional court have corrected certain aspects of the system but recent cases rendered by the European Court of Human Rights[9] require the French legislature to choose between a body of public prosecutor judges with independent status that likens them to a judicial authority, which public prosecutors would like to have, or a body of prosecutors subject to the instructions of the executive branch, separate from the courts and without the power to order suspected offenders to be detained. Most legal systems around the world have opted for this latter solution. In most systems which have a public prosecutor, he does not have judicial authority.

15 – Although the issue of the public prosecutor's status is the subject of debate in France today,[10] even if the law ends up choosing to give prosecutors independent status[11] there will still be confusion in the French system between two very different aspects of independence — on the one hand the statutory independence of judges with special terms for those who are also public prosecutors, and on the other hand the independence of the courts in rendering judgements, which is very different.

16 – The issue of the public prosecutor does not arise for the other levels of courts. There is no prosecutor for the administrative courts or the Constitutional Council.

9 CEDH, *Moulin v. France*, 23 November 2010.

10 Guinchard *et al.* (2009) *supra* footnote 1.

11 Le Monde, Jean-Claude Bécane, 9 December 2011.

From this perspective, the judicial order is treated differently, which is also the case for the place of judicial judges in institutions.

B. *The Place of Judges in the Institutional Environment*

17 – With respect to the independence of the judiciary, the place of the judge in his institutional environment raises two series of questions — career management for judges and the separation between the judicial branch and the other two branches.

1. *The Existence of a Judicial Civil Service*[12]

18 – In France, two-thirds of judges are hired through competitions open to law graduates as soon as they complete their studies and the other third are confirmed lawyers with a few years of practice. Both judges and prosecutors are appointed by decree signed by the President of the Republic and their transfer, change of duties and promotion in the three levels of courts follow the same rule. Throughout their career, such judges are evaluated by the Chief President of the court and, based on their evaluation, they may be promoted to the next court level. A judge's career progresses from the first-level courts to higher courts through successive decisions of the administrative authority, which raises the question of the influence of the executive branch in managing a judge's career and the other political or union influences that come to bear on it.

a. *The Influence of the Executive Branch*

19 – The influence of the executive branch on judges' careers is measured by the government's impact on their training, the management of their careers and their discipline.

Judges' training[13]

20 – The training of judges is entrusted to a school, the *Ecole nationale de la magistrature,* which has the status of a public establishment with relative administrative and management autonomy. Its board is chaired by the Chief President of the *Cour de Cassation* but the other members are designated by the Minister of Justice. The school is also under the tutorship of this member of the government who chooses its director and appoints the instructors. Lastly, the school's budgetary autonomy is relative — the budget is drawn up and submitted to Parliament by the Minister of Justice.

Career management[14]

21 – The power of the executive branch in managing judges' careers is broadly tempered by the intervention of the constitutional body guaranteeing their independence, the High Council of the Judiciary. For basic positions, appointments

12 Perrot (2008) *supra* footnote 5.

13 Id.

14 Id.

are proposed by the Minister of Justice but they must be confirmed by the High Council of the Judiciary. For the positions of President of the court and appointments to the higher court, i.e. the *Cour de Cassation*, the High Council of the Judiciary appoints the judges directly.

Disciplining judges[15]

22 – The High Council of the Judiciary is also the body responsible for disciplining judges. When a judge breaches the duties of his office, the Minister of Justice has a disciplinary investigation conducted by an inspection service, the 'judicial services inspectorate', which answers directly to the Minister. The same minister then refers the matter to the High Council of the Judiciary. Proceedings can also be taken by the Presidents of the appeal courts on which the judge sits. Disciplinary sanctions for judges are decided by the High Council of the Judiciary. For prosecutors, the High Council only issues an opinion, although it is generally followed by the Minister. These sanctions can include removal from office.

23 – Two issues in particular have arisen regarding disciplinary matters. The first was the possibility of an administrative authority, the Ombudsman, in charge of defending the rights of citizens regarding the various government departments, intervening in the taking of disciplinary action against judges. The Constitutional Council[16] has held the provisions of a 2007 statute which provided for such an intervention contrary to the principle of independence of the judiciary and the separation of powers. The second issue involves the possibility of holding a judge liable for a fault in rendering a judgement where he commits a serious and intentional breach of a rule of procedure. On this point, the Constitutional Council has held[17] that in this case the judge could only be prosecuted if the breach was confirmed in a final judgement, which means that the judge's fault must be established by court judgement, not by the disciplinary body.

24 – Treating this second issue differently, a 2010 statute[18] gave every person the possibility of referring a disciplinary complaint against a member of the judiciary to the High Council of the Judiciary through the petitions committee. The Constitutional Council did not consider this provision unconstitutional but it held that when a complaint relates to a matter which is still before the judge, a procedure must be provided for which respects the impartiality and independence of the judge in question vis-à-vis the parties.

---

15 Guinchard *et al.* (2009) *supra* footnote 1.

16 Constitutional Council, Decision No. 2007-551-DC of 1 March 2007.

17 Constitutional Council, Decision No. 2011-611-DC of 19 July 2010.

18 Institutional Act No. 2010-830 of 22 July 2010 respecting the implementation of Article 65 of the Constitution.

The composition of the High Council of the Judiciary[19]
25 – The career and discipline of judges are broadly subject to the guarantee of the High Council of the Judiciary, which raises the issue of the composition of this body and in particular its freedom from political influence. In this regard, the series of statutes which have defined the status of members of the Council of the Judiciary contain specific provisions protecting their independence. The jurisprudence of the Constitutional Council pays particular attention to the effectiveness of this guarantee.

26 – From this point of view, it has been difficult to find a balance in the composition of the High Council of the Judiciary between the influence of political institutions and that of the representation of judges. This body was created by the 1946 Constitution. It was completely transformed by the 1958 Constitution and since then its composition, power and rules of procedure have been changed three times. The latest constitutional reform was that of July 21, 2008, implemented by an institutional act of July 22, 2010. The most notable change was that the President of the Republic, who was its President, and the Minister of Justice, who was its Vice-President, no longer sit on it. The President of the High Council of the Judiciary is henceforth the Chief President of the *Cour de Cassation*, which without question increases the independence of the High Council of the Judiciary and indirectly that of the judges.

27 – By symmetry, there is a section of the High Council of the Judiciary for public prosecutors. However, it only issues opinions about appointments proposed by the Minister of Justice. The two sections may also meet in a plenary session at the request of the President of the Republic or the Minister of Justice to examine certain general questions common to the two categories of judges.

b. The influence of unions[20]
28 – In 2010, during the latest reform, one of the most debated issues was that of the proportion of judges on the High Council of the Judiciary. As recommended by various international reference texts, and in particular those of the Council of Europe, the judges wanted to be in the majority. The opposite solution prevailed for appointment decisions: the council has eight outside members designated by the government and the *Conseil d'État* and seven judges at various levels. However, in disciplinary matters, the judges are in the majority. The issue is that of the power of judges' unions over the mechanisms for controlling judges' careers. They had greater influence before the 2008 constitutional reform, leading certain commentators on the workings of the legal system to criticize the 'corporatist' management of the judiciary.

29 – Paradoxically, the issue of maintaining independence in the management of judges' careers comes up less at the administrative court level. Institutions created

19 Guinchard *et al.* (2009) *supra* footnote 1.
20 Guinchard *et al.* (2009) *supra* footnote 1; Institut Montaigne, *Pour la justice*, 2004.

within the *Conseil d'État*, the highest level of this type of court, suggest appointments and promotions to the Executive, which generally ratifies them.[21]

30 – These issues come up even less frequently for the Constitutional Council, where members are in office for a nine-year, non-renewable term. Appointments are divided into three and made by the President of the Republic and the Presidents of each house of Parliament, the National Assembly and the Senate, and are subject to confirmation by the Houses themselves. During their term of office, members of the Constitutional Council cannot be removed unless they breach the incompatibility rules as determined by the majority.

31 – Finally, for each category of judge there are incompatibility rules designed to prevent conflicts of interest and guarantee their freedom from any outside influence, and in particular from the parties. All judges are also subject to an obligation of discretion in various forms which prohibits them from any perceived political affiliation or position-taking.

2. *The Interference of Public Authorities in the Operation of the Legal System*

32 – Public authorities intervene in the operation of the legal system in two different ways that affect the independence of the judiciary — interference by the legislative branch in judgements and the influence of the executive branch in managing courts' budgets.

a. *Interference of the legislative branch in judgements*

33 – The interference of the legislative branch in judgements arises in civil matters when a statute becomes applicable to ongoing trials[22] (such a possibility is excluded in penal matters unless the new law is less stringent). The legislature thereby changes the course of a civil proceeding by amending the law the judge must apply, generally to avoid the effect of unwanted jurisprudence. This is clearly a breach of the principle of the separation of powers and the independence of the judiciary. On this issue, the jurisprudence of the Constitutional Council[23] contradicts the position of the European Court of Human Rights.[24] It generally allowed the application of new law in pending civil matters whereas the European Court imposed more stringent conditions: to be retroactive, the statute had to be justified by compelling reasons of public order. After a resounding condemnation of France for such practices, which are contrary to Article 6 of the Convention, the Constitutional Council brought its jurisprudence into line by setting very strict conditions of compliance of so-called 'validation' statutes with the Constitution.[25]

21 Guinchard *et al.* (2009) *supra* footnote 1.

22 Jean-François Renucci, *Traité de droit européen des droits de l'homme*, LGDJ, Paris, 2007, p. 398.

23 Constitutional Council Decisions No. 96-375 DC of 9 April 1996, No. 97-393 DC of 18 December 1997, No. 98-404 DC of 18 December 1998; No. 99-425 DC of 29 December 1999.

24 ECHR 28 October 1999, *Zielinski et al. v. France*, Reports 1999-VII, 95 .

25 Constitutional Council, Decision No. 2001-458 DC of 7 February 2002.

b. The influence of the executive branch on court administration and management[26]

34 – I will conclude this first section with the highly debated issue of the budgetary autonomy of the courts. On this point, the solutions adopted by the various States are quite different. Some States confer great management autonomy on the courts, considering it an inherent part of their independence, while other States deny judges any power in this regard, entrusting these duties to administrators answering directly to the government. In France, the situation is somewhere between the two. The courts have funds which they administer themselves but their budget is proposed and discussed in Parliament by the Minister of Justice, who allocates the funds among the courts. Also, expenditures are ordered within the courts jointly by the Presidents and the prosecutors according to a co-management principle, another indication of the government's control over the courts.[27]

35 – The adoption in 2001 of a new system for voting on and implementing the government's budget[28] would have been an ideal opportunity to rectify this situation. However, the issue of the budgetary management of courts in terms of judicial independence was not taken into account and the situation therefore remained unchanged. In a period of budgetary restrictions, the issue of funding for the courts, which is constantly being debated in France, is a pressing one. The least we can say is that, according to the French conception, the independence of the judiciary does not extend to budgetary autonomy. However, the issue is more satisfactory for administrative courts and even more so for the Constitutional Council which, to various degrees, enjoy greater autonomy in establishing and implementing their budget.

36 – Each of these political, administrative and budgetary characteristics which stand in the way of a natural and unambiguous conception of the independence of the judiciary come into conflict with the constitutional guarantees designed to ensure effective protection of the required standard of independence in a democratic society.

3. The effectiveness of the principle of independence in the French legal model

37 – Like most States, the provisions protecting the independence of the judiciary in France are constitutional. In this way, the Constitution itself bears the mark of a specifically French political concept of justice which is rooted in history. The essential aspect of this identity is that since the Former Regime, the judiciary in France has not been considered an autonomous branch equal to the executive and legislative branches. Emanating from royal authority, it was placed under the control and protection of the sovereign, which would be a source of ongoing

26 Institut Montaigne, *Pour la justice*, 2004.

27 Id.

28 Institutional Act No. 2001-692 of 1 August 2001 governing public finance.

conflict among the courts of the Former Regime and the King and, in response, would lead to the weakening of the courts in revolutionary law.[29] As a result, in the institutions of the Fifth Republic, the law was not on an equal footing with the Executive and Parliament; it was an 'authority' and the independence of this 'legal authority' was guaranteed by the President of the Republic.[30]

38 – With this political background in mind, the Constitution contains constitutional standards which guarantee the independence of the judicial authority. Through its decisions since 1958 and especially beginning in the 1980s, the Constitutional Council has given them content which ensures their effectiveness.

A. *Constitutional Provisions Relating to the Independence of the Judiciary*

39 – The constitutional provisions relating to the independence of the judiciary are taken from both the Declaration of 1789 of the Rights of Man and of Citizens, to which the preamble of the 1958 Constitution refers, and the provisions of its Title VIII. The independence of the Constitutional Council is guaranteed by the provisions of Title VII which are specific to it and the independence of the administrative courts stems from a fundamental principle recognized by the law of the Republic, entrenched by the preamble of the 1946 Constitution, which is also included in the constitutional corpus.

40 – Article 16 of the Declaration of 1789 reads as follows: "Any society in which the guarantee of the rights is not secured, or the separation of powers is not determined, has no constitution at all". This is the founding principle of the separation of powers on which the independence of anybody vested with the power to judge is based, regardless its nature, and which prevents the legislature or the government from censoring court decisions, subjecting them to injunctions or substituting their own decisions in the judging of disputes falling under their authority.[31] The independence of the judiciary takes on a new dimension with the affirmation of the former principle according to which no person can be reassigned against his will to a court other than that designated by law.[32] As a result, the law cannot create a special court to decide on a specific trial and no citizen may choose a different court unless it is in the public interest. Conversely, no court may be suppressed without guarantees for both the persons subject to trial and the members of such courts.

---

29 Royer, Jean & Durand (2009) *supra* footnote 2.

30 Th. S. Renoux, Le président de la République, garant de l'indépendance de l'autorité judiciaire?, *Revue Justices*, 1996, no. 3. This conception was expressed in very clear terms by the President of the Republic in a press conference held on January 31, 1964: "In France there is no authority, whether civil, military or judicial, which does not derive its legitimacy from the Head of State ..." (translation by author).

31 Constitutional Council, Decision No. 80-119 DC of 22 July 1980; Decision No. 87-228-DC of 26 June 1987.

32 Article 17 of the Law of August 16-24, 1790; Th. S. Renoux, Le droit au juge naturel, droit fondamental, *RTDciv.* 1993, no 1, p. 33.

41 – Article 64,[33] which deals with the judicial authority, contains substantial provisions involving the principle of independence in the French tradition. Other than pointing out that the President of the Republic is its guarantor, it states that in exercising this part of his power, the President of the Republic is assisted by the High Council of the Judiciary. It indicates here again that the status of members of the judiciary is determined by a category of special laws, institutional acts, voted on according to a strengthened procedure designed to increase the statutory guarantees granted to members of the judiciary[34] and lastly that members of the judiciary, i.e. judges, cannot be removed from office so they cannot be reassigned without their consent, even for a promotion.

42 – Article 65[35] sets out the composition and mission of the High Council of the Judiciary, presided over since 2010 by the Chief President of the *Cour de Cassation*

33 Article 64: The President of the Republic shall be the guarantor of the independence of the Judicial Authority. He shall be assisted by the 'High Council of the Judiciary'. An Institutional Act shall determine the status of members of the Judiciary. Judges shall be irremovable from office.

34 Constitutional Council, Decision No. 2001-445-DC of 19 June 2001.

35 Article 65: The High Council of the Judiciary shall consist of a section with jurisdiction over judges and a section with jurisdiction over public prosecutors.
The section with jurisdiction over judges shall be presided over by the Chief President of the *Cour de Cassation*. It shall comprise, in addition, five judges and one public prosecutor, one *Conseiller d'État* appointed by the *Conseil d'État* and one barrister, as well as six qualified, prominent citizens who are not members of Parliament, of the Judiciary or of administration. The President of the Republic, the President of the National Assembly and the President of the Senate shall each appoint two qualified, prominent citizens. The procedure provided for in the last paragraph of article 13 shall be applied to the appointments of the qualified, prominent citizens. The appointments made by the President of each House of Parliament shall be submitted for consultation only to the relevant standing committee in that House.
The section with jurisdiction over public prosecutors shall be presided over by the Chief Public Prosecutor at the *Cour de Cassation*. It shall comprise, in addition, five public prosecutors and one judge, as well as the *Conseiller d'État* and the barrister, together with the six qualified, prominent citizens referred to in the second paragraph.
The section of the High Council of the Judiciary with jurisdiction over judges shall make recommendations for the appointment of judges to the *Cour de Cassation*, the Chief Presidents of Courts of Appeal and the Presidents of the *Tribunaux de grande instance*. Other judges shall be appointed after consultation with this section.
The section of the High Council of the Judiciary with jurisdiction over public prosecutors shall give its opinion on the appointment of public prosecutors.
The section of the High Council of the Judiciary with jurisdiction over public prosecutors shall give its opinion on disciplinary measures regarding public prosecutors. When acting in such capacity, it shall comprise, in addition to the members mentioned in paragraph three, the public prosecutor belonging to the section with jurisdiction over judges.
The High Council of the Judiciary shall meet in plenary section to reply to the requests for opinions made by the President of the Republic in application of article 64. It shall also express its opinion in plenary section, on questions concerning the deontology of judges or on any question concerning the operation of justice which is referred to it by the Minister of Justice. The plenary section comprises three of the five judges mentioned in the second paragraph, three of the five prosecutors mentioned in the third paragraph as well as the *Conseiller d'État*, the barrister and the six qualified, prominent citizens referred to in the second paragraph. It is presided over by the Chief President of the *Cour de Cassation* who may be substituted by the Chief Public Prosecutor of this court.

for the section with jurisdiction over judges and by the Chief Public Prosecutor at the *Cour de Cassation* for the section with jurisdiction over public prosecutors. At the request of the President of the Republic or the Minister of Justice, it meets in plenary session to express its opinion on any question concerning the operation of justice, including those affecting its independence.

43 – The independence of the Constitutional Council is guaranteed by Article 56 of the Constitution,[36] which determines the number of members and the procedure for appointing them.[37] It has nine members who hold office for a non-renewable term of nine years. Three of its members are appointed by the President of the Republic, three by the President of the National Assembly and three by the President of the Senate. These appointments are subject to the approval of the relevant standing committees of each House, which may oppose them with a majority of at least 3/5 of the votes cast. In addition to these nine members, former Presidents of the Republic are ex officio life members of the Constitutional Council. The President of the Constitutional Council is appointed by the President of the Republic.

44 – Lastly, the independence of administrative courts, which are likened to *Cours des comptes* [courts of auditors], is guaranteed by a fundamental principle recognized by the laws of the Republic.[38] For members of these courts, the rules governing their independence are not found in legislation on the judiciary but in specific rules applicable to them within general civil service regulations.[39]

The Minister of Justice may participate in all the sittings of the sections of the High Council of the Judiciary except those concerning disciplinary matters.
According to the conditions determined by an Institutional Act, a referral may be made to the High Council of the Judiciary by a person subject to trial.
The Institutional Act shall determine the manner in which this article is to be implemented.

36 Article 56: The Constitutional Council shall comprise nine members, each of whom shall hold office for a non-renewable term of nine years. One third of the membership of the Constitutional Council shall be renewed every three years. Three of its members shall be appointed by the President of the Republic, three by the President of the National Assembly and three by the President of the Senate. The procedure provided for in the last paragraph of article 13 shall be applied to these appointments. The appointments made by the President of each House shall be submitted for consultation only to the relevant standing committee in that House.
In addition to the nine members provided for above, former Presidents of the Republic shall be ex officio life members of the Constitutional Council. The President shall be appointed by the President of the Republic. He shall have a casting vote in the event of a tie.

37 Constitutional Council, Decision No. 566-DC of 9 July 2008: "It is implicit from all the provisions of the Constitution that the legislator intended to guarantee the independence of the Constitutional Council" (transation by author).

38 Constitutional Council, Decision No. 80-119-DC of 22 July 1980.

39 Constitutional Council, Decision No. 91-L of 12 March 1991.

B. *Jurisprudence of the Constitutional Council Regarding the Independence of the Judiciary*

45 – Through a series of decisions, the Constitutional Council, which is responsible for deciding whether laws comply with the Constitution,[40] has progressively given effect to each of the constitutional standards we have just mentioned. For courts and the Constitutional Council, the implementation of these texts must be referred to institutional acts[41] which are systematically submitted to it before being enacted. It has therefore been able to systematically oversee the constitutionality of these specific statutes. The organisation and status of other courts are determined by ordinary statute which may be referred to it by political authorities and groups of parliamentarians before being enacted. In addition, since the institution of a constitutionality provision[42] which, during a trial, allows a party to submit the constitutionality of the statute applicable to the dispute to the Constitutional Council upon referral by the judge of first instance and after screening by the *Conseil d'État* or the *Cour de Cassation*, it may be asked to rule on any legislative provision which impairs the independence of the judiciary. This has led to a significant jurisprudential corpus defining the scope and content of the independence of the judiciary, which we will briefly discuss below.

46 – The Constitutional Council thus ensures that the legislature complies with the guarantee of independence, both with respect to its statutory aspect, i.e. the independence of judges, and its institutional aspect, applied to the courts. It exercises this oversight both internally in terms of the operation of justice by ensuring that in rendering judgement, the judge does not receive any instructions from his own superiors,[43] and externally, in terms of the executive and legislative branches, by ensuring that the public authority does not interfere with either judges' freedom to render decisions or the authority of their decisions. This guarantee of independence must also shelter the judge from political and administrative pressure as well as pressure from the parties or private influences. It protects all judges, regardless the court to which they belong, whether they are professional judges or part-time judges hired on an as-needed basis.[44]

47 – The Constitutional Council also ensures that the guarantee of independence applies to all facets of a judge's career, from his appointment,[45] assignment,[46]

40 Article 61 of the Constitution.

41 This requirement stems from Article 64 of the Constitution. Constitutional Council, Decision No. 2002-445-DC of 19 June 2001; Decision No. 2003-446-DC of 20 February 2003.

42 Article 61-1 of the Constitution.

43 Constitutional Council, Decision No. 70-40 DC of 9 July 1970; Decision No. 80-127-DC of 20 January1981; No. 2003-466-DC of 20 February 2003.

44 Regarding *juges de proximité* (local magistrates): Constitutional Council, Decision No. 94-355 of 10 January 1995.

45 Constitutional Council, Decision No. 93-336-DC of 27 January 1994.

46 Constitutional Council, Decision No. 93-336 of 27 January 1994.

the evaluation of his professional skills, remuneration, transfer, promotion[47] and extension[48] to the cessation of his duties.

48 – The Constitutional Council pays particular attention to ensuring that the law efficiently complies with the irremovability of judges and it denounces any proceeding which would move a judge without his prior consent, even in the case of a promotion,[49] or assign him to other duties. It thus carefully examines the status of judges vested with temporary or part-time functions, or rules limiting the time given to exercise certain functions.[50] It gives general scope to the irremovability rule by applying it to both higher court judges and members of administrative courts.[51]

49 – With respect to the requirement of independence, its control extends to legislative provisions relating to the status of members, the rules of procedure of the High Council of the Judiciary, guarantor of the independence of judges, with respect to opinions and decisions regarding appointments, as well as the rules involving disciplinary proceedings and in particular the terms according to which referrals may be made to it by persons subject to trial.[52] The body guaranteeing independence must clearly be sheltered from any influence itself.

50 – Since the judges are elected, like members of labour courts[53] and commercial court judges, the Constitutional Council bases the guarantee of independence, which is an integral part of the exercise of judicial duties, on Article 16 of the Declaration of 1789 rather than on status as member of the judiciary, which does not apply to them. It is important in all cases that those involved be subject to the rights and obligations applicable to all members of the judiciary which give access to court functions, and thus to the same guarantees of independence, subject only to the specific provisions imposed by the part-time or temporary exercise of their duties.[54]

51 – For all categories of judges, the independence guarantee includes verification of their ability to render justice. The law which determines their status must therefore indicate the level of knowledge or legal experience they must have.[55]

47 Constitutional Council, Decision No. 2001-445-DC of 19 June 2001.
48 Constitutional Council, Decision No. 86-220-DC of 22 December 1986.
49 Constitutional Council, Decision No. 67-33-DC of 12 July 1967; Decision No. 80-123-DC of 24 October 1980.
50 Constitutional Council, Decision No. 94-355-DC of 10 January 1995; Decision No. 2001-445-DC of 19 June 2001; Decision No. 2003-466-DC of 20 February 2003.
51 Constitutional Council, Decision No. 80-119-DC of 22 July1980.
52 Constitutional Council, Decision No. 2010- 611-DC of 19 July 2010.
53 Constitutional Council, Decision No. 45-DC of 28 December 2006.
54 Constitutional Council, Decision No. 2003-466 DC of 20 February 2003.
55 Constitutional Council, Decision No. 2003-466 DC of 20 February 2003.

This capacity requirement is based on Article 6 of the Declaration of 1789,[56] from which the principle of equal access to public office is inferred and which, in this case, completes the constitutional sources cited above. The capacities, virtues and talents taken into account must also relate to the functions of a judge and are designed to guarantee equality before the law, a principle which also stems from Article 6 of the Declaration of 1789.[57]

52 – Lastly, the legal requirement of setting up independence guarantees for all judges is controlled both positively, through the censure of legal provisions which breach it, and negatively, where the law fails to provide such guarantees.[58]

4. Conclusion

53 – This brief review shows that the Constitutional Council has built an efficient apparatus for protecting the independence of the judiciary by reconciling the special treatment of the power to judge in our political tradition and the unique context of French legal institutions with the fundamental guarantees set forth in the preamble and body of the Constitution in order to place requirement of judicial independence at the level of international standards. This wish to adhere to universal principles of good legal governance can be seen in particular from the convergence of the decisions of the French constitutional judge with, on the one hand, those of the European Court of Human Rights based on Article 6 of the European Convention on Human Rights and, on the other hand, those of the Court of Justice of the European Union based on fundamental principles of European law.[59] Such a convergence is indispensable in the framework of an European space which requires that justice be rendered in all European Union member States according to identical standards of quality in order to be mutually recognized and executed throughout the European territory.

56 Article 6 Declaration of the Rights of Man and Citizens: "(...) All citizens, being equal in its [the law's] eyes, are equally eligible to all public dignities, places and employments, according to their capacities, and without other distinction than that of their virtues and talents".

57 Constitutional Council, Decision No. 98-336 of 19 February1998.

58 Constitutional Council, Decision No. 2010-10 QPC of 2 July 2010.

59 Renucci (2007) *supra* footnote 22, p. 402.

The Coming of Age of Review of Administrative Action in the Netherlands: A Battle of Effectiveness and the Rule of Law

*Willem Konijnenbelt**

1. Effectiveness and the Rule of Law

Effectiveness, in the context of our subject, essentially means effective review of and protection against administrative action: a procedure that brings the claimant, if he wins his case, the remedy he was seeking. *Rule of Law* essentially means, in this context, a procedure of review that ensures verification of the legality of the administrative action by a court addressing the criteria of Article 6 of the European Convention on Human Rights: in cases where civil rights and obligations are concerned or where a criminal charge is involved – both as understood by the case law of the Strasbourg Court – a review ensured by a court that fulfils the criteria of the Convention with regards to its nature and procedure. One of the essential characteristics required by the Convention is *independence* of the reviewing court. And the implication that the court cannot take the place of the administration.

The question that forms the background issue of the whole article is then: How to reconcile the requirement of effective review of administrative action and the requirement of review by an independent court? The twain, are they compatible or will they never meet?

2. Until the Middle of the XIXth Century

Under the Republic of the United Provinces (1579-1795), all cases against the administration could be brought before the ordinary law courts of the provinces. Following the end of the French period – with its dogmatic separation of judicial and executive powers – in 1814, the newly founded Kingdom of the Netherlands initially retained the ancient system of full competence of the judiciary *vis-à-vis* the administration. The then king, William I (our only autocratic monarch), disapproved of the system and in 1822 the French conflict system was reintroduced. Thus, in civil procedures against a public body before a judicial court, the provincial governor could raise a conflict of competence, as a result of which the court would cease to be competent in the case and the dispute would be decided by the King (who would seek the advice of his Council of State). From 1830 onwards – when

* Dr. W. Konijnenbelt is Emeritus Professor at the University of Amsterdam.

the royal authority had been seriously weakened by his stubborn and authoritarian way of handling the revolt of the Belgian provinces – raising conflicts fell into disuse; in 1844 the *conflict* system was formally abolished.[1]

3. The Rise of Administrative Review

Still, by then one had become accustomed to having, in several cases, a possibility of *administrative* review instead of one form or another of *judicial* review. The reviewing authority would then be an administrative organ: the municipal council (for decisions by the municipal executive or the mayor); the provincial executive (for decisions by municipal or water board bodies); or the Crown (either directly, for decisions made by ministers or by decentralised bodies, or, indirectly, in cases where an appeal could be brought against reviewing decisions by the provincial executive). Whether an administrative appeal would be possible against a certain kind of administrative decision, whether the decision given in review would be subject to appeal to the Crown and to whom such an appeal would be available, all depended on separate provisions in the statute law: in Acts of Parliament, in government regulations; or in provincial, municipal or water board byelaws. Initially, there were no general rules of procedure or generally accepted principles of due process.

The ordinary courts remained competent for "all disputes about property or rights deriving from it, about claims or civil rights", according to a provision of the 1815 Constitution.

From the mid-1840s onwards, the Provincial States of several provinces would vote byelaws providing rules of procedure, such as the obligation to hear both sides. The Provinces Act of 1850 made such rules compulsory. It was not until 1861 that the Council of State Act would give rules of procedure for the proceedings in applications for administrative review by the Crown: all parties concerned would be heard by the Contentious Section of the Council of State, which would formulate a decision in the form of a draft Royal Decree. Should a minister hesitate to follow the opinion of the Section, he had to demand that the section reconsider its draft. The minister could persist in deciding contrary to the draft only if he found the minister of justice willing to countersign the Royal Decree ('contrary decision'). In practice, contrary decisions were extremely rare: they appear in just 1% or 2% of cases.

The case law of the provincial executives and especially the Crown have both made a fundamental contribution to the development of Dutch administrative law by elaborating – long before the courts and the French *Conseil d'État* – the concept of unwritten general principles of law with which administrative decisions must

1 R. Kranenburg, De bescherming tegen onrechtmatig bestuur, *in* C.W. van der Pot *et al.* (eds.), *Nederlandsch Bestuursrecht*, Alphen aan den Rijn, 1932, p. 255.

comply, such as equality, legal certainty and the protection of legitimate expectations, proportionality, prohibition of *détournement de pouvoir* (use of a power in pursuit of wrong ends) and of arbitrariness.

Since the written law would never give specific reasons for granting a review, it was self-evident that these reasons could be both of a legal and of a policy nature. This being the case, and the reviewing authority being an administrative authority itself, if the review were to come down to the annulment of the decision challenged and therefore a requirement that a new decision be made, the reviewing authority would simply replace the annulled decision with its own decision. Hence, this system offered very effective remedies[2] but the rule of law requirement of review by independent courts was not met.

4. End of the 19th Century: Judicial Review, the Exception

By the end of the century, during the eighties, there was much debate – influenced by developments in Germany and France – about the desirability of creating a system of independent administrative courts. Some supported the idea of transforming the Contentious Section of the Council of State into an independent administrative court. The constitutional reform of 1887 made this possible. The French example was not entirely unrelated to this idea. Others were in favour of creating specialised administrative courts; a third suggestion was to add chambers for judicial review of administrative action to the ordinary courts of justice. In the end, no decision could be reached.

From the nineties onwards, some specialised administrative courts were created (*e.g.* taxes, social security, civil service). In many cases, a statute, or a byelaw issued by a decentralised body, would make some kind of administrative review of individual administrative decisions possible, mostly a review by the provincial executive or by the Crown. In other cases, one would have to try and seek access to the ordinary courts with a claim that an administrative decision was 'illegal' and had therefore harmed the claimant. Over the course of the 20th century, the courts would come to accept more and more grounds for the illegality of an administrative decision: not just conflict with written 'private' law but also with public law and with unwritten principles of law, including the principle of due care.

In financial disputes (*e.g.* tax law, social security), the specialised administrative courts would replace an administrative decision, annulled on grounds of illegality, with their own decision. In other kinds of judicial review of an administrative decision, a judgment that found the decision being challenged illegal would be content with annulling the decision, leaving it to the administration to make a new decision. The 'discretionary power' of the administration ought to be respected, both for constitutional reasons (in many cases statute law gives discretionary power to

2 Kranenburg (1932) *supra* footnote 1.

the administration and to the administration only; only administrative authorities can exercise such powers under parliamentary or comparable responsibility) and on practical grounds (in many cases, the courts lack the skills and the tools for making the right decisions). In administrative review, however, the reviewing body would always, as we have seen, able to make the decision itself if need be.[3]

At this stage, review by the specialised administrative courts met the requirements of both effectiveness and review by an independent court. But in many cases the only judicial review available was a tort action before the ordinary courts. This was an independent judge, but effectiveness was assured only insofar as a claimant could be given adequate financial compensation; a 'better' administrative decision was something the judge could not provide though. In the many cases where only administrative review was possible, the effectiveness of the review was assured but the rule of law requirement of review by an independent judge was not met at all; in this respect, the situation showed no improvement.

5. After the Second World War – 1976: 'Arob', Decline of Administrative Review

After the Second World War, new attempts were made to set up a system of review for individual administrative decisions. In 1976 – after a series of intermediate stages – this resulted in the *Wet Arob* (Act on judicial review of individual administrative decisions). The Act upheld the existing possibilities for judicial or administrative review of individual decisions but it created a new independent court for claims with the intention of the annulment of an individual administrative decision for 'illegality', i.e. being (a) contrary to a written provision of law; (b) contrary to the prohibition on the unlawful use of power (*détournement de pouvoir*); (c) contrary to the prohibition of arbitrariness, and (d) contrary to any other general principle of administrative law. This new court was the Administrative Justice Section of the Council of State. In most cases, an objection procedure, based on the principle of fair hearing before the authority that had made the challenged decision, was compulsory.

The new Section, often referred to as the '*Arob* judge', played an important role in the further development of the procedural general principles of administrative law, thus completing the work of the Crown, the pre-existing administrative courts and the ordinary judiciary. The '*Arob* judge' would, in cases where the challenged decision was annulled, mostly content himself with annulling the decision and leaving it to the administration to decide on the consequences of the annulment; only in cases where it was clear that the reason for annulment, had no, or only partial, bearing on the substance of the annulled decision, could it decide that the legal consequences of the annulled decision were upheld entirely or in part.

3 Kranenburg (1932) *supra* footnote 1.

From 1976, the possibility of administrative review of individual decisions was gradually removed from many pre-existing statutes (though not from all). As a result, '*Arob* review' gradually became the standard method of reviewing individual decisions. But three specialised administrative jurisdictions continued to function, each in its own province: tax courts (as part of the common judiciary); a court for social security and civil service disputes and a court for matters to do with economic legislation.[4]

All in all, ever more individual administrative decisions have become potentially subject to review by an administrative court. Where access to the *Arob* judge was made available, the *Arob* judge replaced the ordinary courts; this has not changed the quality of the system in terms of rule of law: one independent judge has given way to another. In terms of effectiveness the change implied some improvement. On the other hand, where the *Arob* judge had replaced administrative review by the Crown, rule of law had won to the detriment of effectiveness; a shift in the balance.

6. Fall of Administrative Review by the Crown

In 1985, the *Benthem* ruling of the European Court of Human Rights in Strasbourg confirmed the opinion of those who had argued that the Dutch administrative review system did not fulfil the requirements of Article 6 of the European Convention on Human Rights, namely that a claimant whose civil rights or obligations are at stake or has a criminal charge against him, is entitled to a fair and public hearing by an independent and impartial tribunal. When the Crown is the final competent reviewing body, there is no independent tribunal to hear the case. In view of that, the competence of the Crown to hear claims against individual administrative decisions was soon abolished; provisionally, the Contentious Section of the Council of State – the same Section that used to hear the cases and that would draw up the draft Royal Decrees that were meant to decide the cases – was declared competent to decide these cases. It could annul a decision on the same grounds, as could its 'sister' the Administrative Justice Section, in *Arob* cases. (In practice, several Councillors of State would be members of both Sections.) A more permanent solution would be introduced a few years later.[5] – A further gain for rule of law, but at the expense of effectiveness in the eyes of the claimants.

7. 1994: The General Administrative Law Act

The second half of the Eighties and the beginning of the Nineties brought a sort of repetition of the debate of one hundred years earlier about review of administrative

4 H.D. van Wijk/W. Konijnenbelt & R.M. van Male, *Hoofdstukken van bestuursrecht*, The Hague 2002, p. 502.

5 Id., p. 503.

action, the only real difference being that an important role for administrative review was no longer an option. Again, three principal models were discussed: (a) the integration of administrative justice into the ordinary judiciary, with the *Hoge Raad* ('High Council') on top as a mere court of cassation; (b) some administrative courts as courts of appeal and, again, the *Hoge Raad* as a common court of cassation for the whole of the judiciary and (c) the retention of the existing system with some adaptations.

Without great enthusiasm on anyone`s part, the third option prevailed. The specialised administrative courts for social security affairs, civil service disputes (and disputes on scholarships) and for economic law disputes were upheld, the tax law chambers remained part of the ordinary judiciary, and the two judicial sections of the Council of State merged into one Section for Administrative Justice. As a rule, a claimant cannot be heard by an administrative court if he has not followed the objection procedure before the authority responsible for the decision which he is challenging. The law concerning the proceedings before the three 'autonomous' administrative jurisdictions was unified; in 2005, these rules of procedure came to apply in tax disputes too.[6]

Recently, the debate has begun anew. The Government seems to be in favour of leaving the system more or less as it is, with improvements where necessary. I should add that there is a constant stream of minor or major legislative improvements, arrangements for a better lay-out of the system and – as we shall see next – improving its effectiveness.

Unfortunately, I must also add some recent setbacks: for not always very convincing reasons, some procedures – especially in the field of construction and road building – have been shortened (the final decision of the court ought now to be reached within six months), resulting, of course, in delays in other matters treated by those same courts; and there is a bill pending before parliament raising the costs of the procedures drastically. There was a chance, however, that the senate would refuse to pass the bill. In the beginning of the year 2013 the new government withdrew the bill; this danger is now over.

8. Effectiveness and the Rule of Law *Revisited*

The tradition of administrative review by the Crown was one of a *substantive scrutiny* of decisions: although questions of procedural law were not completely neglected, the main focus of the reviewing procedure was *what would be the right decision*. If it was thought that the decision challenged was right in the end, the grounds put forward by the claimant would fail; possible faults of a formal nature,

6 H.D. van Wijk/W. Konijnenbelt & R.M. van Male, *Hoofdstukken van bestuursrecht*, Amsterdam 2011, p. 516; R.J.N. Schlössels & S.E. Zijlstra, *Bestuursrecht in de sociale rechtsstaat*, Deventer 2010, p. 1096, 1128.

such as lack of research or failure to hear interested parties, non-convincing motivation etc., would be 'repaired' in the course of the proceedings before the Crown. If it were thought that the decision ought to have been read differently, the decision challenged could be annulled as a whole or in part and the outcome of the proceeding would be the right decision – 'right' meaning both legally correct and appropriate for its purpose. The Crown being itself an administrative organ, it was considered that it had every authority to impose the decision it thought right. The one flaw of the procedure, however, was that the legal scrutiny was carried out not by an independent court but, in the end, by the administration, regardless of the important role of the (independent and impartial) Contentious Section of the Council of State: its role was important, decisive even – but the role was, in law, just an advisory one. Hence, there was non-compliance with Article 6 of the ECHR.

The tradition of the '*Arob* judge', the Administrative Justice Section of the Council of State, was more or less the opposite of the Crown's. The question here was not 'what is or would should have been the right decision?' but 'are the legal complaints of the claimant well-founded or not?'. Very often, if no serious fault of a substantive legal nature could be found, it would appear that the administration had committed one or two formal mistakes and for that reason alone the Section would annul the decision, unless it was sufficiently clear that the mistake had had no effect on the substance of the decision. All in all, it was relatively easy for a claimant to succeed. But very often the victory thus won appeared to be Pyrrhic: the administration, having 'repaired' the reasons for the annulment, could make a new decision, the substance – if not the wording – of which could be an exact replication of the annulled earlier decision. A better founded decision this time, true, but all in all mainly a loss of time.

Under the General Administrative Law Act, 1994, the attitude of the administrative courts has gradually changed. Right from the start the Act, in Article 8:72, stipulated that if an administrative court found a reason to annul the decision challenged, it could, *inter alia*, 'instruct the administration to make a new decision [...] with due observance of its ruling, or it can determine that its ruling will replace the annulled decision or the annulled part of it'. At first, this provision was interpreted rather narrowly: a court was allowed to use its replacement power only if there could be no doubt that only one legally correct decision was conceivable. Gradually, the courts became more lenient. In 2008 they adopted the policy that a court, having annulled an administrative decision and finding that a new decision will have to be made, will make the new decision itself unless there are sound reasons to leave it to the administration. During the hearing, the court may ask the opinion of the parties concerned about possible positive outcomes of the proceeding. There are many possible reasons for leaving the making of a new decision to the administration. For example, the annulled decision was the refusal to grant a written permit, even if it is clear that the permit must be granted now, it may be impossible for the court to establish the conditions attached to the permit. Or the reasons for refusing the permit were insufficient but under the relevant statute law there may be other serious reasons for a refusal and further exploration is needed before a new decision can be reached. In such a case the court will, nowadays, very often set a term for the new decision, possibly with a penalty payment if the administration does not reach its new decision within a given time-limit.

As of 2013, the GALA provides a special procedure where the court may instruct the administration to try and repair the legal defects discovered so far (and maybe, to find a solution that is more favourable to the claimant), so that the court will be able to take the new decision into account before giving its final judgement.[7]

All in all, nowadays the courts will do their utmost to make sure that the procedure will give every indication possible about the consequences of an annulment. From January 1st of 2013 on, Article 8:41a of the General Administrative Law Act obliges the administrative courts even explicitly to strive after final settlement of the disputes they handle.[8]

All this may be so, but it still cannot avoid the fact that judicial review is, and always will be, 'inferior' to administrative review in one respect: a court of law cannot scrutinise the non-legal, policy aspects of administrative decisions (apart from more or less obvious 'misfits', decisions that are manifestly unreasonable from a policy viewpoint – which, fortunately, occur very rarely).

Here a new approach to the objection proceedings, which are compulsory in nearly all cases before the case can be brought before an administrative court, may help. The aim of objection proceedings is that the deciding authority should reconsider its own decision after a fair hearing of all the interested parties. Under the *Wet Arob* of 1976, the Act which made the procedure compulsory, and in view of the more or less formalistic character of the '*Arob* judge's' approach to such matters, a tradition has developed of using the objection procedure as a sort of pre-trial, neglecting, to a large extent, the non-legal aspects of the affair, even when in reality those were predominant for the objector. The committees which, very often, carry out the hearings for the administration and give their opinion on the outcome they think appropriate, have developed a tendency to 'play the little judge'.

For some years now, a campaign initiated by the Ministry of the Interior has tried to convince the various administrative authorities and their advisory committees to adopt a different attitude in the objectives proceedings and to try to find a solution for the complaints of the objectors, paying less attention (but still enough, if a solution cannot be found) to the legal aspects of the affair. This campaign,

7 B.J. Schueler, J. K. Drewes *et al.*, *Definitieve geschilbeslechting door de rechter*, The Hague 2007; J.E.M. Polak, Effectieve geschillenbeslechting: bestuurlijke lus en andere instrumenten, *Nederlands Tijdschrift voor Bestuursrecht* 2011, 2.

8 *Cf.* footnote 6.

welcomed by most, is beginning to bear its first fruit.[9] But much must still be done in this respect; an attitude that is widely spread and has taken root over some decades cannot be completely altered in such a short time.

The new, more 'positive', attitude of the courts, resulting in fewer fruitless annulments and in far more 'leading' rulings, seems solid enough by now; it is strongly advocated by all administrative appeal courts and there is little opposition. Previously, the courts had already made sure that their rulings were delivered promptly, the proceedings before a tribunal of first instance or before an administrative court of appeal seldom take more than one year. In most cases they take six to ten months, and in urgent cases there is a very effective system of preliminary provisions (*'référé administratif'*) available.

If we do succeed in transforming the nature of the objection proceedings into a problem-solving affair instead of 'playing the little judge', the result will be an intelligent combination of 'administrative' and independent judicial review that is both effective and in accordance with the rule of law. So there is hope for the future – but there is still much work to be done!

9 Alex Brenninkmeijer & Bert Marseille, Meer succes met de informele aanpak van bezwaarschriften, *Nederlands Juristenblad* 2011, 1596.

The Function of Judicial Independence in Modern Legal Systems: Preserving the Boundaries of Law

*Martine Valois**

1. Introduction

Since the end of the last century, the general understanding of the separation of powers has changed drastically, especially with respect to the status and function of the judiciary. In 1985, the Supreme Court of Canada had summarised the role of the three branches in the following way:

> ...the role of the judiciary is, of course, to interpret and apply the law; the role of the legislature is to decide upon and enunciate policy; the role of the executive is to administer and implement that policy.[1]

Under that conception, each power had a very narrow and definite role. Among the three branches of government, the legislature was paramount since only that branch had democratic legitimacy. As to the judiciary, its role was limited to the interpretation of statutes according to legislative intent. The situation is very different today. The Supreme Court of Canada teaches us that the constitutional principle of the separation of powers protects the exclusivity of certain functions performed by each of the three powers, in particular those carried out by the courts, and that a law may 'unconstitutionally interfere with courts' adjudicative role'.[2]

These transformation of the function of courts brought with it a general questioning of the role of judges in the production of norms. Paradoxically, the mounting power of judges poses a challenge for judicial independence – the judges' freedom to make decisions based on law without any form of pressure or influence – also had adverse consequences for judicial independence. This is because the increased mobilisation of the judiciary to decide social or moral issues has led to an increase in the criticism addressed to judges and the decisions they render. The rise of criticism towards the judiciary have paved the way to a diminution in the protection afforded to judges.

---

* Dr. M. Valois LL.B., LL.M., LL.D. is a member of the Quebec Bar and Professor of law at the Université de Montreal, Canada.

1 *Fraser v. Public Service Staff Relations Board*, [1985] 2 S.C.R. 455.

2 *B.C. v. Imperial Tobacco Canada Ltd.* [2005] 2 S.C.R. 474, para. 54.

My intention in this paper is to explore these issues using the theoretical framework of Niklas Luhmann systems theory.[3] With the unique perspective of systems theory, issues related to the role of the judiciary in modern legal systems and the concept of judicial independence are given a new significance. Indeed, one may ask if there is yet more worth discussing about judicial independence and the rule of law in legal theory, now that it is universally agreed that the rule of law cannot be guaranteed without judicial independence. On the other hand, the fact that there are still serious threats to the rule of law and judicial independence, even in legal systems where both principles are constitutionally guaranteed, raises the question of the conditions required for judicial independence to be fully implemented.

In this text, I propose a new understanding of the way judicial independence works to guarantee the rule of law. Using the conceptual tools elaborated by Nicklas Luhmann, I will demonstrate that the principle of judicial independence is closely linked to law's independence, that is, the autonomy of the legal system. As an autopoietic system, law observes, reproduces, and conserves itself. Its autonomy is maintained by the self-reflexivity of the system's operations. This autonomy preserves the integrity of the law's key function in differentiated societies – the stabilisation of individual and collective normative expectations over time.[4] The independence of law from political pressure and other irritants can only be guaranteed if this autonomy is preserved. By enforcing the principle of judicial independence, the judiciary participates in the organisational closure of the legal system.[5] This closure is preserved by the boundaries of law, which keep communications from other social systems, particularly the political system, outside the legal system. This is so because these communications are not relevant to the operation of the legal system.[6]

In this text, I will first show the conceptual underpinnings of systems theory and how it can be used to elucidate the legal system's functioning. In the second part of the essay, I concentrate on the role of the courts in modern legal systems. In the last part, I explain how judicial independence contributes to law's organisational closure as one of the essential condition of the maintenance of the rule of law.

---

3 Niklas Luhmann, *Law as a Social System*, Oxford University Press, Oxford, 2004.

4 Id., chapter 3.

5 Martine Valois, *Judicial Independence: Keeping Law at a Distance from Politics*, LexisNexis, Markham, Ontario, 2013.

6 Id., p. 102-103: "It [the legal system] does not pursue imperialist interests to attract as much communication as possible and to retain it in the system. It is not an attracting system. It only predicates: *if* law is to be used, that is, if there is a question of law as to law and injustice, it can be used only *in the terms set by the legal system*. Exactly in this sense the legal system is an operatively closed and structurally determined system."

2. Systems Theory Applied to Law

Before we enter into the fundamentals of systems theory, it must be pointed out that this theory does not pretend to depict the reality 'out there', that is, the reality which can be seen by the normal observer. Systems theory operates in the same way as Weber's ideal types;[7] it is a scientific method which serves to make sense of the contingent and complex reality of social facts. Systems theory places the observer in a second-order observation position.[8] The first observer is only capable of observing the object because its look remains fixed on the object.[9] Systems theory concerns what can be inferred using the observation of the first observer and his observation activity. From the second-order position, the observer can observe how others observe and make distinctions.[10] Furthermore, systems theory makes use of very abstract conceptual tools that are unique to that sociological theory, such as self-referential and autopoietic systems, binary codes, conditional programmes and structural couplings. We shall define those notions as we go on.

Social systems are not made of rules or institutions, or of social interactions between actors, but of communications. These communications convey a meaning that is relevant to the function of the system. Systems theory is thus concerned with societal communications 'that accept or reject statements, interpretations, decisions, theories, policies and so on'.[11] The function of every system is to organise societal communications in a way that all communications may be treated by the relevant system. Systems theory does not assess the performance of a system within society; it only depicts how social systems treat communications that are relevant to their function. In the legal system, the relevant communications are the ones relating to the distinction between what is legal and what is not. To illustrate the nature of legal communications, the authors Michael King and Chris Thornhill give the following examples:

> Law extends to all those communications that are understood as directly relating to the issue of legality or illegality. It extends, for example, to car-drivers arguing about which of them made the error of judgment which resulted in an accident, a customer insisting on his or her rights as a consumer that a shop reimburses him or her for faulty goods, a man refusing to pay maintenance for a child on the basis that the father could have been someone else. In all three examples what is invoked is law rather than some other system of communication.[12]

---

7 Max Weber, *Rudolf Stammler et le matérialisme historique*, Presses de l'Université Laval, Ste-Foy, Québec, 2001, p. 129.

8 Luhmann 2004 *supra* footnote 3, p. 94. Richard Nobles & David Schiff, *Observing Law through Systems Theory*, Hart, Oxford, 2013.

9 Micheal King & Chris Thornhill, *Niklas Luhmann's Theory of Politics and Law*, Hart, Oxford, 2006, p. 18.

10 Id., p. 19.

11 Id., p. 26.

12 Id., p. 36.

It is not because an event can be treated under law that it necessarily falls under the scope of the legal system. It is the legal meaning conveyed through the communications about these events that is relevant to the operations of the legal system. Legal communications are those that serve its societal function, that is, the stabilisation of normative and collective expectations over time.[13] In modern legal systems, law is made of legally regulated decisions. Modern law is thus positive, in the sense that it can be modified by another legally regulated decision, be it a judicial decision or a legislative decision. Only positive law is sufficiently flexible and alterable to respond to the individual and collective normative expectations of differentiated societies.

Social systems are said to be self-referential or autopoietic systems because they use their own reference for the production and reproduction of operations. Hence, a communication is a legal communication if it is treated as such by the legal system. The unity of the system resides in this self-reference since both lawful and unlawful communications are part of the legal system. The self-referential mode of reproduction of law also means that the law does not have to conform to any external authority in order to be considered as valid law by the system. The distinction of system/environment, which is at the heart of the systems theory, entails that the system's operations are closed to the environment of the system. Closure of the system does not amount to isolation;[14] the interaction of the system with the environment exists through structural couplings.

As far as the legal system is concerned, closure of the system means that the system will only use legal standards as programmes for conditional decisions. These decisions are the operations that assign the value legal or illegal. What cannot be treated under the binary code legal/illegal does not belong to the legal system, but to its environment.[15] In other words, the legal system is *normatively closed* but *cognitively opened*. We say that it is normatively closed because only legal communications may be treated internally by the system's operations. It is the system's closure that prevents expectations born out of other social systems from making their way into the legal system.

Every social system operates with a different binary code and structure of programme. The binary code of law is the legal/illegal distinction. This code applies not only to events occurring outside the legal system but also to legal decisions, since the legal system is a self-referential system. The binary code of law excludes the application of a third value, like, for instance, the moral or social acceptability of a court's ruling. The application of a third value would place a risk to the closure

13 Luhmann 2004 *supra* footnote 3, p. 148: "Concretely, law deals with the function of the stabilization of normative expectations by regulating how they are generalized in relation to their temporal, factual, and social dimensions. Law makes it possible to know which expectations will meet with social approval and which not." [footnote omitted].

14 Luhmann 2004 *supra* footnote 3, p. 80.

15 Id., p. 94.

of the legal system. This process is called 'dedifferentiation' by Luhmann. The dedifferentiation of the legal system means that legal norms are supplemented by other considerations irrelevant to the code and programming of the legal system. King and Thorhnhill define dedifferentiation in the following way:

> Where law's institutions (courts, tribunals, statutory drafting, prosecution services), for example, put into effect the policies of the government without giving due consideration to their legal applicability, overtly base their decisions upon the supposed reliability of witnesses who have wealthy connections, delegate responsibility for deciding cases to panels of scientific experts, actively seek to promote people's well-being or protect them from harm or leave matters to be decided by God's will, the legal system will have become dedifferentiated.[16]

Two components of modern law serve to maintain the differentiation of the legal system: a conditional programmes structure of law and organisational closure based on one binary code made up of only two values, legality and illegality. The separation of substantive and procedural law[17] is one of the evolutionary steps in the developments of positive law, which has permitted the introduction of a structure of conditional programmes into law (of the type 'if, then'). The conditional programmes form the architecture of modern legal systems and guarantee the existence of a differentiated legal system. The conditional programmes of law bind judges in their task of making decisions, while limiting their responsibility regarding the consequences of those decisions in the social system. The conditional programmes of law also participate in the stabilisation of law by preventing a change of legal norms even when they fail to respond to their anticipated benefits.[18]

Even when the legal system has achieved the stage of an independent normative order, it is still under the constant threat of dedifferentiation. Differentiated legal systems are constantly subjected to pressure asking for material expectations to be integrated in the normative order. This is so because social systems located in the legal system's environment continuously produce communications that irritate the legal system. The different social systems may not communicate with each other but can 'irritate' one another through their respective environments, which contain every other communication of society. These communications are forcing their way into the legal system to modify the conditional programmes of laws.

Every social system is cognitively open to its environment through the structural couplings it has with other systems. The cognitive openness of systems allows

16 King & Thornhill 2006 *supra* footnote 9, p. 41.

17 Niklas Luhmann, *La légitimation par la procédure*, Presses de l'Université Laval, Québec, 2001, p. 63. The differentiated legal system separates on the one side 'the supply sector of premises to legal decisions', characterized primarily by legislation, and on the other, the source of 'factual premises for decision' situated in the jurisdiction. In this way, the institutions that determine the facts (and therefore truth) and those that establish the law are distinct and socially separated; they are only confronted at the time of the judiciary proceedings.

18 King & Thornhill 2006 *supra* footnote 9, p. 16.

them to learn about expectations coming from other social systems. Structural couplings will occur when the operations of one system trigger a response from another system.[19] In such a case, an event will provoke a response in each system of communication, although it will not be interpreted in the same way because of the difference in coding and programming. Because the system's closure is a semantic closure, communications will not have the same meaning in every system. Legislation is an example of structural coupling between the legal and the political systems.[20] Legislation is communication relevant to both systems but it is not treated in the same way by each of them. While the political system may have a specific policy objective when proposing the adoption of legislation, once this policy is translated into a legal norm, it is treated differently in the legal system where only conditional programmes and a single binary code are allowed.

3. The Courts in Differentiated Societies

Now that we have gone through the essentials of systems theory epistemology, it is time to address the focal point of this paper, that is, whether Niklas Luhmann's systems theory provides a better understanding of how judicial independence can be protected in modern legal systems.

Like many sociologists before him, Luhmann studied the changes in societal evolution over time. He made the postulate of a transformation of the social structure in three successive phases: segmentation, stratification and functional differentiation. For Luhmann, the structure of law followed the transformation of the social organisation and has gone through the same phases of structural changes. Thus, the law has evolved from a state of segmentation where the social structure was essentially based on parental and tribal relationships, to a state of stratification, where law and the exercise of power were ranked according to social prestige, wealth or domination by a superior class over others, to the last stage of differentiation where the social organisation is neither horizontal nor vertical, but functional.

The functional differentiation of law can only be achieved when the production of legal rules are separated from systems of legitimation. The American sociologist Talcott Parsons placed the functional differentiation of law among the few evolutionary universals of societies. For him, the development of an independent normative order is one of the hallmarks of modernity.[21] He defined the independent legal order as follows:

> A general legal system is an integrated system of universalistic norms, applicable to the society as a whole rather than to a few functional or segmental sectors, highly

19 Luhmann 2004 *supra* footnote 3, p. 42-43.
20 King & Thornhill 2006 *supra* footnote 9, p. 44.
21 Talcott Parsons, Evolutionary Universals in Society, *American Sociological Review* 1964, 3, p. 353.

> generalized in terms of principles and standards, and relatively independent of both the religious agencies that legitimize the normative order of the society and vested interest groups in the operative sector, particularly in government.[22]

For Parsons, the establishment of the organisational independence of the judiciary was the crucial symbolic development which accompanied the institutionalisation of an independent normative order. In a universalistic system of rules, symbolised by positive law, the validity of legal norms is not made contingent upon its identification to religious or moral norms. Positive law is a distinctive system of law where the formalisation of procedural rules is independent of substantive legal rules. In democratic societies, the definition of substantive legal rules is the main responsibility of elected legislators, while the judiciary is entrusted with the task of applying substantive legal rules while following a well-defined set of procedural rules.

But in modern legal systems, the legislator often fails to respond to individual and collective normative expectations while the judiciary is pressured into deciding the legality of normative expectations that have been rejected by the legislative system. Normative expectations rejected by the legislative system are trying to make their way into the legal system. Unlike the legislative system, the judicial system does not control the type of cases that are brought before it. Furthermore, because of the prohibition of the denial of justice, the courts are forced to decide the legality of these expectations even in the absence of applicable norms for the solution of the legal dispute. As a result, the distinction between substantive and procedural law, which lies at the very foundation of positive law, becomes blurred by this new role of the courts that formulate the legal norms they have to apply.[23]

In *Law as a Social System*, Luhmann argued that because of the prohibition of the denial of justice, courts are placed in an exceptional position in the centre of the legal system.[24] The prohibition of the denial of justice is present in the French,

---

22 Id., p. 351.

23 *British Columbia v. Imperial Tobacco Canada Ltd.* supra (footnote 2), para. 51: "The judiciary has some part in the development of the law that its role requires it to apply. Through, for example, its interpretation of legislation, review of administrative decisions and assessment of the constitutionality of legislation, it may develop the law significantly. It may also make incremental developments to its body of previous decisions – i.e., the common law – in order to bring the legal rules those decisions embody into step with a changing society": *R. v. Salituro*, [1991] 3 S.C.R. 654, at p. 666.

24 Luhmann 2004 *supra* footnote 3, p. 275.

German and the Swiss civil codes,[25] as well as in the Quebec *Interpretation* Act.[26] Under this principle, judges cannot refuse to decide because of a lack of applicable norms or rules. The courts of autopoietic systems of law are internally different in the legal system. They operate in the centre of the legal system, while other structures (parliaments, lawyers, clients) are placed in the periphery of the system.[27] In this position of relative isolation, the courts regulate the operations of the legal system. These operations are restricted to the code and programmes of law. As we have seen earlier, the application of a third value is excluded. The court's duty is to apply only one or the other side of the binary code, depending on what the conditional programmes of law provide in relation to the specific fact-pattern it has to decide.

In that sense, we can say, as the Supreme Court of Canada in the *Mackin case* did regarding the relationship between courts and others, that the differentiation of courts in the legal system operates an 'intellectual separation'[28] between the norms and the irritants which are trying to make their way into judicial decision making. This separation is even more necessary in democratic societies where the political system controls the legislature and judicial intervention is increasingly sought to force a change in the law.

4. Judicial Independence *versus* Judicial Responsibility

The problem of judicial independence in complex societies lies in the constant requests made to the courts for a change to the law through judicial interpretation. These demands have put a considerable burden on the judiciary. Judges are now faced with the difficult task of deciding conflicts of values and solve problems that should have been dealt with by other social systems. It is not difficult to imagine how the pressure to decide cases even in the absence of applicable legal

25 In article 4 of the French Civil Code, it is stated that the judge cannot refuse to decide (translation) under the pretext of silence, obscurity or insufficiency of the law ("Le juge qui refusera de juger, sous prétexte du silence, de l'obscurité ou de l'insuffisance de la loi, pourra être poursuivi comme coupable de déni de justice."). Furthermore, in article 5, it is expressly stated that the judge cannot act as legislator to overcome the insufficiencies of the law (Il est défendu aux juges de prononcer par voie de disposition générale et réglementaire sur les causes qui leur sont soumises). There is thus a double interdiction placed on the judge, one being to refuse to decide in the absence of law and the other to make general rules.

26 *Interpretation Act*, RSQ, c. I-16: 41.2. A judge cannot refuse to adjudicate under pretext of the silence, obscurity or insufficiency of the law.

27 Nobles & Schiff 2013 *supra* footnote 8, p. 31.

28 *Mackin v. New Brunswick (Minister of Finance); Rice* c. *New Brunswick*, [2002] 1 S.C.R. 405, para. 37: "The concept of independence accordingly refers essentially to the nature of the relationship between a court and others. This relationship must be marked by a form of intellectual separation that allows the judge to render decisions based solely on the requirements of the law and justice. The legal standards governing judicial independence, which are the sources governing the creation and protection of the independent *status* of judges and the courts, serve to institutionalize this separation." (emphasis added).

norms may have on the impartiality and independence of the judiciary. One of the consequences that this combination of the prohibition of the denial of justice and the increase mobilisation of the judiciary to solve political or social conflicts has on judicial independence, is that judges are asked to take into account the effects of their decision in the social system. The tendency to make the justice system and judges 'responsible' or 'accountable' for the consequences of legal decisions threatens the autonomy of the legal system, because it introduces a criterion of social relevancy into decision making.[29] Law is constructed on a conditional programmes structure of the type, if – then[30] which prevents "any future facts, not accounted for at the time of the decision, from being relevant to a decision concerning legal or illegal".[31]

Judicial independence relies on the differentiation of a legal system working in a conditional programmes structure, as opposed to a purpose-specific programmes structure, which is oriented towards the achievement of predetermined outcomes, either political, economic or other. Under such a conditional programmes structure, judges are not requested to consider the objectives pursued by the normative system, nor are they required to verify whether the decisions will achieve the intended results. Furthermore, the legally imposed condition that decisions be made by an independent and impartial judge presupposes that it will be taken by a judge who is free of his other social relationships, whether parental, political, financial, or even moral or religious etc. Since the decision must be based solely on the law and the facts that are presented before the judge, he or she cannot be criticised on the basis of considerations that have not been taken into account in the process leading to the decision. By justifying his decision solely on the basis of written rules and recognised precedents, the judge frees himself from the undesired consequences of his decisions in the social system. Furthermore, by preventing situations where a judge has prejudged of the outcome of the application of the (legal/illegal) binary code in a decision, the principle of impartiality preserves uncertainty as to the outcome of litigation. The guarantee that judges will decide solely on the law and the facts proven before them ensures an almost complete neutralisation of the possible influence of their other social roles.

Judicial independence is both the condition and the consequence of the internal differentiation of courts in the legal system. Courts have to be insulated from the irritations of the environment of the legal system. It is in the centre of the legal system where judges are best protected from the pressures coming from the political system. Judicial independence is also a consequence of this central position where judges who benefit from the essential elements of judicial independence (security of tenure, financial security and administrative independence) can be shielded from criticism regarding the adverse effects of their decisions in the

29 Valois 2013 *supra* footnote 5.

30 Luhmann 2004 *supra* footnote 3, p. 197.

31 Id., p. 198.

social system.[32] Accountability must be reserved for government officials whose decisions are oriented towards goal-attainment objectives and who are elected on the basis that they will implement specific programmes.

Judicial independence also participates in the differentiation of the legal system and the political system. In the 1997 *Provincial Judge Reference,* the Supreme Court of Canada held that the three components of security of tenure, financial security and administrative independence derive from the "constitutional imperative that, to the extent possible, the relationship between the judiciary and the other branches of government be depoliticized".[33] In systems theory, this constitutional requirement is only another way of saying that the legal system is functionally differentiated from the political system and that communications about the legal principle of judicial independence are relevant to the legal system, not the political system. Thus, when courts claim that they guarantee the rule of law, they contribute to the preservation of the differentiation of law. Only an independent judicial system can safeguard the rule of law, because the legislature is too close to the political system, and contract is bound by to the instrumental considerations of the parties interested in the law. As 'central guardians of the rule of law',[34] courts are essential to the maintenance of an independent normative order. Who but the judges can delimit the boundaries between the legal and the political systems? In a recent Supreme Court of Canada's decision concerning the constitutionality of supervised drug injection sites, Chief Justice McLachlin reminded the federal government that once translated into law, governmental policy choices are no longer relevant to the political system and must be treated as communications belonging to the legal system.[35] The Court also pointed out to the government that moral considerations were irrelevant to the issue of the constitutionality of legislation.[36]

32 Id., p. 202: "The more a decision is supported by such purpose-specific reasons, the higher the probability that it is wrong; for the future remains unknown – even to judges. Purpose-specific reasons expose judges to empirical criticism, which leaves only the authority of office and the necessity of decision-making to render judicial decisions valid."

33 *Reference re Remuneration of Judges of the Provincial Court (P.E.I.)*, [1997] 3 S.C.R., para. 131.

34 *Ell v. Alberta*, [2003] 1 S.C.R. 857, para. 31.

35 *Canada (Attorney General) v. PHS Community Services Society*, [2011] 3 S.C.R. 134, para 105: "The issue of illegal drug use and addiction is a complex one which attracts a variety of social, political, scientific and moral reactions. There is room for disagreement between reasonable people concerning how addiction should be treated. It is for the relevant governments, not the Court, to make criminal and health policy. However, when a policy is translated into law or state action, those laws and actions are subject to scrutiny under the *Charter*".

36 Id., para. 102: "The second strand of Canada's choice argument is a moral argument that those who commit crimes should be made to suffer the consequences. On this point it suffices to say that whether a law limits a Charter right is simply a matter of the purpose and effect of the law that is challenged, not whether the law is right or wrong. The morality of the activity the law regulates is irrelevant at the initial stage of determining whether the law engages a s. 7 right."

5. Conclusion

In Weber's sociology of law, the empirical validity is the meaning ascribed to a legal rule by the actors or, in other words, the shared understanding of its validity and enforceability.[37] The sociological validity of a rule can only be determined empirically; precedents or legal rules of interpretation are of no help in that determination, although they might be of great assistance in assessing the juridical validity. To be really effective, the constitutionally guaranteed principle of judicial independence depends on the existence of sociological conditions that serve as empirical foundations to its legal validity. As we have tried to demonstrate, these sociological requisites are the preservation of the conditional programmes of law and the limitation of the judges' responsibility for the consequences of their decisions in the social system. It is under these sociological conditions that the legal principle of judicial independence can acquire its empirical validity in the legal system.

At the level of the legal system, the principle of judicial independence preserves the uncertainty as to the outcome of litigation and contributes to limit the responsibility of judges for the consequences of their decisions in the social system. Judicial independence participates in the autonomy of the judicial system, and in the autonomy of law as a universal, general, and conditional normative order. The keystone to a strong principle of judicial independence is the independence of law from other systems of legitimation such as politics, religion and the market, and a tradition of respect for the judicial role in the legal system. That tradition of respect is one of the most important element in the evaluation of the empirical validity of the principle of judicial independence. As we have seen, in the British legal tradition and in Canada, the lack of a norm of judicial independence in a written constitution was not a bar to the recognition of a strong principle of judicial independence mostly based on tradition.[38]

The determination of the scope of the protection provided by judicial independence is the key to preserving the internal boundaries of the legal system, which keeps courts at a distance from the law's other sub-systems. The norm of judicial independence effects the separation that must exist between the law and the extraneous influences that seek to introduce themselves into judicial decision-making.[39] As guardians of the rule of law, judges are the keepers of this separation between the law and the irritants of the legal system's environment.[40] The autonomy of law depends on this capacity of the judiciary to maintain that buffer zone between

37 Weber 2001 *supra* footnote 7, p. 130.

38 *Valente v. The Queen*, [1985] 2 S.C.R. 673, para. 34: "Lord Sankey, L.C., said in Parliament: The independence and prestige which our judges have enjoyed in their position have rested far more upon the great tradition and long usage with which they have always been surrounded, than upon any Statute. The greatest safeguard of all may be found along these lines for traditions cannot be repealed, but an Act of Parliament can be."

39 *Mackin v. New Brunswick (Minister of Finance); Rice v. New Brunswick, supra*, footnote 28, para. 35.

40 Valois 2013 *supra* footnote 5.

law and politics.[41] The Supreme Court of Canada's decision in the *Insite* case is a remarkable example of how judges can stand up to the politicians. Unfortunately, even in democratic countries, judges do not always dare to do it.[42]

In the *Provincial Judges Reference,* the Supreme Court of Canada established a strong precedent for the protection of judicial independence and the autonomy of law. Despite the harsh criticism directed towards the Court in the aftermath of the decision, the scope given to the principle of judicial independence by the Court was praised for in other jurisdictions.[43] The fear of a 'government of judges' should never make one forget that only courts can enforce the legal limits which check political authority and prevent the abuse of power.

41 Amnon Reichman, Judicial Non-dependence: Operational Closure, Cognitive Openness, and the Underlying Rationale of the *Provincial Judges Reference* – The Israeli Perspective, *in* Adam Dodek & Lorne Sossin (eds.), *Judicial Independence in Context*, Irwin Law, Toronto, 2010

42 In Israel, the Supreme Court upheld the legal validity of a coalition agreement between the Labor Party and Shas which instituted a committee composed of five lawyers and a retired judge whose task was to review judicial decision of the Israeli Supreme Court and determine if it kept in line with the status quo in matters of religion: HCJ 5364/94 *Velner v. Chairman of the Labor Party*, IsrSC 49(1) 758 (1994) referred to in Reichman (2010) *supra* footnote 41, p. 441.

43 Id.

'Markers' vs. 'Makers': Are Constitutional Courts Legal or Political Actors?

*Mauro Zamboni**

1. Introduction

In the opening speech for a theme conference a couple of years ago on judicial activism at Georgetown University, retired Justice Sandra Day O'Connor stated:

> Directing anger toward judges has had a long tradition in our nation... While scorn for some judges is not altogether new, I do think that the breadth of the unhappiness being currently expressed, not only by public officials but in public opinion polls in the nation, shows that there is a level of unhappiness today that perhaps is greater than in the past and is certainly cause for great concern.[1]

This statement by a former Justice of the US Supreme Court reveals an evident and somehow disturbing aspect characterizing the role of the judiciary not only in the US, but in almost all well-established Western democracies: judicial activism, and in general the role judges play in the political game, one of hottest topics of debate inside the legal world.[2] As Justice O'Connor's words show, this discussion not only affects the intricate relations judicial power has with its surrounding environments, but also the (Hartian) normative perspective as to the issue, i.e. the self-vision judges (and the legal world) have of themselves and their role in this network of relations.[3]

Since judicial activism primarily focuses on the point of the relations between law and politics, the main purpose of this article is to evaluate whether Constitutional Courts should be considered as simply 'markers' of the constitution, i.e. legal actors simply enforcing that written by political actors in statutes and constitutions, or as 'makers' of the constitution, i.e. institutional actors with a predominant nature

---

* Prof. dr. M. Zamboni is Professor at the Faculty of Law, Stockholm University, Sweden and Visiting Professor at the Faculty of Law, University of Groningen, the Netherlands.

1 *See* Sandra Day O'Connor, *Importance of an Independent Judiciary* (Conference on the State of the Judiciary), available at <www.law.georgetown.edu/webcast/eventDetail.cfm?eventID=178>.

2 *See, e.g.*, European Commission for Democracy Through Law (Venice Commission), The Binding Effect of Federal Constitutional Court Decisions upon Political Institutions (available at <www.venice.coe.int/docs/2003/CDL-JU(2003)018-e.pdf>).

3 *See* H.L.A. Hart, *The Concept of Law* (2nd Ed.), Clarendon Press, Oxford, 1994, p. 239. *See also* H.L.A. Hart, Problems of the Philosophy of Law, *in* H.L.A. Hart, *Essays in Jurisprudence and Philosophy*, Clarendon Press, Oxford, 1983, p. 103-105.

of being political in determining what the law should say. This investigation considers in particular not only the function Constitutional Courts play as a bridge between law and politics, but also the very positioning of this bridge. These results are of particular importance in determining what the existence of this point of passage between law and politics implies, on one hand, whether these courts are a necessary requirement for the concept of democracy and, on the other, whether primarily 'political' criteria that need to be fulfilled, particularly the requirement of being 'democratic,' are applicable to such courts.

The basic thesis of this work is that Constitutional Courts, though playing a bridging role between the political and legal worlds, from an institutional and functional perspective are still primarily legal actors. These Courts play without doubt a role in the political game; however their location as an institutional actor should be based on the direct effects of their decisions ('outputs') within the legal arena rather than on their indirect consequences ('outcomes') in the political arena. Thus the primary responsibility of Constitutional Courts is towards the legal community and the paradigms governing its discourse. By underscoring the legal nature and function of these courts, it is also possible to offer some criteria for moulding the ideal-typical structure of a Constitutional Court, namely a court that in its formation and working is truly independent from both the political and socio-economic arenas. In order to preserve in particular the legal nature of the Courts towards the political and social actors, this work suggests a shift of focus in the reforms from substantive decisions to more 'democratic' procedures in Constitutional Courts.

This article certainly makes no pretense of providing any final words either in the discussion on judicial activism or as to the relations between the legal and political worlds in general, whatever the 'solution'.[4] The focus here is also solely on Western legal systems. This work has the more limited objective of contributing to clarifying the terms of the discussion, in particular by finding a solid base (at least from a legal perspective) from which to begin the discussion on whether judicial activism is good or bad. In other words, this investigation has primarily a *legal theoretical* task, at least in a loose Hartian meaning of the words: To clarify that meant when the legal discussion deals with the 'political' in the work of Constitutional Courts.

After defining certain key-concepts used in this article, the focus in Part II is on the importance of judicial activism when dealing in particular with Constitutional Courts. Part III views the typical features of Constitutional Courts in well-established Western democracies, i.e. their 'in-the-middle' position between the legal and political arenas. The central Parts IV and V then identify why the characterization of Constitutional Courts, as either legal or political actors, is so relevant from a legal perspective, both in descriptive and normative terms. These parts also explore how it is possible, at least from a legal theoretical perspective, to

4 *See* Jeremy Waldron, *Law and Disagreement*, Oxford University Press, Oxford, 2001, p. 231.

resolve the dilemma of 'legal vs. political actors' by defining Constitutional Courts as legal actors performing a political function.

Based on this legal theoretical characterization, the final Parts VI and VII sketch certain of the consequences as far as concerns the relevance of questioning an 'activist' Constitutional Courts in relation to the idea of democracy. In particular, Part VII examines the necessity of shifting the focus of attention, when dissecting the necessity of Constitutional Courts more in-line with the ideal of democracy, from a substantive perspective to more procedural standpoints.

2. Some Definitions

Before starting, definitions must be clarified with respect to some of the concepts used throughout the text. First, *judicial activism*, though sometimes also referred to under different guises (*e.g.* 'constitutional politics,' 'government of judges' or 'judicialization of politics'), identifies in general the phenomenon, typical (but not only) of well-established Western democracies, when 'courts impose a judicial solution over an issue erstwhile subject to political resolution' by intervening and striking down a part of properly enacted legislation, or by 'legislating' in an area in the absence of legislation.[5] Judicial activism then identifies a judicial activity directed at stretching the formal structures and letter of the law (in particular at the constitutional level) in order to fill gaps left by politicians. This is done by judges in order to implement those values the political actors are unable to sense in the community, or are unable to transform into legislative measures, or simply those that are part of the political baggage of certain judges.

Second, when referring to *Constitutional Courts*, included here are all the highest courts that although under different names (*e.g.* High Council or Supreme Court), have among their legal duties the jurisdiction to evaluate the constitutionality, i.e. the consistency or conflict of legally relevant documents produced in a certain legal system in reference to the basic legal documents of a community. Such courts are also characterized, at least with respect to conducting constitutional reviews, for being positioned somehow outside the ordinary court system and for their work being completely independent (at least in their working modalities) of the other branches of public authority. For this reason, the other fundamental function of Constitutional Courts is often to eventually resolve conflicts between these different branches, in particular in terms of that defined as legally competence according to the constitutional document or fundamental law.

5 David L. Anderson, When Restraint Requires Activism: Partisan Gerrymandering and the Status Quo Ante, *Stanford Law Review*, Vol. 42, No. 6, 1990, p. 1570. *See also* Robert H. Bork, *The Tempting of America: The Political Seduction of the Law*, Touchstone, New York, 1991 and, for a more articulated definition of the term 'activism', Mark V. Tushnet, Tushnet: Comment on Cox, *Maryland Law Review* 1987, p. 147-153 and Greg Jones, Proper Judicial Activism, *Regent University Law Review*, Vol. 14, 2002, No. 1, p. 142-145.

It is worth noting that under this definitional umbrella, several types of Constitutional Courts can find a place. In particular, this definition allows placing under scrutiny both Constitutional Courts that have an abstract review competence (i.e. when a Constitutional Court is asked to decide the compatibility of statutory law with the Constitution at the request of non-judicial public bodies, *e.g.* a law-drafting committee of the National Assembly or a regional government), and those who have a more concrete review power (i.e. when a Constitutional Court's review jurisdiction is activated by a party to litigation pleading that a law violates the constitutional texts).

Third, the definition of political actors adopted here is fairly different from that used by the other discipline that also investigates the role of Constitutional Courts in and towards the political system, political science. While for the latter political actors are more or less identified with all the institutional actors that 'make the law,' by political actors in this article, at least from a legal perspective, is intended a narrower range of institutional entities whose primary goal is to see their values implemented into a community by making use of the legal apparatus and system, *e.g.* political parties or interests-groups. Political actors can (and usually do) have a primary goal of a non-legal nature (*e.g.* economic nature) and therefore mainly take into consideration the surrounding political environment. Moreover, their primary intent is to influence people into adopting a certain model of behavior by means of convincing the addressees of the 'inner goodness' of their model.[6]

Finally, particularly in Western legal systems, legal actors can be defined as those institutional actors primarily aiming at affecting the legal system, and therefore, mainly focusing on the latter's logical structure.[7] Similarly to political actors, the main goal for legal actors is to exercise power, i.e. the concrete capacity of forcing people to do things that they otherwise are not willing to do.[8] As pointed out by Hans Kelsen, both law and politics try to make people do something, the law being 'a social order, that is to say an order regulating the mutual behavior of human beings.'[9] However, that important for a legal actor dealing with a statute or legal precedent is these exist and exercise their (binding) power on the addressees only as part of a larger hierarchical system of norms with a similar (legal) nature,

6 *See* Gunther Teubner, Substantive and Reflexive Elements in Modern Law, *Law and Society Review*, Vol. 17, 1983, No. 2, p. 259.

7 *See* Max Weber, *Economy and Society: An Outline of Interpretive Sociology* (G. Roth & C. Wittich eds.), University of California Press, Berkeley, 1978, p. 657. *See also* Kaarlo Tuori, *Critical Legal Positivism*, Ashgate Publishing, Aldershot, 2002, p. 36-39.

8 *See* Max Weber, *The Theory of Social and Economic Organization* (T. Parsons ed.), Free Press, Glencoe, Illinois, 1964, p. 152.

9 *See* Hans Kelsen, Law, State, and Justice in the Pure Theory of Law, *in* H. Kelsen, *What is justice? Justice, Law and Politics in the Mirror of Science*, University of California Press, Berkeley, 1957, p. 289.

and according to specific (legal) rules to be used for interpretation, application and creation (legal reasoning).[10]

3. The Importance of Judicial Activism by Constitutional Courts

The 'creative' interpretation, or judicial activism, of legal texts is a phenomenon generally characterizing all courts in a legal system, from the lowest county court to the highest court. However, despite that asserted in general by some socio-legal scholars, judicial activism somehow becomes a 'more evident' issue when addressed by and to Constitutional Courts (and all the highest courts in general, *e.g.* the French Court of Cassation).

Using Niklas Luhmann's distinction between the social system and other sub-systems internal to it, it is first possible to see that the judicial activism taking place by Constitutional Courts tends to become more visible because it normally deals with fundamental questions relevant to all the other sub-systems, i.e. questions that by their nature can affect not only the legal or political arenas, but every arena and every person of a national community. Decision-making by Constitutional Courts has as its object the fundamental laws of a community, and one of the features of well-established democracy is the (actual or potential) intrusion of the law in all the aspects of community life.[11] Moreover, the typically high degree of social legitimacy Constitutional Courts possess, i.e. among all actors of a certain community, contributes to rendering every decision taken by these courts more than simply a question of law and politics.

When judicial activism takes place at the constitutional level, as a consequence it potentially reaches out to the social community at large, or at least, using Luhmann's terminology, it creates 'noises' that can somehow 'disturb' the internal work (*autopoiesis*) of all the other subsystems.[12] This is valid both for Constitutional Courts with a jurisdiction of abstract review and also for those with a more concrete review jurisdiction. For example, in a specific euthanasia case, a Constitutional Court's decision can face issues relevant for cultural or religious subsystems, namely the general question of how far the State can interfere with individual rights, or whether the 'right to live' includes also the necessity for the

---

10 *See* Hans Kelsen, *The Pure Theory of Law*, University of California Press, Berkeley, 1970, p. 3-4, 193. *See also* Hans Kelsen, *Introduction to the Problems of Legal Theory*, Clarendon Press, Oxford, 1996 [1934], p. 11: "To comprehend something legally can only be to comprehend it as law."

11 *See* Marc Galanter, Law Abounding: Legalisation Around the North Atlantic, *Modern Law Review*, Vol. 55, 1992, No. 1, p. 13-14. *See also* Lawrence M. Friedman, Total Justice, Russell Sage Foundation, New York , 1985, p. 147-152; Lawrence M. Friedman, *The Republic of Choice: Law, Authority, and Culture*, Harvard University Press, Cambridge, Massachusetts, 1998, p. 15; Niklas Luhmann, *Law as a Social System*, Oxford University Press, Oxford, 2004, p. 273; and Antonie A.G. Peters, Law as Critical Discussion, *in* G. Teubner (ed.), *Dilemmas of Law in the Welfare State*, Walter de Gruyter, Berlin, 1988, p. 252-254.

12 *See* Gunther Teubner, *Law as an autopoietic system*, Blackwell, Oxford, 1993, chapter 5.

public authorities to implement this right against the consensus of the 'owner' of such right.

The second factor underlying the importance of judicial activism by Constitutional Courts has to do to their being the highest judicial body of a legal system. From a more specific legal sub-system perspective, judicial activism is important throughout all the levels of the judicial system. However, in the majority of cases, it is questionable whether lower level judicial law-making, though directly important for the community, can actually in an indirect way influence the higher level. For instance, a county court's law-making interpretation of a specific county council directive on shop-licenses to allow for a certain kind of business in town tends, for natural reasons derived by its limited jurisdiction, to have an impact confined to the local implementing administrative offices. On the other hand, even such a simple issue in the exceptional case can occasionally have reverberations throughout the entire judicial system, for example when it is a question of a pornography shop and freedom of speech.

When it comes to Constitutional Courts, their influence as a rule transcends all lower and intermediate levels, affecting the entirety of the legal structure, i.e. including the lower structure, and a large part of the political world. This influence, and consequently relevance of constitutional judicial activism over all that is legal and political, is both due to the very structure of the legal system (i.e. its being hierarchical) and for the typically high degree of legal legitimacy these types of courts have gained historically from the actors belonging to the legal arena. The centrality of the law-making of the Constitutional Courts is also recognizable in the fact that, when discussing judicial activism, most critical voices, whether in academia, politics or the judiciary, end up in with these Courts as main targets (and not the lower courts).

4. 'Makers' vs. 'Markers': Constitutional Courts as 'in-the-middle' Actors

When dealing with the issue of Constitutional Courts in relation to politics, the first question is where these institutional actors should be positioned on an imaginary map on which there are two ideal-typical continents, namely the legal world and the political world. The role played by the courts in general and the Constitutional Courts in particular is extremely important in every legal system, in both the legal and political systems.[13]

As far as concerns the legal system, Constitutional Courts are ranked at the top, being the supreme and ultimate interpreters of the constitution and consequently, of the constitutionality of different law-making measures, in particular (but not

13 *See, e.g., generally* Bruce Ackerman (ed.), *Bush v. Gore. The Question of Legitimacy*, Yale University Press, New Haven, 2002, where a decision of the Supreme Court is analyzed by looking at its effects both in the legal as well as in the political worlds.

exclusively) statutes. Constitutional review is the legal competence allowing the courts to enjoy an exclusive decision-making power and a legal superiority in relation to the other branches of power.[14]

In addition to this central position within the legal structure, Constitutional Courts also tend to occupy a dominant place in the political building characterizing a democratic form of state. Constitutional Courts are entrusted by the political system (and through it by the community as such) as the ultimate guardians of the basic values that inspired the Founding Fathers and Mothers when writing the fundamental documents (or in establishing the fundamental customs) underpinning and regulating the life of the political community.

If seen from the perspective of the relations of law and politics, however, one can assert that Constitutional Courts actually occupy a third position at a much deeper level, functioning as a sort of transfer point between the legal and political worlds. If one considers the primary (though often implicit in the building of a modern democracy) position occupied by Constitutional Courts, this can be identified as a bridge between values produced in the political world and legal thinking.[15] Due to their 'in-the-middle' position, and their consequent relevance both for the political and the legal worlds, it is not then surprising that Constitutional Courts have been the favorite target of investigations by the discipline primarily concerned with the political world and its surroundings, namely political science.

As previously seen, the primary function of a Constitutional Court is constitutional review, i.e. to continuously monitor the compatibility of legislation and other normative measures with the basic values as announced in the constitution or fundamental law. The basic problem, at least from a legal perspective, is that the constitution is legal in nature, i.e. it is binding towards the addressees. Its message, however, namely the models of behaviors prescribed, is heavily affected by the fact that constitutions are not only written by political actors (as are most legal measures) but that they also often are the product of extremely complex political compromises or very general political statements. Their being a political product, the constitution or fundamental law tends to be written less in legal terms, i.e. in terms of (at least in the intention) 'if-x-then-y' or 'either-or' statements, and more in terms of political messages, i.e. in terms that resemble the political propaganda, where the fundamental goals to be achieved in the community are designed in terms of models of behavior the political actors want to be 'realized' in the community itself.[16]

14 *See, e.g.*, the landmark decision by US Supreme Court in *Marbury v. Madison*, 5 US (1 Cranch) 177 (1803).

15 *See, e.g.*, the debate on the French Constitutional Council as reported by Martin Shapiro & Alex Sweet Stone, *On Law, Politics, and Judicialization*, Oxford University Press, Oxford, 2002, p. 81.

16 "One lesson of American constitutional experience is that words of each provision in the Bill of Rights tend to take on a life of their own, becoming the obsessive catchphrase for expressing everything one might want to say about the right in question.", *see* Waldron 2001 *supra*, p. 220.

On the other end, constitutional documents are regarded for historical reasons as the highest sources of law in Western legal systems. This means that they are treated as legal documents, having the strongest binding force on all the national law-making and law-applying agencies and the community as well. In other words, constitutions or fundamental laws in general have a content that tends to be dominated by the logics of the political discourse, but is inserted into a shell which has the form of a law, shaping and somehow determining the agenda for the entire legal arena of a certain community.[17]

Since the primary goal of a Constitutional Court is somehow to 'guard' such documents, how this institutional actor tends to end up being a sort of 'in-the-middle' actor is easily understood. Three different features affect Constitutional Courts, rendering it an actor that though they have their feet in the legal world, they tend to lean heavily towards the political arena.

First, Constitutional Courts are an 'in-the-middle' actor from an *institutional perspective*, i.e. from the perspective of where these courts are positioned among the different organizations in a certain community having the primary goal of governing the behavior of individuals, characterized for being permanent as well as making and enforcing rules governing human behavior. Constitutional Courts are in the middle in the sense that their institutional position as an intermediary link between the political actors, is represented in particular by the various assemblies with law-making powers, and the legal actors, mostly in the forms of judges and all the legal apparatus, having as a primary duty the implementation of the product of the political law-making.

A Constitutional Court has the position of being a legal institution, i.e. an organization constructed for taking care of certain important legal issues from a legal perspective, namely the constitutional review of statutes and other legal documents, and not, for example, the political opportunity of statutes. At the same time, a Constitutional Court indirectly places the activities and operations of political actors, such as national or local assemblies, under scrutiny. It is true that its evaluation is directly legal in nature, but it is also true that the main voice political actors have, at least in a democratic form of a state that has adopted rule of law, is the law. Each time Constitutional Courts modify, approve or even remain silent as to that which political actors have expressed through the law, the courts operate in the political institutional arena, particularly by allowing or disallowing certain political actors to produce statements that are directly relevant and binding for the entire community from which such actors have been (directly or indirectly) chosen. In other words, Constitutional Courts are 'in-the-middle' institutional actors because they are gate-keepers, allowing the actors operating in the political world to be heard (or not) in the legal world.

17 *See* Waldron 2001 *supra*, p. 221-222, calling for not formalizing rights into a fixed constitutional document due to their very political nature (and therefore adaptable to the wishes of the representative institutions).

At the side of this institutional factor, i.e. concerning the very location of Constitutional Courts among the different actors, a second factor operates from a *structural perspective* in such a way as to render Constitutional Courts as 'in-the-middle' actors between the political and legal arenas; this factor has to do with the element characterizing the configuration of these highest courts as different from that of other types of courts.

It has previously been mentioned how Constitutional Courts reside outside of the ordinary court system and are independent from other branches of the public authorities. However, Constitutional Courts always tend to present a certain 'structural cohesion' with the actors belonging to the political arena. By this is meant that almost all Western legal systems have foreseen that political actors, either as legislators or within the executive branch, can have partial (as in Italy) or total (as in the US) control as far as concerns the individuals who are to sit as justices in the Constitutional Courts. As a consequence, the political arena and the ideologies prevailing within it, by means of the legal power to decide who will be justices, affect and somehow overlap the very structure of the courts and their fundamental components.

Despite this important political influence in deciding the structure of Constitutional Courts, these courts cannot be considered as having a pure and exclusive 'political structure'. This type of structure, when it occurs at least in Western legal systems, is of an exceptional nature, such as for revolutionary courts (*e.g.* during the French revolution) or for 'people courts' in totalitarian states (e.g. in Germany during the last years of World War II). On the contrary, though they can (and often are) politicized individuals. The predominant feature of individuals sitting on Constitutional Courts normally is that they are always chosen from among lawyers or individuals with formal education in law.

In other words, even when all justices are chosen based on political considerations, and according to their personal political ideologies and affiliation, the selection process is limited (either by law or by constitutional customs) to individuals trained at least formally in the art of law, *e.g.* holding a law degree. Moreover, most (but not all) of the time the recruitment procedures require that the candidates have spent some years working in the judiciary branch at a high level.

Finally, Constitutional Courts can be defined as being 'in-the-middle' actors between the political and legal arenas from a *functional perspective*, i.e. by observing the function these courts play in the relations between lawyers and politicians. In this work, function refers to the function-as-effects of a certain institution on a certain environment, in this case, the concrete outcomes that the work of Constitutional Courts have on structures in both the legal and political worlds.

Viewed from this functional perspective, one can note how Constitutional Courts perform an intermediary function between these two arenas. As briefly sketched above, one of the major contributions of Constitutional Courts to the community is mediating between the highly political statements present in the constitution, i.e. statements dominated, from a legal perspective, by the substantive rationality of the political discourse, and the 'legally relevant' concepts and categories, i.e. concepts binding public officials and the community in general due to their observance of the parameters of formal rationality required by a certain community from a legal system.

This mediating role played by Constitutional Courts is not only in the direction towards the legal world in defining for its actors in legal terms what the general statements of goals enunciated in the constitutional documents or practices mean, for example, by guiding a justice in the interpretation of constitutionally questionable statutes or parts thereof. The mediating role is also played in the direction towards the political arena as the decisions of Constitutional Courts set the legal frameworks that the political actors in their law-making ought to respect, for example by extensively discussing the right of 'due process' with regards to a new administrative procedural statute.

This mediating role has not only a horizontal dimension, i.e. among different arenas in the same system, but also a vertical one. In particular, it is worth briefly noting how Constitutional Courts play a decisive role in mediating the values produced at international or supranational levels into the national legal arena. A classic example is the US Supreme Court's decision in *Lawrence vs. Texas*, or several of the decisions taken by different European national courts in order to further implement the values of the EU fundamental charters.[18]

Since a constitution is the product of the will of a community (through their political representatives), at least in theory, Constitutional Courts in a democratic state play the function of mediating to the community and, in particular, to its political representatives, the value-message that this very community and its political actors originally adopted, but now in terms of a legal message, i.e. a message also and primarily directed to the actors endorsed with the duty of implementing the legal rules as 'interpreted' (or accepted) by the Constitutional Court. As the American legal realists and Alf Ross pointed out, judges in general play a decisive role as the point of passage where the 'law-in-books' becomes 'law-in-action,' i.e. the normative apparatus of rules felt as binding by the population or by the officers.[19]

In this case, Constitutional Courts have the primary function of translating into binding norms for the political actors and the community the law-in-books that the very latter have enacted. Constitutions tend to be documents where the political

18 *See*, the US Supreme Court decision in striking down the sodomy law in Texas with *Lawrence v. Texas*, 539 US 558 (2003). In particular, Justice Anthony Kennedy, citing a European Court of Human Rights' case (*Dudgeon v. United Kingdom*, 1981, signs an opening of the 'parochial character' of some parts of the American legal system, in particular at the State level, to the political globalizing political values, *e.g.* equality regardless of sexual orientation).

19 *See* Ronald Dworkin, *Freedom's Law: The Moral Reading of the American Constitution*,: Harvard University Press, Cambridge, Massachusetts, 1996, p. 7-15; and Waldron 2001 *supra*, p. 262.

origins of the law, a typical feature of contemporary law, surface more clearly than in other legal documents (*e.g.* a statute regulating taxation law). Constitutions are often used not only as a legal document grounding a new legal system, but also as a primary form of a 'political symbol', i.e. as a message to the community by the political actors as to which fundamental values the state/community is based. Moreover, and as a consequence of this partial political nature, legal language in the Constitution tends to be interspersed with the political language. A classic example in this sense is the article of the Italian constitution stating that property ownership is guaranteed by the law as long as it fulfills its social function.[20]

This being the situation, where judges by their nature are the intermediaries between the 'paper-law' and 'real-law,' and the 'paper-law' being the Constitution, a mixture of political statements and legal concepts, it is then not surprising that more than in the other branches of the judiciary, Constitutional Courts become the 'makers' by being the 'markers.' As already pointed out by many legal theoretical approaches focusing on the legal discourse, regardless of whether their competence is of concrete or abstract constitutional review, the adjudication power that is typical for every court, therefore even for the Constitutional Courts, tends to become a law-making power. The very text to 'mark' is so vague that the 'marking' of its content and of its border becomes a 'making' (at least if seen from a legal perspective) of the law directly applicable in concrete cases (as for the concrete constitutional review) or in general (as for the abstract constitutional review).[21]

In summary, Constitutional Courts, for all the reasons mentioned above, are a special type of institutional actor that positions themselves among the 'markers' of the law, i.e. they are mostly actors aiming at interpreting and applying the law, but at the same time largely overlap with the 'makers' zone, i.e. through interpretation Constitutional Courts shape the very law.[22] This being the situation, the question naturally arises as to whether and why it really is necessary, from a legal perspective, to insert Constitutional Courts into a box with either 'legal actors' or 'political actors' labels.

5. Why Is A Definition, either Legal or Political, So Important For Constitutional Courts?

Shifting attention to the central question of this work, namely whether Constitutional Courts should be defined as either primarily legal or political actors, a

20 Italian Constitution, Art. 42: "Property is public or private. Economic assets may belong to the State, to public bodies or to private persons. Private property is recognized and guaranteed by the law, which prescribes the ways it is acquired, enjoyed and its limitations so as to ensure its *social function* and make it accessible to all" (emphasis added).

21 *See* Gunther Teubner, And God Laughed... Indeterminacy, Self- Reference and Paradox in Law, *in* J.-P. Dupuy & G. Teubner (eds.), *Paradoxes of Self-Reference in the Humanities, Law and the Social Science*, Anma Libri, Stanford, 1991, p. 31.

22 *See* Luhmann 2004 *supra*, p. 235.

first reaction can be to question the importance of this very issue. It appears to be a purely terminological question as the competence and jurisdiction accorded to Constitutional Courts tend, at least in well-established Western democracies, to be the same from a legal perspective, regardless of whether they are considered more political or more legal actors operating inside a certain system of powers. Regardless of whether they are considered primarily as legal or political actors, justices sitting in the highest benches will always be in charge of deciding the constitutionality of statutes and, by doing this, will always be influenced by the political environment and their political ideologies.

However, this is not simply a definitional or academic problem.[23] As often happens for legal matters, defining something or someone means attributing it with certain legal areas of competence and jurisdiction and, at the same time, limiting its capacity to operate in other legal areas.[24] In other words, when it comes to legal issues, the classification of either a problem or a subject matter means shaping it and, at the same time, reducing it.[25]

If one considers in particular Constitutional Courts and the definition of their nature as actors working in a certain environment, it has been previously seen that among their central tasks is 'controlling' that the transformations of ideologies or values into law are done according (or at least not grossly contrary) to the basic and often politically formulated principles enumerated in the constitution or fundamental law of a certain community.

The characterization of Constitutional Courts as either being legal or political actors brings with it the identification of fundamental criteria, or in Max Weber's terminology, 'rationalities,' that ought to govern this control of the constitutionality of the law-making taking place in a certain legal system.[26] By defining the nature and function of Constitutional Courts, it then is possible to answer the following normative question that is fundamental for every democratic legal system: What is the fundamental criterion that ought to guide a Constitutional Court when performing its task of constitutional review?

Considering the fact that Constitutional Courts operate as 'in-the-middle' actors between the legal and political worlds, it is possible to identify two fundamental criterion, or rationalities, inspiring Constitutional Courts in their work. First, at

23 *See* Waldron 2001 *supra*, 229.

24 *See* Timothy Andrew Orville Endicott, Law and Language, *in* J. L. Coleman & S. Shapiro (eds.), *Handbook of Jurisprudence and Legal Philosophy*, Oxford University Press, Oxford, 2002, p. 935-968.

25 *See, e.g.*, Linda L. Berger, Applying the New Rhetoric to Legal Discourse: The Ebb and Flow of Reader and Writer, Text and Context, *Journal of Legal Education*, Vol. 49, 1999, No. 2, p. 155. *See also* Peter Goodrich, *Legal Discourse: Studies in Linguistics, Rhetoric, and Legal Analysis*, Palgrave Macmillan, London, 1988, p. 2-3. *See, e.g.*, Roberto Mangabeira Unger, *The Critical Legal Studies Movement*, Harvard University Press, Cambridge, Massachusetts, 1986, p. 50-51.

26 *See* Weber 1978 *supra*, p. 650-658.

least when seen from a legal perspective, Constitutional Courts have the option to primarily embrace a substantial rationality in order to resolve issues of constitutionality. In order to reach the 'best' solution, justices then regard the legal system as primarily instrumental to the fulfillment of certain goals external to the system itself. In other words, Constitutional Courts ought to be ready to 'sacrifice' the internal rationality and rules traditionally superseding Western legal systems and reasoning, if and as long as this capitulation is directly functional to reaching the political, social and economic values the courts intend, on various grounds, to insert into a certain community.

However, there is another possible ideal-type rationality or criterion that ought to guide Constitutional Courts in their work. As pointed out by Weber, in modern capitalist societies, the fundamental criterion inspiring the work of legal actors is formal rationality, i.e. they reach a decision or a legal solution according to the criteria of internal logical criteria and for the maintenance of the consistency of the legal system, regardless of the actual effects in the surrounding environments. This respect for formal rationality (or 'legality') is and ought to be, as Weber continues, because it is directly functional and fundamental for legal actors (and judges in particular) in order to gain and maintain 'legitimacy,' i.e. a high degree of probability that their decisions will be concretely followed by the majority of addressees because they are considered 'correct' and therefore binding.[27]

The characterization of a certain actor as legal or political then is always fundamental, at least from a legal perspective, in order to attach to a certain actor a certain criterion (or type of rationality, as in this work) that should guide it in its operations. This definition, however, is even more important in the case of Constitutional Courts due to the position these types of courts occupy in modern democratic forms of political organization.

Constitutional Courts are certainly not the only actors whose nature can be and is widely disputed. For example, the legal nature of in-house attorneys is often heavily questioned, they are treated as facilitating simply a legal cover-up of purely economic and political programs; the same can be said of general practitioners or law professors.[28] However, the theoretical issue of defining Constitutional Courts is fundamental because, among both legal and political actors of a modern democracy, the decisions of these courts (and consequently the criteria inspiring them) are those that can shape the fundamental legal, but also political and social, features of an entire community, sometimes even more than the decisions taken in the democratically elected assembly. For example, in deciding *Brown v. Board of Education* (1954), the Supreme Court of the United States shaped (at least as much as the Congress did ten years later with the 1964 Civil Rights Act) the future of an

27 *See* Weber 1978 *supra*, p. 654-658.

28 *See, e.g.*, Neil MacCormick, *H.L.A. Hart*, Stanford University Press, Stanford, 1981, p. 126.

entire national community as far as concerned unlawful structural discrimination based on ethnicity.[29]

It is also true, by using Dworkin's famous metaphor, that Constitutional Courts write just one chapter in the chain novel that constitutes the valid law, since, after their decisions, their words will then be interpreted by all the other actors, *e.g.* legal scholars, lower judges and law-makers.[30] However, even if the subsequent actors write a 'different' continuation of the novel, it is the Constitutional Courts that have the privilege of setting the agenda for future discussion. Using the previous example, with *Brown v. Board of Education* the US Supreme Court definitely opened the door to de-segregation, i.e. it gave a heavy push to put into the trash can all the attempts to retain in American society the racist principle 'separate-but-equal.'

Many other aspects, both political and legal, underscore the necessity of coming forward with a clear definition of which kind of actors Constitutional Courts are. From a political perspective, the definition of a Constitutional Court is important as it clarifies, and therefore partially prevents, possible points of collision between the highest powers in a community. By pointing out the basic features and criteria that should inspire the work taking place in the courts, this clarification allows for a better and more precise control of the activity of the courts by political authorities, *e.g.* in the form of offering a clear matrix to parliamentary committees or investigators against which to evaluate certain constitutional judicial decisions. In other words, this legal theoretical definition more clearly locates a fundamental actor on the political map, either as primarily promoting certain and different in-time ideologies (if defined as a political actor) or primarily as attempting to maintain one single and established legal ideology, namely the rule of law (if defined as a legal actor).

The necessity of characterizing the nature of Constitutional Courts is also important from a legal perspective as this maneuver allows us to normatively fix what type of rationality Constitutional Courts ought to follow in their work. Justices sitting on the highest bench can be defined primarily as legal actors. As a consequence from a legal perspective, the legality of their decisions in 'hard-cases' can and should be questioned, even by lower courts, when their legal reasoning is mainly grounded on the goal of implementing values they consider as immanent in a community, although they do not explicitly appear in the constitutional document or fundamental law.

This critique of the legality of their decisions can and ought to be done in particular when the realization of values is done at the expense of the traditional criteria superseding the legal reasoning (*e.g.* consistency or respect for previous decisions on similar matters), i.e. the only type of reasoning on which legal actors

29 *See Brown v. Board of Education*, 347 U.S. 495 (1954).

30 *See* Ronald Dworkin, *Law's Empire*, Belknap Press, Cambridge, Massachusetts, 1986, p. 228-238.

in modern democracy have a legitimate domain. For example, if a court decides in diametrical directions in similar cases or issues, it can be directly criticized from a legal perspective for violating a fundamental principle of Western legal systems as such, namely treating individuals equally under the same circumstances.

On the other end, in the event Constitutional Courts are defined primarily as political actors, the possibility of holding them responsible from a legal perspective for doing something 'illegal' is more restricted. If they are considered political actors, while it is always possible to legally criticized Constitutional Courts for violating certain basic rights guaranteed in the constitution through a certain decision, it is not possible to 'force' the courts to decide in accordance, or at least consequent, with previous decisions. One privilege accorded to political actors in general is the fact that they can indeed change their value system without being held responsible (at least legally) for this. If a political party or national assembly decides to pursue values other than those originally planned, it cannot be criticized or held responsible from a legal perspective for such.

Finally, another element stresses the importance of questioning the nature of Constitutional Courts in Western legal systems. Constitutional Courts somehow symbolize and stretch to the limits an underlying feature typical of most legal actors operating in contemporary Western legal systems: their 'middle' position between the political world where values (or models of society) are created and the legal world, through which those values have to pass in order to be implemented into a community. Each one of the concrete individuals forming the skeletal structure of the legal actors is formally educated in the law and such an education is almost always a formal requirement to becoming a part of this group of actors. The individuals composing the legal actors, in other words, are all educated in the idea that law, although highly politicized, keeps certain features that distinguish it from pure political propaganda.[31]

On the other end, for justices working in Constitutional Courts, most legal actors operate within the legal system but with a face also turned to the outside world, to the world where non-legal (in the sense of value-oriented) ways of reasoning dominate. They work within the legal system, but they do this with the knowledge that law is instrumental in order to introduce into a community models of behaviors or values embraced by their political reference (*e.g.* for legal experts working in political parties) or by economic reference (*e.g.* in-house attorneys for large corporations).

This characteristic feature of the law and legal system in the Western legal system, i.e. their always being functional to something else, then forces legal actors in

31 *See, e.g.*, Karl N. Llewellyn, On Reading and Using the Newer Jurisprudence, *Columbia Law Review*, Vol. 40, 1940, No. 4, p. 589 and Alf Ross, *Towards a realistic jurisprudence: a criticism of the dualism in law*, E. Munksgaard, Copenhagen, 1946, p. 72. *See also* Neil MacCormick, *Legal Reasoning and Legal Theory*, Clarendon Press, Oxford, 1978, p. 188.

general to always take into consideration the ideologies, or value systems, affecting the origins, development and final environment in which the law-making or law-applying is taking place. In short, the importance of defining Constitutional Courts as either legal or political actors lies in the fact that such institutional actors represent better than others the difficult situation in which lawyers operate nowadays: educated in law and employed in order to build, interpret and apply the law, but under an extreme non-legal pressure that wants them to disregard that considered the characterizing elements for a legal system (predictability, certainty, rule of law and so on) in order to instead fulfill political goals.

6. A Possible Legal Theoretical Solution

Part III (*'Makers' vs. 'Markers:' Constitutional Courts as 'In-the-middle' Actors*) showed how Constitutional Courts can be considered as actually positioning 'in-the-middle', between the legal and political worlds. Part IV (*Why Is the Definition 'Either-Legal-Or-Political' So Important For Constitutional Courts?*) pointed out that for several reasons, it is important to somehow 'insert' the Constitutional Courts into either one of these two ideal typical boxes, i.e. to establish which of the two natures (political *vs.* legal) dominates Constitutional Courts and should be used as basic point for investigating and (if warranted) criticizing their decision-making.

A possible perspective from whence to begin the journey to answer this fundamental question is certainly legal theory. Due to the central position and function Constitutional Courts play in contemporary legal systems, legal theory has devoted many and important writings on this topic. From the modern natural law theories to legal positivism, from critical legal thinking to legal-sociological approaches, most contemporary legal theories have tackled the issue of what Constitutional Courts are, somehow being forced to take issue with this question due to the impact of these courts decisions on the law and society at large.[32]

Though along legal theoretical paths, it is helpful here to start, however, by resorting to a sociological distinction made between the institutional position of a certain actor and the function-effects of that actor's work. By the first is intended the position given to a certain actor operating inside a larger environment. This positioning, as far as concerns judicial bodies, is mainly a combination of the operating of two (often overlapping) factors: the degree of legitimacy that judicial bodies enjoy, indicating where in the spectrum of power judges are inserted (vertical positioning); and the distribution of power as sanctioned in the law, which indicates where, at the stage assigned by the legitimacy, the judicial body is located (horizontal positioning).

32 *See, e.g.*, the decision of the US Supreme Court in *Brown v. Board of Education*, 347 U.S. 495 (1954) or by the German Federal Constitutional Court in *Wünsche Handelsgesellschaft* (BvR 2, 197/83; 1987 3 CMLR 225), (1986) (Solange II).

When speaking of function-effects of an actor's work, this simply refers to the impacts that the work of the actor has on the environment. These effects can be of different ideal-typical natures. They can be *intended*, where they correspond to the original goal the actor had in mind when starting the work, or *unintended*, where they do not (totally or partially) correspond to the original motive of the action. Effects can also be in the form of either *outputs* or *outcomes*.[33] Outputs are the impacts (intended or unintended) a certain action has inside the ideal-typical arena in which the action has taken place (*e.g.* effect of a decision of a court on the legal right of the condemned to appeal). Outcomes, in contrast, mark the effects (intended or unintended) such impacts have on the surrounding environment (*e.g.* the effect of a court decision on the economic situation of the condemned's family).

In reality, these different ideal-types almost always tend to be mixed with each other, *e.g.* in the form of court decisions that have intended and unintended effects or outputs and outcomes simultaneously. Despite this, such ideal-types can be useful analytical tools in order to reveal specific tendencies in an actor as to operating in one environment instead of another in order to gain certain effects, and then choosing the type of rationality more suitable for that purpose.

If one considers Constitutional Courts in light of these distinctions, between institutional position and function-effects (and among the different types of effects), one can see how the dominant features of the courts are of a legal nature. Starting from the institutional position, Constitutional Courts first of all are 'courts.' This means that their decisions are what they are, namely considered binding by the vast majority of the addressees, and not because of the content of the decisions, i.e. the models of behaviors they aim to impose on a community. They are considered binding because they are legal normative decisions, that is decisions that ought to be obeyed because they are produced by a legally formed body, entrusted with the legal power to produce such type of binding decisions. In other words, the major institutional position of the Constitutional Courts, i.e. their being a 'dispute-resolving' actor, is given to them by the legal legitimacy such courts enjoy in the modern form of a democratic state.

In contrast to political actors such as political parties or lobby groups, the consideration and respect for the work of Constitutional Courts is not so much based on the intrinsic values promoted by the very decisions, for example, such as the 'popularity' of a certain political program. The respect, or legitimacy, is given to the decisions by the legal form they take, and by the forms that have been observed while producing the decisions and choosing the individuals (i.e. judges) in charge of taking such decisions. In other words, Constitutional Courts keep their position

33 This separation of outputs from outcomes is actually an adaptation of the results reached by a long series of studies developed in political science. *See, e.g.*, Joel A. Thompson, Outputs and Outcomes of State Workmen's Compensation Laws, *Journal of Politics*, Vol. 43, 1981, No. 4, p. 1132; or Francis G. Castles, *Comparative Public Policy. Patterns of Post-war Transformation*, Edward Elgar, Northampton, Massachusetts, 1998, p. 248-292.

and 'job' in the community as the highest dispute-resolving actor as long as they are able to maintain their legal legitimacy, i.e., legitimacy gained in Western legal systems mostly by observing the paradigms of formal legal rationality.

Naturally, this does not mean that Constitutional Courts lack political sympathies. However, even when justices are strongly politicized, they still have to operate taking a look at and being forced into the barriers and limits as set by the legal system or, if in more modern terms, by the principles or paradigms established by the dominating legal culture (*e.g.* rule of law, bill of rights, separation of powers, due process and so on) in order to not lose their legitimacy among the addressees.

As to their function, if one starts by considering the *intended* and *unintended outputs* of a certain decision by a Constitutional Court, the primary arena of operation of Constitutional Courts here is the legal one. A Constitutional Court, per definition, evaluates legal issues, in particular the possible unconstitutionality of a statute or acts of law-making agencies. The outputs of the courts' deliberation are to decide whether certain legal rules of a lower dignity can still be considered as 'binding and therefore existing' legal rules. In particular, Constitutional Courts 'prove' the existence of these rules by evaluating whether they are compatible with the fundamental rules and principles enumerated in (or somehow derived from) constitutions and fundamental laws. This, as pointed out before, is a typical legal problem since it is created exclusively by axiomatically accepting the legal principles presupposing an ascending structure of rules, where the lower rules, in order to exist as legal (and therefore to be binding) rules, cannot be in conflict with the higher.

As pointed out by Hans Kelsen, and also by other legal scholars (even natural law theoreticians), this idea is typical of the legal arena.[34] In contrast, the hierarchical structure in the political arena, though present (*e.g.* basic values vs. tactical choices), is not fundamental in order to give 'validity' to the lower types of decision. Tactical decisions taken by a congressional party are still considered 'valid' for the political line of a certain party, even if contrary to the fundamental values contained in the party program and even if such tactical decisions can perhaps 'shape' the support the party's leader enjoy in the same party.

In contrast to political actors, Constitutional Courts are not totally freed in their reasoning from what can be defined as the 'external' borders of legal reasoning. By 'external borders', or 'minimum content of natural law' in Hart's terminology, are identified in particular the no-cross limits of the legal culture of a certain community, limits which have to exist in order for the legal system to exist as such.[35] In a democratic free-market regime, for example, these no-cross borders can be

34 *See, e.g.*, Hans Kelsen 1970 *supra*, p. 3-4, 19. *See also* Neil MacCormick, Natural Law Reconsidered, *Oxford Journal of Legal Studies*, Vol. 1, 1981, No. 1, p. 108.

35 *See* H.L.A. Hart, *The Concept of Law*, Clarendon Press, Oxford, 1961, p. 189-195. *See also* Hart 1983 *supra*, p. 112.

defined as the fundamental legal principles (*e.g.* protection of freedom of expression and private property) expressing the substratum of political, cultural, and economic forces by which the system itself is created and to which it is functional.

Political actors do not necessarily have to respect such external borders of the legal reasoning. Actually, for many political parties, the primary and fully politically legitimized goal of their existence is to change or shift such external borders, for example by heavily restricting freedom of expression or by eliminating legal protection accorded to private property.

The situation changes if one moves the focus to the *outcomes* of the decisions taken by Constitutional Courts, i.e. the effects (intended or unintended) that their decisions have on the (non-legal) environments surrounding the one in which the courts operate (the legal one). It is easy to note here how the legal feature characterizing the function played by the Constitutional Courts tends to disappear. Decisions by Constitutional Courts almost always have effects outside the legal world or, using Luhmann's terminology, in the other sub-systems composing a society: in the cultural, economic, and political life of a community. In other words, it goes without saying that as far as concerns the outcomes of their decisions, Constitutional Courts present certain similarities with political actors such as, for example, the government or national assemblies. As for the latter, Constitutional Courts with their decisions also attempt in the end (consciously or unconsciously) to impose certain models of behaviors or values upon a community.

Despite this sliding into the political arena, Constitutional Courts should be considered as having primarily a legal nature, i.e. primarily being a legal actor. First, the grouping of an actor under a certain terminological roof has to be done primarily according to both its institutional location and the function-effects of its work, in particular the intended outputs its actions produce. If one should look at the outcomes, the very analytical possibility of grouping actors in ideal-typical arenas, and the consequent possibility to identify some normative criteria according to which evaluate and criticize their work, would disappear. Outcomes of decisions almost always tend to spread in different directions and, especially for unintended outcomes, it is often not even possible to determine in which area a certain action has had its major impact particularly after a long period of time. For example, a decision taken by large corporations can have relevant outcomes in the religious or cultural fields, but it would be quite strange to define such corporations (and consequently evaluate their work) as primarily religious or cultural actors.

The fact that Constitutional Courts are legal actors does not rule out the possibility that they still can (and often do) play a political function. As said, all legal decisions have certain outcomes, but generally, Constitutional Courts make their decisions by looking (or at least by reasoning according) to the legal outputs, namely the constitutionality or not of certain provisions. Justices sitting on the highest bench certainly can (and often do) have a political agenda, but they are still forced to confront it with the legal system and the principles dominating within it. A reversed example can be found in individuals sitting in the Parliament. They are without doubt political actors with a clear political agenda, but they still sometimes play a very relevant legal function, and this is done according to a specific legal agenda, i.e. according to certain model of how the legal system or part of it should look. This is the case, for example, when members of Parliament in a special committee evaluate the legal limits of criminal liability attached to the highest position of the State, such as the President of the Republic or the Prime Minister.

Moreover, and connected to the latter, the legal feature attached to Constitutional Courts is traceable to the fundamental ideology shaping their work. Justices working in Constitutional Courts live in an environment which, though with many political passersby, has a primary legal task: to be the guardian insuring that the law-making taking place in a certain state is done, or conflict among the highest public authorities is decided, according to the highest rules fixed in the constitutional documents or fundamental law.

This task of Constitutional Courts is legal in the sense that it consists of dealing with legal rules. When justices sit on the bench, they primarily work with checking the 'constitutionality' of certain legal rules, i.e. with the possibility that, from a legal discourse perspective (i.e. with the traditional rules regulating the legal reasoning), such legal rules can fit into the legal system as designed in the constitutional documents or fundamental laws. Obviously, justices are often well aware of the indirect political effects of their decisions (outcomes), an awareness that sometimes affects their very reaching a certain solution instead of another. However, regardless of any hidden agenda behind a certain decision, justices are always forced to somehow 'squeeze' their politically-motivated decisions into boxes of legal justification.[36]

In the end, Constitutional Courts must always speak the language of the law, not the one of politics, even if they want to send political messages. As pointed out by Michel Foucault, among others, language in modern society is power, and by classifying a political problem and a political solution according to legal terminology, the choice of language immediately imposes on the issue the domain and limits set by the legal discourse and, at the same time, tends to exclude all features and limits set by the other types of discourses, among them the political one.[37]

---

36 For instance, the doctrine of stare decisis is primarily a legal doctrine, though it certainly presents both political roots and political effects on the political world. *See, e.g.* Lawrence B. Solum, The Supreme Court in Bondage: Constitutional Stare Decisis, Legal Formalism, and the Future of Unenumerated Rights, *University of Pennsylvania Journal of Constitutional Law*, Vol. 9, 2006, p. 160-176; and Ronald Dworkin, *Justice in Robes*, Belknap Press, Cambridge, Massachusetts, 2006, p. 147-50.

37 *See* Michel Foucault, *The Archaeology of Knowledge and the Discourse on Language*, Pantheon books, (New York, 1972, chapter 2. *See also* Alan Hunt & Gary Wickham, *Foucault and Law: Towards a Sociology of Law as Governance*, Pluto Press, Chicago, 1994, p. 7-12, 41-43; and Anne Barron, Foucault and Law, *in* J. Penner *et al.* (eds.), *Introduction to Jurisprudence and Legal Theory: Commentary and Materials*, Butterworths, London, 2002, p. 955-997.

Now that the fundamental nature of Constitutional Courts, at least from a legal theoretical perspective, has been established, it is now time to move back to the original issue, namely the law-making activity by Constitutional Courts and in particular, the possibility of evaluating it according to a political criterion such as its (present or absent) 'democratic' character.

7. Constitutional Courts as Legal Actors and The Idea of Democracy

One of the major criticisms against judicial activism is that it allows non-elected legal actors (highest courts) to substitute themselves for duly elected political actors (legislatives) and, therewith, destabilizing the very idea of democracy. In general, most legal theories describing or prescribing what democracy is, or better, the fundamental elements for having a democratic form of state are, have problems with 'fitting in' the position and function played by Constitutional Courts in their theoretical portrait of a democratic law-making.

With all the specifications taken, one of the basic elements for a democracy, at least when dealing with law-making, is that the ultimate agency empowered to enact laws (or to somehow 'sanction' the legitimacy of certain normative statements as legally binding) resides in the political actors. This is because only the latter are the elected (and therefore legitimate) representatives of the ultimate actor from which all power in a democracy emanates, namely the people.

This being the case, it is quite consistent that it is difficult for most democracy theoreticians (both inside legal and political scholarships) to somehow insert in their idea of how a law-making works in a democratic country the fact that some older men and women, not chosen or directly sanctioned by popular vote, have the power to stop a statute or a decision taken by the legally highest representative of the people, either the Congress or President of a nation. While (more or less) shared solutions have been reached as to similar limits imposed on the law-making and political actors by the legal concept of human rights (mostly by incorporating the latter into the very idea of democracy), it is still very difficult for most democracy theories to somehow accept the fact that a non-elected actor actually has an institutional position higher than the representatives of the people, a position that allow justices to always have the final word in legal matters. Even where Constitutional Courts are not especially 'active', they still retain a law-making power of striking down new pieces of legislation enacted by the political representative of a certain community.

The definition of Constitutional Courts as legal actors then reveals a central question once considered from the perspective of the democratic form of state. One fundamental feature of democracy shared by the majority of contemporary legal theories is that the political powers of the state organization are chosen (directly or indirectly) by the community. Moreover, there ought always to be a possibility for the representatives of the people to somehow control and decide the course of action of all the other non-political actors belonging to the state apparatus. In addition to all accepted specifications (*e.g.* Robert Dahl's theory of economic democracy), the adopting by a modern state of democracy ideology still takes with it the axiom of the prevalence of the political discourse and its main actors above all the other discourses, either religious, cultural, or legal.[38]

In contrast to the current political discourse, which in order to exist as such needs a legitimacy built on the acceptance (even by the most extreme ideologies) of the concept of 'support' (explicit or implicit) by the majority of people, legal discourse is by nature undemocratic. This feature is given to the legal discourse in particular by its very way of working its primary source, the law, the latter being based on the 'authority' of certain decisions taken by certain unelected persons, regardless of whether they are supported by the majority of people.

If one defines Constitutional Courts as legal actors, the question that can be raised then is the following: As Constitutional Courts are not democratically elected by the majority of a certain community, is it undemocratic that they retain the highest legal power among the public authorities, a power allowing them to virtually stop every legal measure taken by political actors who are representative of the people? Isn't the fact, that through Constitutional Courts, the 'undemocratic' legal discourse prevails over the 'democratic' political discourse, against the very concept of democracy?

These are significant issues and it certainly is not feasible to answer them by the end of this short essay, as this would probably take more than a few pages. However, based on the results reached by the analysis developed above, it is perhaps possible to at least identify the correct perspective from which to start answering whether Constitutional Courts fit without major problems in an ideal democratic form of state.

When talking about democracy, one refers to a form of primarily political organization, namely a form to organize the 'striving for a share of power or for influence on the distribution of power.'[39] The idea of democracy is either a picture mirroring the reality (for the descriptive theories) or a painting of how the reality should be (for the normative theories) and it zooms directly on the organization, structuring and sharing of political power. In other words, the characterization of a democratic

38 *See* Adam Smith, *Lectures on Jurisprudence* (R.L. Meek, D.D. Raphael & P.G. Stein (eds.)), Oxford University Press, Oxford, 1978 (1762-1763), p. 200. *But see* Hart 1961 *supra*, p. 72-74; *cf.* Wolfgang Friedmann, *Law in a Changing Society* (2nd Ed.), Stevens & Sons, London, 1972, p. 505-506. Another explanation can be traced back to Machiavelli's idea as to the modern state in general (and not necessarily in a democratic shape), where one can observe the growth and dominance of political reasons and categories over almost all other kinds of discourses. *See, e.g.* George H. Sabine, *A History of Political Theory* (3rd Ed.), Holt Rinehart & Winston, New York, 1964, p. 344-347.

39 Max Weber, The Profession and Vocation of Politics, *in* P. Lassman & R. Speirs (eds.), *Max Weber: Political Writings*, Cambridge University Press, Cambridge, 1994, p. 311.

form of state is ascribed to it primarily by the specific way the power is distributed in a certain community. Of course, this structuring and sharing of political power is usually done by means of using certain legal instruments and legal institutions (such as an elected legislative assembly).

However, while the presence of certain forms of political organization is fundamental for defining a certain state as democratic (*e.g.* the presence of competing political ideologies represented in the political discourse), the presence or absence of the usual legal instruments normally attached to a democratic form of state can be not essential. Using a previous example, while it is certain that a democracy has to protect human rights, it is still highly controversial which human rights are to be protected (*e.g.* the right to private property), their extent (*e.g.* right to life) and whether the public authorities should act 'actively' for their implementation (*e.g.* right to work).[40]

Similarly, different political communities in the Western hemisphere in particular, share a common denomination of democracy, but this does not necessarily imply the presence of the same legal institutions with the same legal powers, and in particular of a Constitutional Court with the jurisdiction of constitutional review. A typical example can be found in a parallel observation of the United States and Sweden. Both these systems are considered as a political form of democracy. However, as far as concerns the organization of their legal systems, fundamental differences are detectable, in particular as to the presence of a highest court with jurisdiction in constitutionality matters.

The United States has a highest court with the specific power to check the constitutionality of statutes and when necessary, the legal possibility to directly strike them down. Sweden (as most of the other Nordic countries) has a high organ, composed of well-experienced judges, with the jurisdiction to perform a constitutional review prior to the passage of legislation, the Council on Legislation. However, this body cannot be considered a Constitutional Court, since its decisions are not legally binding to the addressees (namely the Parliament and the Government in this case); it is more a constitutional council, working as legal advisor for the political actors but unable to stop them, even in cases of gross violations of fundamental laws. It is true that courts, either general or administrative, have the power to strike down acts of the Swedish Parliament as unconstitutional, but this power is strictly limited only to the case in question, and only if the error is 'manifest' (in Swedish, *uppenbarhetsrekvisitet*). This power has only been used in a handful of cases in recent decades. Moreover, this power has been granted comparatively recently in comparison to that of the United States Supreme Court (thirty years

40 *See* Waldron 2001 *supra*, p. 224-225 as to the very complexity of the legal concept of 'rights' already in its philosophical underpinning.

compared to the almost two hundred since *Marbury v. Madison*), and certainly long after Sweden was considered a well-established democratic form of State.[41]

Moreover, if one looks at the procedures used in selecting justices, extremely different processes exist, different in particular as far as concerns the role political actors and political culture play. Existing procedures are stretched across a broad spectrum. At one extreme is the US Supreme Court, where justices are directly nominated by the President (a political actor) with the approval of the Congress (another political actor) after hearings in which the candidate's position on various (and often very hot) political issues are 'tested.' Somewhere in the middle is the Italian procedure of choosing constitutional judges (and to some extent also France's), where political actors and their 'political scrutiny' play a relevant role (by electing one-third of the judges). The legal world and its dominating culture also matter, one-third of the judges elected being among the most qualified judges, appointed directly by the Supreme Organ of the Judicial Body, the highest internal instance of the judicial body. Sweden can be positioned at the other extreme end of the spectrum, where, though political 'affiliation' plays a certain role (due in particular to the fact that the appointment of the justices is entirely by political actors), the criteria and reasons of choosing one justice over another are based mainly on evaluative criteria 'internal' to the judicial body. The criteria used in this Scandinavian country are almost of a purely 'judicial bureaucratic' nature and do not consider the 'link' between the political value of the justice and the political representatives of the community.

As the procedures for choosing justices are so different among well-established political democratic regimes, as is also the role political culture plays in them, the simple conclusion can be drawn that a necessary *sine qua non* relation between the selection of the justices and the participation of the representatives of the people in the process does not exist; or, to put it in another way, a democratic political system does not necessarily require a direct link between political actors and the justices sitting in Constitutional Courts in order to guarantee the 'democratic' representation of the latter.

Another element considered essential to Western democratic regimes from which Constitutional Courts depart is the position of political rights (*e.g.* the right to vote) as essential for a constitution and the work of Constitutional Courts in protecting them.[42] If, as for the previous example, one considers the US Supreme Court and the Swedish Supreme Court as two different ideal-typical Constitutional Courts, one can notice a deep divergence of positions on this issue. First, the consideration and progressive 'refinement' of political rights enumerated in the Constitution has occupied quite a bit of space of the US Supreme Court's work, being followed

41 *See* Instrument of Government (in Swedish, *Regeringsformen*) (Ch. 11, § 14, 1974). *Compare* to *Marbury v. Madison*, 5 U.S. (1 Cranch) 137 (1803).

42 *See* Martin Shapiro, Judicial Review in Developed Democracies, *Democratization*, Vol. 10, 2003, No. 4, p. 11-13.

in this (but only to a certain extent) by several European Constitutional Courts, such as the German Federal Constitutional Court or the Italian Constitutional Court. In the Swedish form of democracy, the primary role of the Supreme Court (and the constitutional texts) has been, at least until recently, mostly concentrated on distributing and delimiting political power among the various institutional actors. Until very recently, the protection and interpretation of most basic political rights have been left instead to extra-parliamentary agreements among the actors of the political, legal and social arenas; when addressed by statute, political rights tend to fall under the domain of administrative law and administrative courts more than that of constitutional law. Similar to Sweden, the French Constitutional Council has only from the early 1970's taken a strong stand in positioning basic political rights in the central part of the constitutional map.[43] In both cases, however, Sweden and France have been considered democracies long before the constitutional recognition of political rights took place.

Finally, from a legal perspective, one aspect that the different Western Constitutional Courts at least have in common, as pointed out in Part II (*Some Definitions*) is that all Constitutional Courts are courts with the specific legal competence to check the constitutionality of statutes or acts. This being the case, when one starts evaluating the actual use or implementation of such legal power, a broad range of positions can be detected, however, going from the frequent striking down of the constitutionality of the work of the political actors (as in the US or many of European countries) to the almost constant 'constitutional-guarantee' stamp for every word produced in the political world (as in Sweden or, until the early 70's, in France).

Naturally, one can maintain the idea that Constitutional Courts in Sweden (or in France) do not go against the law-making by political actors because the latter were more 'cultivated into legal matters' and 'obedient' to the law than in other Western countries. However, a more realistic assessment, at least from a legal perspective, is that in the Swedish (and to some extent French) form of democracy, the control of constitutionality by a specific court does not belong to the legal underpinning necessarily required by a Western democratic political regime, legal underpinnings to which, for instance, one can ascribe legal rules safe-guarding freedom of expression, freedom of association or private property.

This brief comparative analysis shows one important fact: Constitutional Courts in the well-established democracies can, in relation to the political world, present fundamental differences as to their legal jurisdiction, as to the procedures for their formation (and the role political actors play in it), as to the areas of focus of most of their work, and even as to the 'actualization' of their judicial review jurisdiction. As the issue of whether both the United States and Sweden are fully considered and legitimized as Western democratic forms of state is not debated, the conclu-

43 *See* Constitutional Council of France (in French, *Conseil Constitutionnel*), Décision n° 71-44 DC of 16 July 1971.

sion then must be drawn that the presence or absence of a Constitutional Court, with binding decision-making power as to constitutional review, cannot be considered a *conditio sine qua non* for a democracy. As recently pointed out in an article by Lee Epstein *et al.*, Constitutional Courts can play a decisive role in 'reinforcing' already democratic political regimes, but not in 'establishing' them.[44] In other words, having a Constitutional Court is helpful but is not a fundamental requirement for a community in order to be considered as living in a democracy.[45]

A fundamental bias can then be detected in the accusation against a certain legal system or legal culture in general for being undemocratic because there is space for judicial activism that a legal actor, as a Constitutional Court, can control, limit and somehow modify the decisions taken by a democratically elected political power. This charge presupposes that the concept of democracy necessarily incorporates Constitutional Courts, an incorporation that the empirical observation of the realities of the legal systems in the Western world does not support.

At the same time, this accusation of operating as political actors paradoxically starts with the implicit presupposition that Constitutional Courts should be political. It begins with the premise of attaching to Constitutional Courts the wrong kind of legitimacy, namely legitimacy based on the idea that, as for the political actors, it is given by the content of their decision ('the decision is against the majority's will, therefore it shakes the legitimacy of the court'). However, Constitutional Courts are primarily legal actors and, as pointed out by Weber at least for Western legal systems, the fundamental criterion according to which their legitimacy is acquired and maintained is not by following the substantive rationality, but the formal one.[46] This means that the formal legitimacy of Constitutional Courts is not based on how 'democratic' their message is, but on the observance of the pre-established rules regarding how the decision should be taken, according to which procedures and by whom ('the decision is done following the proper forms, therefore it reinforces the legitimacy of the court').

In the end, criticism against the judicial activism of Constitutional Courts is shown to be a paradox, or better yet, confusion as to which kind of legitimacy is and should be attached to these courts. Critics attack court activism for destabiliz-

---

44 *See* Lee Epstein, Jack Knight & Olga Shvetsova, The Role of Constitutional Courts in the Establishment and Maintenance of Democratic Systems of Government, *Law & Society Review*, Vol. 45, 2001, No. 1, p. 138-148.

45 *See* Robert Barros, *Constitutionalism and Dictatorship: Pinochet, the Junta, and the 1980 Constitution*, Cambridge University Press, Cambridge, 2002, chapter 6, as an example of possible coexistence of a dictatorial political regime and a functioning Constitutional Court.

46 *See* Weber 1978 *supra*, p. 37 ("Today the most common form of legitimacy is the belief in legality, the compliance with enactments which are *formally* correct and which have been made in the accustomed manner"). *See also* Gianfranco Poggi, *The Development of Modern State. A Sociological Introduction*, Stanford University Press, Stanford, 1989, p. 132; Immanuel Kant, Die Metaphysik der Sitten, *in* I. Kant, *Immanuel Kants Werke Band VII 25-26*, (B. Kellermann ed.), Bruno Cassirer, Berlin, 1916 (1797), p. 122 and Philippe Nonet & Philip Selznick, *Law and Society in Transition: Toward Responsive Law*, Harper and Row, New York, 1978, p. 51-52.

ing democracy due to the political content of their decisions, and in the long run, for endangering one of the central axioms of democracy, namely a system of courts legitimized as purely law-applying actors. However, this criticism of being 'political' presupposes that the work of courts and their decisions ought to be evaluated (and legitimized) from the same perspective as for other political actors' decisions, namely from the presence (or not) of a content which is supported (directly or indirectly) by the majority of the people.

Once the constitutional document has been written and its legitimacy as such accepted and, in particular, the premise that an independent Constitutional Court should exist with the primary legal task of controlling that the law is done and applied according to the constitution is accepted by the political actors, it would be against the very idea of certainty of the fundamental law to ask Constitutional Courts to play according to a different criterion, namely the political evaluation of the democratic level of certain decision instead of their legality.

8. Towards A More 'Democratic' Model of Constitutional Court

It is necessary to point out one thing before concluding this article. The point of this article is not to totally 'disconnect' Constitutional Courts from the ideal of democracy. The basic point instead has simply been to stress that Constitutional Courts are not necessarily present in every Western democratic political system or, in other words, the institution of Constitutional Courts does not belong to the legal substratum typical for every democratic regime. However, as pointed out above by Epstein *et al.*, Constitutional Courts can (and usually do) help a community reinforce the democratic form of organization: democracies can exist without Constitutional Courts, although it can be seen to be better if democracies are assisted by Constitutional Courts.[47]

In other words, the point made here is that the debate on judicial review, in particular at the constitutional level, does not have to end by claiming that courts (and their judicial review) and democracy do not belong together. On the contrary, based on the consideration of the legal nature of Constitutional Courts and the primary political nature of the concept of democracy, the aim is to re-set the terms of the debate of 'democracy' and 'judicial review,' at least from a legal theoretical perspective.[48]

---

47 *See* Lee Epstein, Jack Knight & Olga Shvetsova 2001 *supra*, p. 155-156.

48 *See, e.g.* Samuel Freeman, Constitutional Democracy and the Legitimacy of Judicial Review, *Law and Philosophy*, Vol. 9, 2004, No. 4, p. 353-354; Gunther Teubner, Substantive and Reflexive Elements in Modern Law, *Law and Society Review*, Vol. 17, 1983, No. 2, p. 254; and Andrew Halpin, The Theoretical Controversy Concerning Judicial Review, *Modern Law Review, Vol. 64*, 2001, No. 3, p. 500. *But see* Waldron 2001 *supra*, p. 283.

Most of the debate as to constitutional judicial review starts from the request to the courts to be a more 'integral part' of the democratic form of state, the position then being different as to what is expected by 'democratic' courts (*e.g.* strict obedience to the legal rules laid down by the representatives of the people vs. 'activism' in searching of the 'true meaning' behind the legal text). However, as seen up to now, by defining Constitutional Courts as essentially legal actors, there is a need to shift the perspective from which the evaluation (and eventually criticism) of the work of the Constitutional Courts originates, at least in the legal debate: from the political standpoint (*e.g.* majority's support to a certain decision) to the legal standpoint (*e.g.* respect to the traditional rules dominating the legal reasoning).[49]

Specifically, since Constitutional Courts are not part of the conceptual hard-core of 'democracy', but usually play a relevant function in the establishment of democracy, the re-setting of the debate on constitutional judicial review and democracy should then not be in the direction of absorbing one element (Constitutional Courts) into the other (democracy), but instead in proposing an 'ideal' of Constitutional Courts more aligned or compatible with the elements characterizing a democratic form of state.

As an example of this search for compatibility between Constitutional Courts and ideals of democracy, one can begin with the definition of democracy developed, among others, by Jürgen Habermas: Democracy is that form of state striving for the participation of all the community (or specific part of it) to the formation of the decisions which have effects on the community (or on the specific part of it).[50] If one starts from this definition of democracy, then changes to the Constitutional Courts in order to make them more 'compatible' to a democratic system should be in the direction of their procedural aspects, and less on the material content of their decisions, i.e. in the direction of making the addressees of the decisions more participatory in decision-making processes.

The first step to be taken is certainly one of adopting a process of selection of the candidate justices similar to the one used for the US Supreme Court. In particular, the 'hearings' procedure in front of the national Assemblies would allow not only a more specific control of the judges by the representatives of the people. More importantly in the modern information society, public hearings also allow the

49 As typical representative of the political standpoint from which to investigate the idea of democracy in relation to the role of Constitutional Courts, *see* Waldron 2001 *supra*, p. 283.

50 *See* Jürgen Habermas, *Between Facts and Norms: Contributions to a Discourse Theory of Law and Democracy*, MIT Press, Cambridge, 1998, p. 134, according to whom the democratic discourse is the one allowing the citizens "to test whether a contested norm can or could obtain to acquiescence of all those who might be affected". *See also* Samuel P. Huntington, *The Third Wave: Democratization in the Late Twentieth Century*, University of Oklahoma Press, Norman, Oklahoma, 1991, p. 8-9. *But see* the substantive idea of democracy as expressed by Dworkin 1996 *supra*, p. 17, for whom the most fundamental aim of genuine democracy is not to pass laws in accordance with certain procedural requirements, but to treat "all members of the community, as individuals, with equal concern and respect".

community (in particular through the mass media) to have a larger set of information as to the people occupying such an important position as a justice. Unlike that which happens now in most European Constitutional Courts, in this way the community will have access to greater information and, hopefully, a clearer idea of 'who represents what' or of the specific political culture each justice carries.

This solution, of course, does not prevent justices from playing a less 'political' function, a function that as seen above is somehow connected with the 'in-the-middle' position of Constitutional Courts. However, public hearings give the addressees, or their representatives, a better way of participating in fundamental decisions affecting them, certainly better than the 'behind-closed-doors' procedures vastly used in Europe and at the European Union level.

A general preference for the typology of concrete instead of abstract review is a further procedural element adapting the Constitutional Courts better to the ideal of democracy. The concrete review typology, by allowing the parties of a case to raise a possible question of constitutionality, implements a relative 'socialization' of the constitutional review. By this expression is meant that, though in relative terms due to the filtering presence of the court invested by the case, concrete constitutional review gives the possibility for a wider spectrum of actors in a certain national community to stimulate the control and the respect of the constitution.

Instead of leaving the entire commencement procedures in the hands of public authorities (as for the abstract review typology), concrete review better fits in the idea of democracy by transferring the starting mechanisms to the hands of those who are the direct addressees of a certain provision thought to be unconstitutional. This transfer to the social arena provided by the concrete review typology is furthermore strengthened if it is paralleled by the extension of the number of institutional actors that can access and promote the judicial constitutional review. In particular, Constitutional Courts are more aligned with the ideal of democracy if the procedures governing their work allow 'groups of interests' relevant for the case (*e.g.* NGOs in human rights issues) to participate and help private parties in cases in front of the Constitutional Courts. Moreover, this 'democratization' of the constitutional review procedures can be strengthened by parallel reforms of procedural law allowing these groups of interests to participate in various trials where the issue of constitutionality can be then raised.

Another aspect to consider is introducing the mechanism of dissenting opinions. In this way, the various positions of justices, somehow mirroring the complexity of the issue among the community, can be represented entirely behind the legal reasoning leading to a certain decision. Introducing the mechanism of dissenting opinions also allows the legal discourse to get closer to those discourses in the other sub-systems. In controversial questions (*e.g.* euthanasia), in particular, the legal discourse, which tends to operate in a binary way ('either-or'), will be structurally more in touch with the other kind of discourses (*e.g.* cultural discourses), which can present a range of possible intermediate solutions. Moreover, as shown for example by US constitutional law history, the dissenting opinion of today can become the majority opinion for tomorrow or, in other words, it can lead the path for future decision-making and law-making developments.

A final suggestion in the direction of making the work of Constitutional Courts more in-line with the ideal of democracy here assumed, should be in the direction of opening to the public (and to the media in particular) the very proceedings of discussion of constitutional review. This, for instance, can be done by modeling the phase of debate as more similar to a 'normal' trial than as to the usual 'behind closed doors' decision-making process, the latter being closer to the political parties or group interests' way of taking fundamental decision (i.e. political actors).

In summary, pointing out the 'undemocratic' nature of decisions taken by justices is a never-ending debate, and probably, a question without a concrete solution, as justices are legal actors who will, and should, always play a political function. Instead, by focusing on the procedural aspects surrounding the work of Constitutional Courts, the above-mentioned suggestions open the courts to the scrutiny of and availability to larger segments of the community, and in the end, render the entire system of constitutional judicial review closer to the ideal of participative democracy.[51]

9. Conclusion

In the light of the debate as to judicial activism, in particular at the constitutional level, this work has investigated the issue of whether Constitutional Courts should be considered primarily legal or political actors and whether they really should be targeted for the political accusation of being 'undemocratic.' After having stressed in Part II the importance of Constitutional Court 'activism' inside the general issue of judicial activism, Part III pointed out the reasons why Constitutional Courts in established Western democracies can be seen as occupying an 'in-the-middle' position between the legal arena and the political arena. The central Parts IV and V then stressed the importance of the reasons why Constitutional Courts can be defined, from a legal theoretical perspective, as legal actors, though playing a political function. Part VI sketched certain of the consequences of this 'legal' characterization of Constitutional Courts, in particular as far as concerns the wrongfulness of absorbing judicial activism at the constitutional level (and the work of Constitutional Courts in general) in the general discussion about democracy. Finally, Part VII presented some possible examples of making the work of Constitutional Courts more 'compatible' with the Habermas ideal of democratic form of political organization, in particular focusing on the need of shifting from a 'democratic' Constitutional Court decisions to a 'democratic' Constitutional Courts procedures.

51 *See* Waldron 2001 *supra*, p. 276: "[P]rocedural rules... make participation possible, by setting out a matrix of interaction in which particular contributions can take their place and 'register'."

In conclusion, criticizing Constitutional Courts for not fulfilling the democracy criterion is like criticizing a soccer referee for not being democratic because he or she does not follow the teams' beliefs on controversial decisions during a match. As for political parties, the teams' belief can eventually become a criterion in choosing a certain referee (as for justices in the United States), or in adopting certain types of basic rules at the beginning of the tournament or in the deciding of playing a certain tournament or even in later changing the rules of the game. However, once the teams have decided to be in the tournament and to play by the fundamental rules, while playing the match the teams' belief systems cannot and ought not to be used in evaluating how the referee should apply the fundamental rules of the game: a soccer referee can be criticized for having applied the wrong rule or of having misjudged the situation to which the rule was applied, but not for being 'undemocratic.'[52]

As for soccer, one of the essential elements for having a real, functioning, and fair to everybody democracy perhaps is having 'undemocratic' chosen referees for the match, who apply during it rules felt as 'undemocratic' both by one team's players and fans.

52 *See* Stephen Holmes, *Passion and Constraint: On the Theory of Liberal Democracy*, University of Chicago Press, Chicago, 1995, p. 163-164, as to the different types of constitutive rules and regulative rules. *But see* Waldron 2001 *supra*, p. 277.

II – Independence and Accountability of Judges and Adjudicators

Adjudicative Independence: Canadian Perspectives

*John Evans**

1. Introduction

Judicial independence is for judges what academic freedom is for professors. Both are generally acknowledged as indispensable. Judicial independence is the bedrock of the rule of law in a democratic society because it allows for the impartial adjudication of disputes according to law, free from external influences. Academic freedom protects the dispassionate pursuit of truth through research, writing, and teaching. These principles preserve the legitimacy of the institutions and activities to which they relate and thereby protect the fundamental public interests in justice, and in advancing our understanding of the world, society, and the human condition.

Both concepts are, however, contingent and contested at the margins. Governments are tempted to rail against judicial decisions that do not conform to their policy preferences or political interests, and to call into question the legitimacy of decision-makers who are neither elected, nor politically accountable to the Legislature or the Executive. It is never too difficult to arouse a suspicion in the public that judicial independence and academic freedom are merely devices created by judges and professors to ensure that their privileges and policy preferences are beyond the reach of the public at large and its elected representatives.

On the other hand, judges and professors can stretch the concepts of judicial independence and academic freedom beyond their intended goals; they are not all about us, but about the respective public interests that they serve. To be frank, we are both rather good at persuading ourselves, if not others, that our professional and personal interests are one and the same as the public good. The danger is that unduly expanding these concepts will discredit them and render them incapable of performing their essential functions.

Judicial independence and academic freedom must also be dynamic concepts if they are to remain functional. They must evolve in response to new demands and challenges relating to, for example: the proper roles of the judiciary and the academy in contemporary society; competing and growing demands for public

* J.M. Evans is Judge in the Federal Court of Appeal, Canada. He wishes to thank Kathrin Furniss, his law clerk for the judicial year 2011-12, for her substantial contributions to the preparation of this paper. Her work here, as in all other aspects of her professional responsibilities, is characterized by diligent research and perceptiveness.

accountability in the exercise of power and use of scarce resources; and changing demographics and societal values.

In Canada, the independence of the judiciary has traditionally and principally been concerned with protecting judges from attempts by the government to improperly influence the course or outcome of litigation, whether or not the government is a party. Another important aspect of judicial independence concerns the institutional independence of courts. While the Executive retains overall financial control by setting courts' budgets, some aspects of the operation of courts are so closely linked to the adjudication of cases that judicial independence requires that they be left within the control of the court itself, normally acting through its chief justice.[1] These core areas of judicial administration include: the assignment of judges to cases; the sittings of the court; the establishment of court lists; the allocation of courtrooms; and the direction of the court staff engaged in carrying out these and other functions connected to the performance of judges' adjudicative responsibilities. Institutional independence as an aspect of judicial independence is not discussed further in this paper.[2]

Maintaining the confidence of the public in the impartial and independent character of the judiciary is of vital importance to the rule of law. The legal arrangements for securing judicial independence must therefore be sufficiently robust to satisfy a sceptical public that its judges will decide cases according to law, without fear or favour. The legal test of judicial independence is objective: would a reasonably informed person, having thought the matter through in a practical manner, conclude that the judge was independent?[3]

Political culture and public opinion give judicial independence its vitality; both the Legislature and the Executive (and particularly its political heads, the Ministers) must be mindful not to trespass on terrain of the Judiciary and thus bring into question its independence. They should, for example, not voice criticisms of individual judicial decisions that, because of their content or tone, might appear to members of the public as likely to intimidate judges and thus to call into question their independence. This, of course, is in no way to say that judges and their decisions are above or immune from vigorous criticism from public and politicians alike. But there are lines that, in the interests of maintaining judicial independence, should not be crossed.

The first half of my paper gives a brief account of the constitutional framework within which judicial independence is secured in Canada, and compares judges and members of administrative tribunals in this regard. The second part describes three contemporary pressure points where judicial independence comes up

1 See *R. v. Valente*, [1985] 2 S.C.R. 673 (*Valente* case).

2 See further, Fabien Gélinas, Judicial Independence in Canada: A Critical Overview, in Anja Seibert-Fohr (ed.), *Judicial Independence in Transition*, Springer, Heidelberg, 2012, p. 567.

3 *Valente* case *supra* footnote 1, paras. 21-22.

against the competing principle of accountability: the processes for the appointment of judges, for the determination of judges' salaries and pensions, and for the disposition of complaints of judicial misconduct. The Constitution does not deal expressly with any of these issues, although the constitutional guarantees of judges' security of tenure and financial security form an essential backdrop. And it is to this that I now turn.

2. The Constitutional Framework

1. *The Judiciary*

If political culture and public opinion provide the necessary vitality to judicial independence, the law and the Constitution provide its essential form and structure. Canada is a federation and is in some respects very decentralized; however, compared with the United States, the federal level of government plays a relatively small role in the regulation of trade and commerce. For example, only last year, the Supreme Court of Canada declared unconstitutional a federal Bill creating a federal scheme for the regulation of the capital market and securities industry.[4]

However, the *Constitution Act, 1867*, which sets out the division of powers between the provinces and the central government, does not rigorously apply the federal principle to the judiciary, unlike the Constitutions of the United States, and Australia for example. Thus, section 96 confers on the federal government the power to appoint the judges of the superior courts and courts of appeal in each of the ten provinces and the three territories, which administer both provincial and federal law within their borders. Section 101 also authorizes the federal Parliament to create additional courts for the administration of federal law (currently, the Tax Court of Canada,[5] the Federal Court and Federal Court of Appeal[6]), and "a General Court of Appeal for Canada" – the Supreme Court of Canada, our national court of last resort from provincial courts of appeal and the Federal Court of Appeal. The federal government appoints the judges of the section 101 courts, and is responsible for paying the salaries and pensions of the all the judges it appoints.

4 *Reference re Securities Act*, 2011 SCC 66.

5 Formerly the Tax Review Board, the Tax Court of Canada principally hears appeals by taxpayers from federal income tax and goods and services tax (analogous to VAT) assessments.

6 The Federal Courts were established in 1971 by the *Federal Courts Act*, R.S.C. 1985, c. F-7. They decide disputes governed by wide areas of federal law, including disputes between individuals and the federal government and its agencies (federal administrative law), taxation appeals, intellectual property, Aboriginal law, maritime law, and any issues of constitutional law arising therefrom. In contrast, the Supreme Court of Canada, also a statutory court and created in 1875, determines disputes involving constitutional law, provincial laws (statutory and non-statutory, the civil law of Quebec and the common law of other jurisdictions), and federal laws, including the *Criminal Code*.

On the other hand, the administration of justice in the provinces is the responsibility of the provincial level of government.[7] This includes the creation, operation, and financing of the courts in the province (including those in which federally appointed judge sit) and the appointment of judges to the courts below the level of the superior courts. Provincially appointed judges decide all but the most serious criminal cases, as well as cases involving aspects of family law and the welfare of children. There is a right of appeal from the provincial court of a province to its superior court.

Drawing on the British *Act of Settlement* of 1701, Canada's *Constitution Act, 1867* sets out the three basic safeguards of independence for the judges of the superior courts: tenure in office until the age of 75 during good behaviour; dismissal from office only on an address passed by both Houses of the federal Parliament; and a salary and pension provided by Act of Parliament.[8]

These explicit protections of the independence of superior court judges do not apply to judges of the lower courts appointed by provincial governments.[9] However, in 1997, the Supreme Court extended to provincial court judges the protections of the basic principles of security of tenure, salary, and pension.[10] It held that judicial independence is an unwritten principle of the Constitution that extends beyond its specific provisions; guarantees of security of tenure, salary, and pension analogous to those of superior court judges apply to all judges.[11]

7 *Constitution Act 1867* (UK), 30 & 31 Victoria, c. 3, s. 92(14).

8 The relevant text of the *Constitution Act 1867, ibid.*, reads as follows:
"99 (1) Subject to subsection two of this section, the Judges of the Superior Courts shall hold office during good behaviour, but shall be removable by the Governor General on Address of the Senate and House of Commons.
(2) A Judge of a Superior Court, whether appointed before or after the coming into force of this section, shall cease to hold office upon attaining the age of seventy-five years, or upon the coming into force of this section if at that time he has already attained that age.
100. The Salaries, Allowances, and Pensions of the Judges of the Superior, District, and County Courts (except the Courts of Probate in Nova Scotia and New Brunswick), and of the Admiralty Courts in Cases where the Judges thereof are for the Time being paid by Salary, shall be fixed and provided by the Parliament of Canada."

9 Nor is it altogether clear that these provisions apply to judges of the courts created by federal legislation under section 101. Section 11(d) of the *Canadian Charter of Rights and Freedoms*, Part I of the *Constitution Act, 1982*, being Schedule B to the *Canada Act 1982* (UK), 1982, c. 11 (*Charter*) provides that those charged with offences are entitled to a trial before an independent and impartial tribunal. This provision applies to provincial courts when exercising their criminal, but not their civil jurisdiction.

10 *Reference Re Remuneration of Judges of the Provincial Court of Prince Edward Island*, [1997] 3 S.C.R. 3 (*Judges' Remuneration Reference*). If judges of the federally created courts are not within the express provisions of the *Constitution Act, 1867*, they are certainly covered by this decision.

11 See *supra* footnote 9.

2. *Administrative Tribunals*

Unlike judges of the courts, members of administrative tribunals, whether federal or provincial, enjoy no constitutional protection for their independence.[12] This may seem particularly surprising given that governments, both federal and provincial, are parties to most administrative proceedings in Canada, and often have a stake in the outcome that goes well beyond the particular case.

Nonetheless, in *Ocean Port Hotel Ltd. v. British Columbia (General Manager, Liquor Control and Licensing Branch)*[13] the Supreme Court of Canada held that administrative tribunals are part of the Executive branch of government because their function is to implement government policy in the context of particular facts. Accordingly, members of administrative tribunals do not enjoy the kind of protection of their independence that in the *Judges' Remuneration Reference* the Supreme Court found implicit in the Constitution for judges not covered by the specific provisions of the *Constitution Act, 1867*.

Ocean Port has been the subject of much critical commentary by scholars and others who have pointed out that the bright line drawn by the Supreme Court between courts and administrative tribunals is too stark. While some administrative bodies certainly fulfil the policy implementation function described by the Supreme Court in *Ocean Port*, others are better described as "rights tribunals" and are much more akin to courts. It is thus arguably inappropriate to deny to members of *all* administrative tribunals any constitutional guarantee of independence to protect tribunal members from improper interference by government with their decisions.[14] The criticisms made of *Ocean Port* include the following.

---

12 The only hint of constitutional guarantee of the independence of all adjudicative decision-makers appears in subsection 2(e) of the *Canadian Bill of Rights*, S.C. 1960, c. 44, which provides that individuals' legal rights and obligations must be determined by a "fair hearing in accordance with the principles of fundamental justice". The *Bill of Rights* was enacted by the Parliament of Canada in 1960, and was a precursor of the *Charter, ibid.*, which is a part of Canada's formal Constitution. While described as having 'quasi-constitutional status', the *Bill of Rights* is a federal statute and therefore does not apply to legislation, administrative acts, or institutions of provincial governments. Before the *Charter*, the courts construed the *Bill of Rights* narrowly; since the *Charter*, it has been largely ignored. Nonetheless, it is still in force and contains some provisions, such as the enjoyment of property described in section 1(a), which are not found in the *Charter. See generally* Peter Hogg, *Constitutional Law of Canada* (5th ed.), Thomson Reuters, Toronto, 2007, chapter 35 (loose-leaf, consulted on 8 May 2012). The procedural fairness of a decision of an administrative tribunal may also be challenged in judicial review proceedings on the ground that the tribunal was not independent. However, since this is a common law rule, it may be excluded by statute either expressly or by necessary implication. See Brown & Evans, *Judicial Review of Administrative Action in Canada* (6th ed.), Canvasback, Toronto, 2011, chapter 11 at p. 21-25, 69-74 (loose-leaf, consulted on 14 May, 2012).

13 2001 SCC 52, [2001] 2 S.C.R. 781 (*Ocean Port* case).

14 *See e.g.* Ron Ellis, Fair Hearings in an *Ocean Port* World: A Textured Concept, *Journal of Law and Social Policy*, Vol. 18, 2003, p. 46; Ron Ellis, The Justicizing of Quasi-Judicial Tribunals. Part I, *Canadian Journal of Administrative Law & Practise*, Vol. 19, 2006, No. 3, p. 303 & Ron Ellis, The

First, there is little functional difference between what courts and many administrative "rights tribunals" do. Both adjudicate disputes between individuals (including the government) and determine their rights and obligations on the basis of findings of fact, apply the relevant law to those facts, and exercise their discretion over the award of the appropriate remedy or some other aspect of the dispute.

Second, these functional similarities are reflected in their decision-making processes. The common law rules of natural justice and the duty of procedural fairness, or their statutory codifications, provide for participatory procedures that are to a large extent simplified versions of the procedures followed by the courts.

Third, whether a legislature entrusts the resolution of disputes arising from a statutory scheme to a court or a specialist tribunal may be more a question of practicality than principle. Further, whether an adjudicative body is called a court or a tribunal is little guide to its functions, powers, or formality. For example, the chair of the Competition *Tribunal* is a Federal Court Judge, as are some of its members, and its powers and procedures closely resemble those of courts. On the other hand, provincial small claims *courts*, which deal mainly with consumer disputes involving small sums of money, are highly informal.

Fourth, many administrative tribunals deal with matters involving relatively small amounts of money (social assistance, employment insurance, workers' entitlement to vacation pay or minimum wage, and disputes between landlords and tenants, for example). However, small sums of money may be very important to those of modest means. The larger sums of money at stake in commercial disputes that end up in a superior court are not necessarily more important to the parties concerned.

Some administrative tribunals regularly adjudicate disputes involving constitutional rights: the Immigration and Refugee Board,[15] the National Parole Board, mental competency tribunals, and human rights tribunals,[16] for instance. Indeed, most adjudicative tribunals also have express or implicit jurisdiction to decide questions of constitutional law necessary to dispose of a matter properly before them, to determine the constitutional validity of provisions of the statute under which they operate, and to fashion an appropriate remedy for breach of an individual's constitutional right.[17]

Justicizing of Quasi-Judicial Tribunals. Part II, *Canadian Journal of Administrative Law & Practise*, Vol. 20, 2007, No. 1, p. 69.

15 A determination by the Board to accept or reject a person's claim for refugee status in Canada may literally be a question of life or death.

16 Human rights tribunals adjudicate disputes arising under anti-discrimination legislation. These disputes often have constitutional overtones, in the sense that they may raise issues very similar to those arising under the constitutional guarantee of equality and freedom from discrimination in section 15 of the *Canadian Charter of Rights and Freedoms*, *supra* note 8. The *Charter* was added to the Canadian Constitution in 1982.

17 *R. v. Conway*, 2010 SCC 22, [2010] 1 S.C.R. 765 (*Conway* case).

The truth of the matter is that administrative tribunals are immensely varied in the functions they perform, the powers they exercise, and the seriousness of the impact that they have on the rights and interests of individuals. Tribunals are normally specifically created and designed to decide disputes arising from the administration of a particular statutory program or a cluster of programs in a given area ("land use planning" or "social justice", for example).[18] While some are truly adjudicative ("rights tribunals"), others render individual decisions, or make general rules and policies, that are governed more by the exercise of broad discretion and public policy choices than by the application of more or less precise statutory standards to individual facts.

On the other hand, tribunals created to regulate an area of economic activity (telecommunications, energy, foreign investment, and securities, for example) typically render their decisions on the basis of broad statutory grants of discretion which call for the balancing of competing interests in order to determine where the public interest lies. It may be appropriate to keep those exercising these powers on a shorter political leash. One model of independence may well not fit all administrative decision-makers. Critics argue that the *Ocean Port* decision fails to acknowledge this.[19]

I should note here one constitutional interface between the courts and administrative adjudication, which relates to the independence of courts and the lack of similar guarantees for administrative tribunals. The Canadian Constitution does not expressly guarantee a right to judicial review of decisions made by administrative bodies affecting individuals' legal rights, even though the decision-maker is not independent of the Executive and, like decisions made by courts, the decision turns on the interpretation of legislation and the finding of facts.[20]

However, the Supreme Court has held that provincial legislatures may not entirely exclude decisions of administrative tribunals from judicial review in the superior courts.[21] The Court inferred this limitation from the power of the federal government under section 96 of the *Constitution Act* to appoint judges to the superior courts in the provinces. The Court reasoned that it would make a mockery of this

18 The province of Ontario recently 'clustered' adjudicative tribunals working in similar areas through the *Adjudicative Tribunals Accountability, Governance and Appointments Act*, 2009, S.O. 2009, c. 33 Schedule 5, ss. 15-19.

19 See *supra* note 14. It is also notable that the Supreme Court subsequently appeared to recognize the varied character of administrative bodies (see *Bell Canada v. Canadian Telephone Employees Assn.*, 2003 SCC 36, [2003] 1 S.C.R. 884 at paras. 21-22). The issue of administrative independence has not been fully resolved.

20 Of course, if the decision affects a person's constitutionally protected rights, it is always possible to challenge the decision in a superior court. Tribunals' decisions engaging the constitution are always subject to review.

21 *Crevier v. Attorney General for Québec*, [1981] 2 S.C.R. 220 (*Crevier*). Previously, courts had narrowly interpreted clauses limiting judicial review so that they did not preclude decisions that were beyond the tribunal's 'jurisdiction'. The preclusive clause considered in *Crevier* was held to exclude all judicial review, even of decisions outside the tribunal's jurisdiction.

appointing power if provinces could remove the core jurisdiction of the courts in which federally appointed judges sit and give to a provincial tribunal the power to decide the limits of its own jurisdiction without the possibility of review in the superior courts.

Nowadays, this constitutional right to judicial review is viewed as based on the rule of law, rather than on the division of powers between the federal and provincial levels of government. In particular, it reflects the notion that no one's legal rights or duties may be conclusively determined by an administrative body (whose members may not have the essential protections of independence) without some level of scrutiny by an independent court.[22]

3. Three Current Pressure Points

Judicial independence is not an absolute value, but must be balanced against other constitutional principles. As mentioned earlier, in recent years judicial independence has been important in Canada in three areas: the processes for appointing judges, fixing the level of judges' compensation, and for disciplining judges for misconduct. In each instance, the task has been to design a process that appropriately balances judicial independence and political or public accountability.

1. *Judicial Appointments*

If judicial independence were an absolute principle, then judicial appointments would be free from all political influence. However, democratic principles require political accountability for the appointment of senior public office-holders, including judges. In a parliamentary system of government such as Canada's, political accountability is secured through the Minister responsible for making the appointment. The question is how to find a process that strikes a satisfactory balance between these competing principles.

The approximately 1,100 judges of the superior courts in Canada are appointed by the federal government from members of the Bar of the Province or Territory where they are to sit.[23] The legal profession in Canada is organized on the common law model, in the sense that law students do not elect a career as a judge or an advocate. Candidates for judicial appointment must have been qualified to practise law for at least ten years.[24] In their pre-judicial lives, most judges will

22 Since *Crevier*, *ibid.*, administrative law has seen the virtual disappearance of the concept of 'jurisdictional' provisions in an enabling statute. It is therefore difficult to define how much judicial review is constitutionally guaranteed. For most purposes, it may extend only to administrative tribunal decisions that can be shown to be unreasonable. With or without a preclusive clause limiting judicial review, courts normally defer to tribunals' interpretation of their enabling legislation unless it is unreasonable.

23 *Constitution Act, 1867*, ss. 97 and 98.

24 *Judges Act*, R.S.C. 1985, c. J-1, s. 3. In fact, most appointees have been lawyers for at least twenty years.

have been in private practice as lawyers; government lawyers and, more rarely, law professors (like me) are also appointed from time to time.

In Canada, the appointment process for all federally appointed judges, other than judges of the Supreme Court of Canada, has three stages. First, under a non-statutory process introduced in 1988, an advisory committee in each province assesses the qualifications of lawyers who have applied for a judicial appointment. On the basis of a candidate's letter of application, and informal and confidential consultations within the profession, the committee determines whether to recommend or not recommend the candidate as suitable for a judicial appointment. These committees comprise judges, lawyers, and non-lawyer nominees of the federal Minister of Justice. The committees' confidential recommendations are sent to the Minister of Justice. About 40% of applicants are recommended.

Ministers are not in law bound by the committees' recommendations. However, they have undertaken not to appoint candidates whom a committee has not recommended. Nonetheless, this is a relatively small restriction of the Government's appointment power because at any given time the number of those recommended by an advisory committee for judicial appointment exceeds the number of judicial vacancies. In addition, the present Government instructed the advisory committees that candidates were to be put into one of only two categories: recommended or not recommended for judicial appointment. Previously, candidates had been ranked as highly qualified, qualified, or not qualified.

At the second stage, the Minister recommends to the Cabinet the name of a person to be appointed to a particular position. At this stage, political "jockeying" may occur among "recommended" candidates. Third, the Minister recommends to Cabinet the appointment of a particular person to a vacancy. Cabinet usually, but by no means always, accepts the Minister's recommendation.

This process has attracted much criticism recently, not because of the quality of those appointed as judges, but because it is non-transparent and overly politically partisan.[25] Although not traditionally seen as relevant to the post-appointment independence of judges, the present appointment system has also been criticised on the ground that it puts the perceived independence of judges into question in two respects.

25 See e.g. Lorne Sossin, Judicial Appointment, Democratic Aspirations, and the Culture of Accountability, *University of New Brunswick Law Journal*, Vol. 58, 2008, p. 11; Troy Riddell, Lori Hausegger & Matthew Henniger, Federal Judicial Appointments: A Look at Patronage in Federal Judicial Appointments since 1988, *University of Toronto Law Journal*, Vol. 58, 2008, p. 39. It is also said that the current appointment process has resulted in the recent appointment of too few women and members of visible minorities (*see e.g.* Jeff Bassett, Minority lawyers demand diversity among appointed judges, *The Globe and Mail* (8 March 2012), <m.theglobeandmail.com>). The legitimacy of the exercise of judicial power depends in part at least on judges being representative of the population as a whole.

First, it might be thought that a judge appointed through political connections is likely to be disposed to find in favour of the government who appointed him or her, as a matter of gratitude or loyalty. Judicial security of tenure after appointment only goes so far by way of ensuring judicial independence. Loyalties may be seen as persisting after appointment, and the possibility of promotion to a higher court may be regarded as an additional inducement to favour the government side in litigation.[26]

Second, it may be thought that Governments will tend to appoint judges who share their particular ideology on, for example, law and order, environmental issues, or labour relations. The independence or impartiality of such judges may be regarded as suspect because of their ideological inclinations.

Not surprisingly, commentators complain that the determination of a litigant's legal rights, or the length of a prison sentence imposed on a person convicted of a crime, should not depend on whether a case comes before Judge *X* who was appointed by one Government, or Judge *Y* who was appointed by another. Indeed, a recent academic study has attracted public attention because it purports to show a wide disparity among judges of the Federal Court in the frequency with which they have granted leave to applicants seeking judicial review of tribunal decisions in immigration and refugee cases.[27] The author argues that his study suggests that judges appointed by the present Government are more likely to find in favour of the Minister than those appointed by previous Governments.

I express no view on the validity of the methodology employed in this study or on the soundness of its conclusions. I would only say that judging is as much art as science; finding the facts, formulating the legal rule relevant to a given case, and applying it to the facts, are far from being mechanical exercises. Judges inevitably bring to these tasks, especially in close cases, a perspective shaped by their life experiences, values, and personal philosophy.

Provinces have their own processes for appointing judges to provincial courts. The process in Ontario, Canada's largest and most culturally diverse province, is widely admired.[28] Vacancies are advertised and applications are invited. The selection committee conducts formal interviews with candidates and places three names before the provincial Attorney General, who is normally expected to select from this list. The process is believed to have greatly reduced the role of partisan political influence in judicial appointments and to have resulted in a Bench that is not only very competent, but also closely reflects the gender, ethnic, and racial

26 The promotion of judges to higher courts is entirely a matter for the Minister of Justice. Might a reasonably informed person think that judges interested in promotion would be reluctant to make decision that would displease the Government?

27 Sean Rehaag, Judicial Review of Refugee Determinations: The Luck of the Draw?, *Queen's Law Journal*, Vol. 38, 2012, No. 1, p. 1-58.

28 Ontario's appointment process is described in: Judicial Appointments Advisory Committee, *Annual Report for 2010*, Ontario Court of Justice, Toronto, 2011, p. 13-20 www.ontariocourts.ca>.

diversity of the Province, and is perceived as independent. Giving the Minister the power to select from among three names ensures an appropriate level of political accountability.

The appointment by the federal government of the nine judges to Canada's highest court, the Supreme Court of Canada, has attracted much media attention in recent years, largely because of the public's awareness of the Court's increased powers following the addition of the *Canadian Charter of Rights and Freedoms* to the Constitution in 1982, which has brought many controversial issues to the Court. *Charter* cases have included challenges to the validity of legislation concerning the refugee determination process, a woman's right to an abortion, child pornography, and collective bargaining rights.[29] The *Charter* has also been the basis for challenging the validity of Ministers' decisions to close a safe injection drug facility, and to refuse to request the United States to return a Canadian citizen detained in the Guantanamo Bay facility.[30]

Nonetheless, appointments to our Supreme Court have not so far been ideologically-driven to anywhere near the same extent as in the United States, where law and order, racial equality, reproductive rights, religion and the state, and sexual orientation are highly divisive political issues.

Recent changes to the process for appointing judges to the Supreme Court of Canada are designed to make it more transparent. Although the precise details of this non-statutory process remain in flux, the essential elements seem to be as follows.[31]

First, after consulting broadly in the legal community, the Minister of Justice identifies six or more candidates to fill a vacancy on the Court. Second, these names go to an all-party advisory committee composed of Members of Parliament, which consults broadly and evaluates the candidates identified by the Minister and reduces the Minister's list to three names. Third, the prime minister nominates

29 See *Singh v. Minister of Employment and Immigration*, [1985] 1 S.C.R. 177 (refugee process); *R. v. Morgentaler*, [1988] 1 S.C.R. 30 (abortion); *R. v. Sharpe*, 2001 SCC 2, [2001] 1 S.C.R. 45 (child pornography); *Health Services and Support – Facilities Subsector Bargaining Assn. v. British Columbia*, 2007 SCC 27, [2007] 2 SCR 391 (collective bargaining).

30 See *Canada (Attorney General) v. PHS Community Services Society*, 2011 SCC 44, [2011] 3 S.C.R. 134 (safe injection); *Canada (Prime Minister) v. Khadr*, 2010 SCC 3, [2010] 1 S.C.R. 44 (return of Guantanamo detainee).

31 See Sossin 2008 *supra*; Benjamin Alarie & Andrew Green, Policy Preferences and Appointments to the Supreme Court of Canada, *Osgoode Hall Law Journal*, Vol. 47, 2009, No. 1, p. 6-12. The composition of the nine-judge Supreme Court of Canada is regional. That is, three judges must by law come from the Province of Québec (Canada's only civil law and francophone jurisdiction); and by convention three come from Ontario (Canada's most populous province), and one from British Columbia, one from the three provinces of Alberta, Saskatchewan or Manitoba, and one from the Atlantic region provinces of Nova Scotia, New Brunswick, Prince Edward Island, and Newfoundland and Labrador. When a judge retires, his or her successor will be appointed from the same region.

one of these candidates. Fourth, the chosen candidate appears at a televised hearing held by an all-party parliamentary committee, at which he or she makes a statement of their judicial philosophy and answers questions from Parliamentarians. Fifth, the prime minister makes the final selection and the person is appointed by order in council.

It is too early to say how broadly acceptable this process will prove to be. Suffice it to say that critics complain that it still leaves too much power in the hands of the Executive and provides too little by way of accountability for its exercise. In my view, the larger question is whether judicial independence requires a more radical de-politicisation of the appointment process for all federally appointed judges.

I suspect that the time may be ripe for a serious conversation in Canada along these lines. Ontario's appointment process, in both design and operation, offers a very attractive alternative model. It appears to have produced high quality judges and strengthened judicial independence, while retaining with the Minister the ultimate power to appoint and effective political accountability for its exercise. In my opinion, the processes for the appointment of judges by the federal government should be tilted more to enhancing judicial independence, and political power (and hence accountability) reduced.

2. *Judicial Compensation*

Financial security is an important aspect of judicial independence. Hence, section 100 of the *Constitution Act, 1867* requires that judges be paid such salaries and pensions as are prescribed in a statute enacted by the Parliament of Canada. However, section 100 is silent on the process by which the appropriate level of statutory compensation is to be determined. In a parliamentary system of government, such as Canada's, the Executive effectively determines the levels of judicial compensation as part of its responsibility for the expenditure of public funds, at least when it has a parliamentary majority. The challenge is to design a process for determining judges' compensation that both safeguards judicial independence and recognizes governmental accountability for the expenditure of public funds.

Here is the problem. In one form or another, the federal government is a frequent litigant before the superior courts. Indeed, no other litigant appears as frequently in either the Federal Courts or the Supreme Court of Canada. The fact that judges are dependent on a frequent litigant for maintaining or increasing their levels of compensation may lead to a public perception that judges are likely to find in favour of the government in litigation, especially in politically sensitive cases, in order to protect their own financial interests.

The Constitution provides no mechanisms for dealing with this delicate issue. However, this did not deter the Supreme Court of Canada in the *Judges' Remuneration Reference* from establishing the governing principles. The case concerned the validity of legislated reductions of the salaries of provincial court judges in three provinces, as part of across-the-board cuts to remuneration in the public service in the provinces concerned.

The Court stated that it was entirely inconsistent with judicial independence for judges to negotiate with the Executive over compensation increases, decreases, or freezes. On the other hand, the Court also recognized that it would be unfair to require judges to wait passively for whatever the Government might decide to do, if anything, with respect to judicial compensation. To allow governmental inaction over time to reduce the purchasing power of judicial compensation is inconsistent with the spirit, if not the letter, of section 100 of the *Constitution Act* which provides that the salaries and pensions of superior court judges must be fixed by Act of Parliament. The Court resolved the tension between the Executive's responsibility for public expenditure and judicial independence by inferring from the "unwritten constitutional principle" of judicial independence the institutional mechanisms for determining judicial compensation, which Parliament has now codified.[32]

Every four years, an independent commission is struck to make recommendations to the government, on the basis of objective criteria, on the levels of judicial compensation.[33] One member of the commission is appointed by the federal Government, and one by the Superior Court Judges Association; the chair is appointed by the other two members. The parties make written and oral submissions to the commission, and adduce evidence, on the basis of which the commission makes recommendations to the Government in a published report. The Government must respond within six months. Governments are not bound to implement these recommendations because they are ultimately responsible for public finances. However, if they do not accept a commission's recommendations, they must provide reasons for their decision. Similar provisions have been enacted by provincial legislatures for dealing with the salaries of judges appointed by the provinces.

It was anticipated that governments would normally implement the recommendations of an independent and well-informed commission. But this is not how it has worked out. Commission reports have generally been regarded as carefully researched and reasoned, and balanced in their recommendations. However, governments have given them relatively little deference. The present federal Government has twice significantly reduced the salary increases recommended by two commissions. Judges of the superior courts are yet to follow the example of some provincial court judges and applied for judicial review of the legal-

32 *Judges Act*, R.S.C. 1985, c J-1, ss. 25-26.3.

33 If, mid-way through a four-year cycle, economic conditions require a reduction in judicial salaries a part of a broader program of public sector wage restraint, the government would convene a commission and obtain its recommendation. The *Judges' Remuneration Reference* also held that the government could not reduce judicial salaries to a point that judges' independence was in jeopardy. The concept of a constitutionally guaranteed wage for judges, and defined by judges, has provoked some skepticism among commentators!

ity of the Executive's exercise of its statutory discretion not to accept commission recommendations.[34]

It is obvious that the system is not working well. In my view, the Commission process is unduly formalistic, expensive, and adversarial. The results are too often unacceptable to the ultimate paymaster. The not uncommon applications by provincial court judges for judicial review by superior court judges of government compensation decisions are frankly embarrassing. The public may be right to be sceptical of a system for determining judges' pay in which the judges write the rules, referee disputes, and are players of the game![35] This is an area in which, in my opinion, the concept of judicial independence has been stretched too far.

3. *Judicial Discipline*

Superior court judges may only be dismissed from office for misconduct following a Parliamentary resolution.[36] No superior court judge has ever been dismissed, although there have been a few "pre-emptive" resignations when dismissal seemed a real possibility. Security of tenure is at the heart of judicial independence. A legal system in which judges fear dismissal if they render a decision that displeases the Government does not comply with the rule of law. The appeal process is the

34 See e.g. *Alberta Provincial Judges' Association v. Alberta* (1999), 177 D.L.R. (4th) 418 (Alta. C.A.) (the Alberta Government's reasons for departing from the commission's recommendations with respect to remuneration of provincial court judges were not rational; the Court ordered implementation of the recommendations); *Manitoba Provincial Judges Assn. v. Manitoba (Minister of Justice)* (2001), 2001 MBQB 191, 202 D.L.R. (4th) 698 (Man. Q.B.) (commission's recommendations rejected by the government ordered implemented because the reasons for rejecting them were either irrelevant, unsupported by economic facts, did not respond to the specific recommendation, or did not provide a proper analysis with respect to the Committee's concerns); *Mackin v. New Brunswick (Minister of Finance)*, 2002 SCC 13, [2002] 1 S.C.R. 405 (legislation abolishing supernumerary (part-time) judges unconstitutional because the change was not approved by an independent compensation commission); *Bodner v. Alberta*, 2005 SCC 44, [2005] 2 S.C.R. 286 (the reasons given by New Brunswick, Ontario, and Alberta for departing from the recommendations were rational; however, the Quebec government needed to reconsider the issue, their reasons having been rejected as unreasonable).

35 The Supreme Court's decision in the *Judges' Remuneration Reference* has been subject to considerable negative criticism by commentators. They have argued, among other things, that the Court constructed out of whole cloth a legal process for reviewing changes to judges' salary levels that was extremely detailed, cumbersome, and based on dubious legal principles. The Court, it was said, had gone too far to protect judicial salaries, for reasons not reasonably connected to judicial independence. *See e.g.* Robert G. Richards, Provincial Court Judges Decision – Case Comment, *Saskatchewan Law Review*, Vol. 61, 1998, p. 575; Tsvi Kahana, The Constitution as a Collective Agreement: Remuneration of Provincial Court Judges in Canada, *Queen's Law Journal*, Vol. 29, 2004, p. 445; Peter W. Hogg, The Bad Idea of Unwritten Constitutional Principles: Protecting Judicial Salaries, *in* Adam Dodek & Lorne Sossin (eds.)., *Judicial Independence In Context*, Irwin Law, Toronto, 2010, p. 25; Lori Sterling & Sean Hanley, The Case for Dialogue in the Judicial Remuneration Process, *in* Adam Dodek & Lorne Sossin (eds.), *Judicial Independence In Context*, Irwin Law, Toronto, 2010, p. 37.

36 Judges of provincial courts enjoy similar protections, though an address by the legislature is not required: *Judges' Remuneration Reference* at para. 115.

normal, public method of correcting errors in the way in which a judge decided a case or conducted the proceeding.

However, judges should also be accountable to the public for behaviour, in and out of court, that falls short of the standards expected of judges, even if it is not so serious as to render them unfit to hold office and thus liable to dismissal. The tension between judicial independence and accountability has increased with the decline of public deference to authority figures, including judges, and a more democratic culture.

Not all kinds of judicial misconduct can be appropriately remedied through the appeal process, such as: allegations of racist or sexist comments; a pattern of chronic delays in rendering judgments or of rudeness to participants in a trial; a criminal conviction for driving under the influence of alcohol; and sexual harassment of court staff.

The Canadian Judicial Council (CJC) is a statutory body composed principally of chief justices and associate chief justices.[37] Its mandate is "to promote efficiency and uniformity, and to improve the quality of judicial service, in superior courts ...".[38] As part of this mandate the CJC receives complaints of judicial misconduct from members of the public.[39]

A member of the Judicial Conduct Committee of the CJC reviews each complaint. Most complaints are dismissed summarily because, for example, they are about a judge's decision rather than his or her conduct, or concern a provincially rather than federally appointed judge.

If a complaint is not immediately resolved in this manner, it is the subject of further investigation, sometimes by independent counsel. The report of the investigation is considered by a Review Panel of three or five judges. If the Panel finds the complaint to be unmeritorious, it is dismissed. If the Panel is of the view that the complaint has merit, but is not serious enough to warrant possible dismissal, the Panel will dismiss the complaint but may express concern or, with the judge's consent, recommend counselling. Up to this point, the process is not public.

However, if the Panel is satisfied that the complaint is sufficiently serious that it could result in a finding that the judge is unfit to hold office, it refers the complaint to the CJC's Inquiry Committee. The Committee holds public hearings on the complaints referred to it and prepares a report for the full Council of the CJC. If the Council concludes on the basis of this report that the judge's conduct constitutes

37 *Judges Act supra* footnote 32, s. 59.

38 *Id.*, s. 60(1).

39 For an overview of the complaints process, see Gélinas 2012 *supra*, p. 15-19. The CJC has published a handbook or guide for judges, which is couched in general terms: Canadian Judicial Council, *Ethical Principles for Judges*, Canadian Judicial Council, Ottawa, 1998.

misbehaviour for the purpose of section 99 of the *Constitution Act, 1867*, it may recommend to the Minister of Justice that a resolution be put before Parliament that the judge be dismissed from office.

Very few complaints have proceeded to a hearing before the Inquiry Committee; most are disposed of summarily by a member of the Judicial Conduct Committee without a formal investigation or, less often, by the Review Panel following an investigation. For example, in the 2010-2011 fiscal year, the CJC received approximately 150 complaints, closed 140 complaint files, and had 45 complaint files under review at various stages of the process.[40] Only 8 complaints have been referred to the Inquiry Committee since the CJC's inception.

These arrangements have attracted criticisms from different quarters. For example, some commentators have criticised the process up to the point that a complaint is referred to the Inquiry Committee, on the ground that it is overly confidential. When the CJC describes in its annual reports the work of the Judicial Conduct Committee it does not publish the names of the judges against whom complaints have been dismissed. However, publication of more details may undermine a judge's ability to continue in office, even if the complaint is dismissed. Others go further and argue that the public can have no confidence in a discipline system in which, for the most part, judges investigate each other; disciplinary bodies for other professions typically include representatives of the public.

Some judges have also expressed doubts about the complaints process, on the ground that the judge against whom a complaint is made is not sufficiently informed about the progress of the investigation; some have even questioned whether the whole process is compatible with the constitutional guarantee of judicial independence.

All I would say is that balancing judicial independence and public accountability in this context is extremely delicate; how much information should be made public, and at what stages of the process, can be a difficult judgment call. Further, both complainants and judges have an interest in seeing that complaints are processed promptly and in a manner that is fair to both. Lay members should also be included in the discipline process to prevent it from seeming unduly protective of judges. Like any other administrative scheme, the CJC's discipline process would benefit from regular, independent audits. Finally, it is widely acknowledged that the judicial irascibility and routine discourtesy to advocates, parties or their witnesses is nowadays a relative rarity.

40 Canadian Judicial Council, *A Strong, Effective and Efficient Judiciary: Annual Report 2010-2011*, Canadian Judicial Council, Ottawa 2011, <www.cjc-ccm.gc.ca>.

4. Conclusion

As the above examples show, it is never easy to achieve the right balance between judicial independence and accountability. In some situations, judicial independence can be underweighted and in others, it is given too much importance. In order to achieve an appropriate balance regular review and recalibration is required.

Judges and the Executive in Britain: An Unequal Partnership?

*Robert Hazell**

1. Introduction

The judiciary is often characterised as the least dangerous branch of government; with the implicit (and sometimes explicit) corollary that the executive is the most dangerous branch – especially to the judiciary.[1] Depicting relations between them might be expected to be a tale of tensions and recurrent conflict. But in practice the development of judicial policy and the running of the judicial system in the UK has long been managed as a partnership between government and the judiciary, which works because of mutual respect and understanding for each other's roles.

Those roles have changed significantly following the greater separation of powers introduced by the Constitutional Reform Act 2005. The purpose of this chapter is to explore how this changed the nature of the partnership between the executive and judiciary, and what impact it has had on their respective responsibilities for upholding judicial independence and ensuring proper judicial accountability. Both in upholding judicial independence and in ensuring judicial accountability, the executive will be found to play a stronger role than most lawyers and judges might have expected.

No country has a complete separation of powers. But the phrase is simplistic and not particularly helpful. (Even in the United States, Supreme Court Justices are dependent on the Executive for their appointment and Congress for their funding). It may be more useful to think in terms of division of powers and functions between the different branches of government; and also to be aware of shared responsibilities and overlapping functions, as implied by the 'partnership' proclaimed between the Lord Chancellor and Lord Chief Justice.[2]

---

* Prof. R. Hazell is Professor of Government and the Constitution, School of Public Policy, University College London, England.

1 In *The Federalist* no. 78, Alexander Hamilton suggested that the judiciary would always be the "least dangerous branch" of the federal government, since it had "no influence over either the sword or the purse" and had "neither force nor will, but merely judgment".

2 Para 1.1 of the 2011 Framework Document for HM Courts and Tribunals Service; but for other references to partnership, *see e.g. para.* 28 of the 2004 Concordat between the Lord Chancellor and Lord Chief Justice.

The UK flouted the separation of powers particularly badly, until big constitutional reforms in 2005 which created much greater separation between the Judges and the Executive. The Judiciary are now a more separate branch of government, and senior judges have more direct responsibility for the leadership and management of the Judiciary. This chapter will describe and analyse those reforms, and will ask:

- How much separation has there actually been? Who does what in the new division of powers and functions?
- Does the new system strengthen or weaken judicial independence, and judicial accountability?
- Have the Judges become more powerful? In what ways? And has the executive become less powerful as a result?

The chapter is primarily about the greater separation of powers in England and Wales, which is the main legal system in the UK: there are separate legal systems in Scotland and Northern Ireland. It focuses on the changed relationship between the mainstream judiciary and the Executive, not the new Supreme Court.

2. The 'old' Lord Chancellor

Until 2005 the Head of the Judiciary in the UK was a Cabinet minister, the Lord Chancellor. The Lord Chancellor was responsible for the judicial appointments system, and appointed the judiciary; he determined their pay and pensions; he was responsible for investigating complaints against judges, and imposing discipline; he could dismiss junior judges; he provided and managed the Courts Service. In an extraordinary breach of separation of powers, he could also sit as a judge in the highest court: the last Lord Chancellor to do so was Lord Irvine, in 2001.[3] And, equally extraordinarily, he presided over the second chamber of Parliament, the House of Lords. He was a senior member of all three branches of government. The judiciary accepted this state of affairs, because they liked the head of the judiciary being a senior member of the government, who was able to defend their interests in Cabinet.

3. Greater Separation of Powers in 2005

In June 2003 Lord Irvine was dismissed by the Prime Minister Tony Blair. Blair also announced plans to abolish the office of Lord Chancellor, establish an independent Judicial Appointments Commission, and a new Supreme Court. The Lord Chancellor was to be replaced by a Secretary of State for Constitutional Affairs, who need not be a lawyer, and could sit (like most government ministers) in the House of Commons. The sudden announcement of these reforms, and in particular the proposal to abolish the ancient office of Lord Chancellor, with no

3 In the case: *Uratemp Ventures Ltd v Collins [2001] UKHL 43.*

consultation, caused the Judges great alarm. The Lord Chief Justice Lord Woolf postponed his retirement to moderate the proposals and negotiate a new settlement, and the result of his negotiations with Lord Falconer (the new Secretary of State for Constitutional Affairs) was published in a document known as the *Concordat* in January 2004.[4]

The *Concordat* set out the key responsibilities of the new Secretary of State and the Lord Chief Justice. Its contents and coverage can be judged by the headings of its different sections: Judicial Independence; Judicial Posts held by the Lord Chancellor; Leadership of the Judiciary in England and Wales; Oath-taking; Provision of Resources; Deployment of Judges; Judicial 'Leadership' Posts; Appointments to Committees, and Similar Bodies; The Making of Procedural Rules for Judicial Fora; Rule Committee Appointments; Practice Directions; Education and Training; Judicial Complaints and Discipline; Judicial Appointments Commission – Process, and Membership.

One half of the Concordat was devoted just to the last two headings: the process for handling judicial complaints, and the new process for judicial appointments were covered in great detail.[5] The rest was dealt with more succinctly. Under each heading the *Concordat* stated a general principle, and then explained how that principle would be applied in practice. For example:

> **Judicial Independence**
> **Principle:**
> 5. The new arrangements should reinforce the independence of the judiciary.
> **Application:**
> 6. A general statutory duty will be imposed on the Government, all those involved in the administration of justice and all those involved in the appointment of judges to respect and maintain judicial independence.
> 7. In addition, there will be a specific statutory duty falling on the Secretary of State for Constitutional Affairs to defend and uphold the continuing independence of the judiciary.

The *Concordat* provided the basis for the subsequent legislation enacted as the Constitutional Reform Act 2005. It was in effect the White Paper which preceded the legislation. The only change was that the office of Lord Chancellor survived in attenuated form. The Act removed the roles of the Lord Chancellor as head of the judiciary and Speaker of the House of Lords, but otherwise left the office in being, albeit reduced by the transfer of functions to the Lord Chief Justice. The Act set out in detail the functions to be transferred to the Judiciary, implementing the agreement struck in the *Concordat*. The Act came into force in 2006, together

4 *The Lord Chancellor's judiciary-related functions: Proposals*, commonly referred to as 'the Concordat'.

5 40 paragraphs are devoted to judicial complaints and discipline (paras. 73-113), and 30 to judicial appointments (paras. 114-144).

with the independent Judicial Appointments Commission created by the Act. The new Supreme Court (also created by the Act) came into being in 2009, when their new building was ready. The division of powers between the Executive and Judiciary was further refined in 2008 in a Framework Document for the management of the Courts Service (revised and updated in 2011 to incorporate the Tribunals Service). The *Concordat*, the 2005 Act and the 2011 Framework Document are the main documents setting out the new relationship between the Judges and the Executive.

4. Division of Powers between the Executive and the Judiciary

Under the *Concordat* and the Constitutional Reform Act 2005, the division of powers is as follows. The *Lord Chancellor*[6] is responsible for providing the courts system, and is accountable to Parliament for the efficiency and effectiveness of the system. He sets the framework for the organisation of the courts system, such as geographical and jurisdictional boundaries.[7] He determines the overall number of judges, after consulting the Lord Chief Justice, including the number required for each region and at each level of the judiciary.[8] He is also responsible for supporting the judiciary in enabling them to fulfil their functions; and he provides the staff and resources for the Courts Service, and for the Lord Chief Justice. He sets the pay, pensions and terms and conditions of the judiciary.

The *Lord Chief Justice*[9] is responsible for the deployment of the judiciary, the roles of individual judges, and the allocation of work within the courts. After consulting the Lord Chancellor, he decides which individual judges should be assigned to which region, district or court; and he can authorise judges to sit in levels of court other than their usual level.[10] He nominates judges to posts which provide judicial leadership, again in consultation with the Lord Chancellor. The judges are responsible for deciding on the assignment of cases before particular courts, and the listing of those cases before particular judges.[11] The Lord Chief Justice also has a general responsibility for the well-being and training and providing guidance for the judiciary.[12]

6 The Lord Chancellor's responsibilities are set out in paragraph 4(a) of the Concordat, Part II of the CRA 2005 & paragraph 1.3 of the 2011 Framework Document.

7 Concordat para. 26.

8 Concordat para. 29.

9 The Lord Chief Justice's responsibilities are set out in paragraph 4(c) of the Concordat, Section 7 CRA 2005 & paragraph 1.2 2011 Framework Document.

10 The Lord Chief Justice's allocation responsibilities were first laid out in paragraphs 29 – 33 of the Concordat ,and further in Section 7 (2) & Schedule 4 Part 1 paragraph 129 CRA 2005.

11 Concordat para. 36 & Schedule 2 Part 2 paragraph 6(6)(a) CRA 2005.

12 Section 7(2) CRA 2005.

5. Complaints and Discipline

Responsibility for judicial complaints and discipline is a joint responsibility of the Lord Chief Justice and the Lord Chancellor.[13] They are supported by a complaints secretariat (the Office for Judicial Complaints, staffed by civil servants), and the Lord Chancellor is accountable to Parliament for the effective and efficient operation of the complaints and discipline system. The OJC may filter out complaints, but refer serious ones to a nominated judge, who is a further filter; then an investigating judge. If the Lord Chief Justice and Lord Chancellor are considering disciplinary action, they must refer the case to a review body, composed of two judges and two lay members. They must decide jointly on any disciplinary sanction,[14] but cannot take disciplinary action more severe than that recommended by the review body. If the sanction is removal from office, the Lord Chancellor will invite both Houses of Parliament to approve dismissal of High Court judges and above. Judges below this level can be removed by the Lord Chancellor. Complainants or judges can complain about the handling of a complaint to the Judicial Appointments and Conduct Ombudsman, but he can only review the process, not the merits of the decision.[15]

6. Judicial Appointments Commission

Judicial appointments used to be a field in which the Lord Chancellor had complete discretion. He was restricted only by the statutory criteria specifying the minimum level of experience for each post; and the strong convention that he would consult the senior judiciary before making any appointment. Now he has almost no discretion. Judicial appointments are regulated by an independent Judicial Appointments Commission (JAC),[16] which has 15 members, of whom six are lay members, and five are judges, plus a magistrate, barrister, solicitor, and tribunal member.[17]

The JAC runs competitions for judicial vacancies, and submits a single name to the Lord Chancellor.[18] The Lord Chancellor can appoint, request reconsideration, or reject the JAC's candidate. But the grounds on which he can reject or request reconsideration are strictly limited by statute, and he must give reasons in writing. He is also strictly limited in the number of times he can reject or request

13 Concordat para. 73 & Section 115 CRA 2005.

14 Concordat para. 80 & Section 108(2) CRA 2005.

15 Section 102 of CRA 2005.

16 Established by Section 61 CRA 2005.

17 This membership composition is set out in Concordat para. 132 & Schedule 12 Part 1 para. 2 CRA 2005.

18 The 'single name' rule applies to all levels of judicial appointments, for example see Section 70(3) CRA 2005 (in relation to appointing Lord Justices of Appeal).

reconsideration (a maximum of twice for each appointment).[19] In practice, in the 2,500 or so judicial appointments made between 2006 and 2012, the Lord Chancellor rejected just one nomination, and requested reconsideration twice.

The judiciary are closely involved in judicial appointments. They have five members on the JAC, whose views carry disproportionate weight. Judicial members are included in all the JAC's selection panels. For appointments to the Supreme Court there is a special selection committee, composed of the Court's President and Deputy President, and the chairs of the JACs for England, Scotland and Northern Ireland.[20] For appointments to the Court of Appeal the selection panel is the Lord Chief Justice, another senior Court of Appeal judge, the chair and a lay member of the JAC.[21] The Lord Chief Justice must be consulted before any selection process is initiated, and he must be consulted before any name is submitted to the Lord Chancellor. So the judiciary have a very strong input. When we interviewed members of the JAC, none could recall any appointment being made against the wishes of the Lord Chief Justice. Indeed, Ken Clarke as Lord Chancellor would not accept a recommendation from the JAC unless it had been approved by the Lord Chief Justice.[22]

7. Management of the Courts Service

The judiciary also have stronger input into the management of the Courts Service. Under its 2011 Framework Document the Courts Service 'operates on the basis of a partnership between the Lord Chancellor and the Lord Chief Justice'.[23] The Lord Chancellor remains responsible to Parliament for the efficiency and effectiveness of the courts,[24] tribunals and the justice system. Staff of the Courts Service are civil servants, but they have a joint responsibility to the Lord Chancellor and the Lord Chief Justice for the effective, efficient and speedy operation of the courts and tribunals.[25] All members of the judiciary have a similar responsibility to work with the staff to deliver these objectives. Staff work subject to the directions of the judiciary in matters such as listing, case allocation and case management.[26]

The Framework Document provides that the Lord Chancellor and Lord Chief Justice will not intervene in the day-to-day operations of the Courts Service. They have placed responsibility for overseeing the leadership and direction of the Courts Service in the hands of its Board, and the Chief Executive is responsible

---

19 Again the Lord Chancellor's power to accept/reject/request reconsideration applies to other levels, for example see Sections 73-75 CRA 2005.
20 Schedule 8 CRA 2005.
21 Section 71 CRA 2005.
22 Interviews with MoJ officials.
23 Para. 1.1 Framework Document.
24 Para. 1.2 Framework Document.
25 Para. 2.4 Framework Document.
26 Para. 2.5 Framework Document.

for day-to-day operations and administration.[27] Three senior judges are on the Board, which has ten members,[28] and the selection panel for the Chief Executive includes a senior judge.[29] The judicial members are accountable to the Lord Chief Justice for their conduct as members of the Board,[30] and the other members are accountable to the Lord Chancellor;[31] but the Board have agreed to act collegiately, and not in representative capacities.[32]

For determining the budget of the Courts Service, the Framework Document provides that the Lord Chancellor must keep the Lord Chief Justice informed about his department's resourcing discussions with the Treasury. The Lord Chief Justice may write to the Lord Chancellor representing the views of the judiciary, and the Lord Chancellor must forward any letter to the Treasury.[33] If the Lord Chief Justice has concerns about the budget allocated to the Courts Service, he may record his position to the Lord Chancellor, and to Parliament.[34]

The Courts Service produces monthly performance data for the Board on the workload and efficiency of each court centre. The judicial members of the Board take this data back to the Lord Chief Justice, and he or his deputies can talk to judges about improving the performance of their courts. This may involve talking to individual judges about their performance in terms of case management, delays etc. The Judiciary do not feel that this trespasses on judicial independence, so long as it is senior judges managing judicial performance, not court administrators. The Framework Document provides: "Performance measures that have an impact upon the judiciary only bind the judiciary when the Lord Chief Justice has expressly agreed that they do so. No performance measure fetters the exercise of judicial discretion or the interests of justice in any individual case".[35]

8. The Executive Works to Uphold Judicial Independence

Lawyers tend to view the Executive as a threat to judicial independence; but this account shows how the Executive works systematically to support and uphold judicial independence, in a range of different ways.

First, the Lord Chancellor, all government Ministers and everyone with responsibility for the administration of justice is under a statutory duty to uphold judicial

27 Para. 1.6 Framework Document.
28 Para. 4.5 Framework Document.
29 Para. 3.5 Framework Document.
30 Para. 4.11 Framework Document.
31 Para. 4.12 Framework Document.
32 Foreword from the Chairman to Annual Report of HM Courts and Tribunals Service 2011-12.
33 Para. 7.1 Framework Document.
34 Para. 7.2 Framework Document.
35 Para. 7.17 Framework Document.

independence.[36] Ministers are specifically enjoined not seek to influence particular judicial decisions through any special access to the judiciary.[37] Other guardians of the rule of law and judicial independence within the Executive include the Attorney General, as the government's senior Law Officer; Parliamentary Counsel, in their drafting of legislation; and the Government Legal Service, who will remind Ministers if they risk crossing the line.

The Lord Chancellor has additional duties to have regard to the need to defend judicial independence, and the need for the judiciary to have the support necessary to enable them to exercise their functions.[38] 'Defending' judicial independence means defending the judges and their role when they come under attack, from the media or from ministerial colleagues who publicly criticise a judicial decision. The defence can be in public or in private. The Lord Chancellor's officials will be alert to forthcoming court decisions which might embarrass the government, and seek to dissuade ministers in other departments from venting their frustration in public. If they fail, the Lord Chancellor will privately have a word with the minister, to discourage a repeat offence; he will not reprimand a minister in public. A difficulty arises when the offending minister is the Prime Minister, as has happened with both Tony Blair and David Cameron. The Lord Chancellor can still try, and has done so; but it is difficult to admonish a political superior.

Second, the Executive has designed and introduced a new system for judicial appointments which removes any scope for political patronage. The Lord Chancellor's discretion is extremely limited, and although he is nominally still the decision maker, when presented with a single name he effectively has very little choice. [*insert Ken Clarke quote ?to Lords Const Cttee*] The judges have a lot of involvement, and influence, by being directly involved in devising the selection processes and sitting on the selection panels which produce the single name. Judges have criticised the cumbersome and slow nature of the new process, but they all recognise how the independence of the Judicial Appointments Commission helps to underpin the independence of the judiciary. Critics on the other side say that the new system has tilted power too far towards the judges, who are now dominant in the selection process; and that the Executive has lost the ability to take effective action to promote more diversity in the judiciary.[39]

Third, there are stronger systems in place to ensure that the courts and the judicial system will be adequately resourced, that the judges are consulted about resourcing, and involved in the allocation of resources through their involvement in the management of the Courts Service. The Lord Chancellor is under multiple

---

36 Concordat paras. 5, 6, 7, Section 3(1) CRA 2005 & Paras. 1.2, 2.3 Framework Document.

37 Section 3(5) CRA 2005.

38 See Section 3(6)(a) & (b) CRA 2005. The Lord Chancellor also swears this as part of an oath, see s17(1) CRA 2005.

39 Alan Paterson & Chris Paterson, *Guarding the Guardians? Towards an independent, accountable and diverse senior judiciary*. CentreForum, London, 2012.

statutory duties to ensure that there is an effective system of courts and tribunals, and that the judges have the support they need.[40] Under the Framework Document, he must keep the Lord Chief Justice fully informed about his discussions with the Treasury. This does not mean that the courts are immune from budget cuts; but the judges have the opportunity to spell out in advance any adverse consequences for judicial independence, and through their representatives on the Board of the Courts Service they have the opportunity to minimise the damage.

Fourth, the independence of the judiciary is reinforced by the creation of new bodies whose function is to help protect judicial independence. That is clearly the role of the Judicial Appointments Commission, which is required to select candidates solely on merit. That is clearly the role of the Judicial Appointments Commission, which is required to select candidates solely on merit. It is also the role of the Office for Judicial Complaints, with its three stage process, each stage involving an independent judge, to ensure that judges judge the conduct of other judges, and ensure that judicial independence is preserved. And it is also in part the role of the Judicial Appointments and Conduct Ombudsman. Disappointed candidates can complain to the Ombudsman; and judges who have been unfairly complained against, or unfairly disciplined, can also complain. In all these cases the independence of the new body helps to buttress the independence of the judiciary.

9. The Executive Helps to Ensure the Accountability of the Judiciary

The Executive also plays an important role in ensuring the accountability of the Judiciary. The judiciary is not purely self-regulating, but is held to account by the other two branches of government. The role of the Executive in checking the judiciary is recognised in statute. The same section which requires the Lord Chancellor to defend judicial independence and provide the judiciary with adequate support, goes on to require him to have regard to the public interest in decisions affecting the judiciary or the administration of justice.[41] The statute does not spell it out, but the public interest is different from the interests of the judiciary: in terms of pay and pensions, it includes what the nation can afford, as well as what the judges might want to have. Similarly with the programme of court closures: the courts exist for the convenience of the public, not the judges. In terms of judicial recruitment, it includes the need for greater diversity, as well as appointment on merit. The Lord Chancellor is the ultimate judge of the public interest, and accountable to Parliament for his decisions on where the public interest lies.

Accountability involves giving an account (explanatory accountability), and being held to account, and possibly paying a penalty (sacrificial accountability). The judiciary give an account of their work through publishing annual reports, which the

40 Section 1 Courts Act 2003, Section 3(6)(b) of the Constitutional Reform Act 2005, Section 39 of the Tribunals, Courts and Enforcement Act 2007.

41 Section 3(6)(c) CRA 2005.

Lord Chancellor lays before Parliament. So the Supreme Court produces an annual report for the Lord Chancellor, which also goes to the First Ministers in Scotland, Wales and Northern Ireland (whose governments help to fund the court).[42] Below that level the annual reporting has become more ragged since the Lord Chief Justice became head of the judiciary. Whereas there used to be annual reports by the Civil and Criminal Divisions of the Court of Appeal, by the Commercial and Admiralty Courts, and the Technology and Construction Court, together with regional reports by the Crown, County, Family and Magistrates Courts, now only two of those produce an annual report.[43] The Lord Chief Justice produces a review of the administration of justice every two years or so, but it is a selective, high level account, and the irregular basis makes it impossible to compare performance with earlier periods.[44] The annual report of HM Courts and Tribunals Service does not bridge the gap, being mainly financial.[45] For detailed information on the workload of the courts, the reader must turn to the Judicial and Court Statistics produced by the Ministry of Justice. They reveal the management challenge from changing workloads: whereas the number of cases in the Crown Court in 2011 was little different from 2001, in the country court the number of claims brought fell by 25% between 2006 and 2011.

The Judicial Statistics and Courts Service reports are important tools for external scrutiny, with data on waiting times, costs per sitting day, etc. They provide essential information for the Executive to work with the judges in seeking to improve the efficiency of the courts, and judicial performance. Court performance and judicial performance are closely linked; but to preserve judicial independence, improving judicial performance is seen as the judiciary's business. The Executive acts as constructive critic, and coach, and there are many different forums in which it can make suggestions and put its point of view across, from the formal Board meetings of the Courts Service to the informal meetings which take place every month between the Lord Chancellor and Lord Chief Justice. The Executive can also offer help and advice, as it has done recently over introducing appraisal systems for evaluating individual judicial performance; and developing more systematic succession planning for recruitment to the senior levels of the judiciary. These are matters where the judiciary have no experience, but the Executive have valuable expertise.

In terms of regulating misconduct in the judiciary, the Executive still plays a central role. The Lord Chancellor used to be solely responsible for investigating complaints and imposing discipline. He now shares that responsibility jointly with

---

42 Section 54 CRA 2005.

43 Court of Appeal (Criminal Division), and Technology and Construction Court.

44 There have been three such reports, covering the periods April 2006 to March 2008; April 2008 to February 2010; January 2010 to June 2012. The intention is to bring these onto an annual basis, perhaps matching the annual Business Plan produced by the Judicial Office.

45 The budget of HMCTS was reduced by 9 per cent in 2011-12. The annual report contains five pages on Workload and Performance Summary, and six on Performance Review; with over a hundred on the annual accounts, and notes to the accounts.

the Lord Chief Justice, under detailed procedures set out in the *Concordat*[46] and implemented in the Judicial Discipline (Prescribed Procedure) Regulations 2006. Under those procedures all decisions on complaints and discipline have to be taken jointly. But at the end of the process only the Lord Chancellor may formally remove a judge from office[47] (and only Circuit judges or equivalent and below: High Court judges and above are removable only by resolution of both Houses of Parliament). And as the new head of the judiciary, the Lord Chief Justice can impose lesser penalties: suspension, or a formal warning, reprimand or advice. The Lord Chief Justice may do this only with the agreement of the Lord Chancellor.[48] Agreement is not merely formal: the Lord Chancellor has adjusted penalties both upwards and downwards.[49] So in terms of complaints and discipline, the judiciary is more self-regulating than it used to be; but the system operates under the close eye of the Lord Chancellor, who must agree to any disciplinary sanction, and only he can impose the ultimate sanction of removal from office.

Finally brief mention should be made of the accountability of the Judges to Parliament. That is not the focus of this chapter, but again it is more than just a formality. Parliament has shown a lot of interest in the work of judges and the courts: especially the House of Commons Justice Committee, and the House of Lords Constitution Committee. The Lord Chief Justice regularly appears before those two committees, but that is not all. Since 2003, eight different Select Committees have heard oral evidence from judges on some 80 different occasions, and from around 80 different judges. The topics covered include judicial appointments, human rights legislation, the family justice system, asylum and immigration, delays, and sentencing policy.

10. Have the Judges Become More Powerful? In what Respects?

The final part of this chapter considers whether the judges have become more powerful as a result of the constitutional changes described above. It is widely accepted that British judges have become more powerful as a result of other factors: the relentless growth of judicial review, the introduction of EU law, the Human Rights Act 1998. But this analysis focuses just on the changes flowing from the Constitutional Reform Act 2005, and the establishment of the judiciary as a more separate and autonomous branch of government.

Asking whether the judges have become more powerful requires a conceptual definition of power. It is a complex concept, much debated in the politics literature. Power was originally related to concepts of authority and the use of force, and

46 Concordat paras. 73-113 & Section 115 CRA 2005.
47 Concordat para. 81 & Section 108(1) CRA 2005.
48 Section 108 CRA 2005.
49 Information from interviews.

defined as the ability to carry out one's will.[50] But it has since been understood in more subtle ways. Steven Lukes identified three faces of power: the ability of governments to make decisions; to set and control the agenda; and to influence people's thinking.[51] The last two are forms of what Nye has called soft power.[52]

These more subtle definitions provide a better framework for understanding judicial power. But to apply them empirically, we need something with a sharper edge. That can be supplied by Rhodes' resource-dependency model of power.[53] In Rhodes' model power is a function of the resources available to the different actors: but building on the earlier definitions, he uses 'resources' in a wide sense to include authority, information etc. His model also involves a concept closely related to power, that of autonomy: a party possesses autonomy if it is able to exercise power in relation to its own functions without requiring the support of the other party in doing so.[54] Weaving together these different models, power can be said to consist of the following main elements:

Constitutional autonomy. (a) Autonomy from interference by another branch of government; (b) power to alter internal arrangements without reference to another branch of government.

Legal and hierarchical authority. The ability to set the agenda; initiate and make policy; issue directions or guidance to others; and make final decisions.

Resources. Having sufficient finance and staff to discharge core functions; the ability to adjust resources between functions; and to select and direct staff.

Informational power. Understanding the thinking of other branches of government; and having the ability to shape their thinking, and influence public debate.

Each element of power will be considered in turn, asking how much power is possessed by the Judiciary, and how much by the Executive, in determining judicial policy, running the justice system, and upholding judicial independence and accountability. In terms of *constitutional autonomy*, the Judges are clearly more autonomous now that the Lord Chancellor is no longer head of the Judiciary. The Lord Chief Justice is their head,[55] and exercises internal and external leadership. He leads the judiciary with the advice of the Judicial Executive Board, selected by him, and supported by the Judicial Office, which in 2012 had grown to 200 staff. But he has little power to alter the internal structures or arrangements of the

50 M. Weber, *The Theory of Social and Economic Organisations* (T. Parsons ed.), Free Press, New York, 1947.

51 S. Lukes, *Power: A Radical View* (2nd ed.), Palgrave Macmillan, 2004.

52 J. Nye, *Soft Power: The Means to Success in World Politics*, PublicAffairs books, New York, 1974.

53 R.A.W. Rhodes, *Control and Power in Central-Local Government Relations*, Gower, Aldershot, 1981, chapter 5.

54 A. Trench, *Devolution and Power in the United Kingdom*. Manchester University Press, 2007, p. 17.

55 Para. 11 of the Concordat & Section 7(1) CRA 2005.

courts, or the judiciary. The Executive, through the Lord Chancellor, still determines the geographical distribution of the courts, and the jurisdiction of each court. The Executive determines the number of judges, and sets their terms and conditions. It is only over judicial appointments that the Judiciary has more power than the Executive: the Executive still formally makes the appointment, but the Judiciary now has a lot more influence over the selection process. And in future the Judiciary will itself make all appointments at the level of Circuit Judge and below.[56]

The size of the judiciary and the extent of its constitutional autonomy has been vastly extended by the creation of the Tribunals Service, and its incorporation into the Courts Service in 2011. This development is so recent that its implications have not yet been fully realised. The inclusion of the tribunals judiciary has increased the total size of the judiciary from 3575 to 5635.[57] And the inclusion of tribunals in the justice system has increased the total number of civil cases handled each year from 1,643k to 2,524k.[58]

The Executive by contrast has greater constitutional autonomy: as seen in the decision by the Executive to create the Tribunals Service, and then merge it into the Courts Service. The Prime Minister has full autonomy to alter the structure of the government, and to create, merge or close departments. That was vividly seen in the 2003 decision to abolish the office of Lord Chancellor, and the 2007 decision to bring responsibility for prisons and the criminal justice system into the new Ministry of Justice. The judges disliked both decisions, and succeeded in modifying the first; but they recognised the Prime Minister has the right to make such decisions.

Generally the Executive suffers from little interference by the Judiciary, save for the constant pinpricks of judicial review to ensure that it follows due process. The pinpricks clearlyhurt, to judge from the occasional howls of ministerial outrage; but they seldom prevent the Executive from doing what it planned to do – with rare high profile exceptions, like the court decisions after 2001 curbing the detention of terrorist suspects. Empirical research suggests that just under half of judicial review cases against central government are successful, but only a quarter to a third of successful cases call for changes in procedure or the government's approach to decision-making.[59]

In terms of *legal and hierarchical authority*, the Executive is also more powerful. The Judges are primarily reactive, both in their judicial work, in terms of the cases that come before them, and in terms of policy. Even on judicial matters,

56 Under the Crime and Courts Bill 2012 Part 2 clause 19.
57 Judicial Appointments for England and Wales by type, April 2012.
58 HMCTS Business Plan 2012, pp. 12-13.
59 Initial findings from Essex University/Public Law Project research on the effects of judgements of the Administrative Court 2010-12. Final results expected May 2013.

the lead on policy generally comes from the Executive. The Executive leads on macro policy, or policy involving other government departments or external stakeholders. So the 2010 Norgrove review of family justice was initiated by Jack Straw as Lord Chancellor, and confirmed by his successor Ken Clarke, and its central recommendation of a single Family Court was included by the government in the Crime and Courts Bill 2012. But some policy reviews are initiated by the judiciary, such as the 2009 Jackson review of civil litigation costs, which was ordered by the Master of the Rolls. But whatever the genesis of a review, the Executive will consult the judiciary, or *vice versa*, to ensure that a review will not be opposed, and that its results are likely to be implemented. And on small things like guidance for the courts, the majority of guidance comes from the Executive: the power to allow and disallow Court Rules rests with the Lord Chancellor.[60] The judiciary make final decisions in court cases; but under the UK doctrine of parliamentary sovereignty, it is always open to the Executive to reverse those decisions by passing amending legislation through Parliament.

By contrast the legal and hierarchical authority of the Executive is immense. It sets the agenda on most legal and judicial policy; it can make policy through legislation, as it has done through successive Courts Acts, restructuring the courts system; or by legislating in fields like family law; and it has wide authority to issue directions or guidance.

As for *resources*, here too the Executive is more powerful. The Lord Chancellor determines the budget for the courts system, not the Lord Chief Justice. The Lord Chief Justice can go public if he considers the budget insufficient, but that is recognised as a weapon of last resort. It is only in relation to the allocation of the budget within the Courts Service that the judges have an equal say, through their participation in the management and operation of the Courts Service as a partnership between the Lord Chancellor and Lord Chief Justice. The judges do not choose the staff of the Courts Service, and do not choose the staff working in the Judicial Office (save for the chief executive). All staff in the Judicial Office are civil servants, as are the staff working for independent bodies like the JAC, OJC and JACO. The Executive chooses the staff, and the Executive is responsible for their careers, deployment and promotion.

However once posted to the Judicial Office the staff's primary loyalty is to the judiciary. As more and more functions have been transferred across from the Ministry of Justice to the judiciary, the staffing of the Judicial Office has grown and grown. The 'old' Lord Chief Justice before 2005 had a private office of half a dozen people. In 2006 the Directorate of Judicial Offices serving the 'new' Lord Chief Justice opened with 145 staff; in 2012 it had over 200.

This gradual transfer of staffing and expertise has meant that in relation to power as *knowledge and information*, the playing field is a bit more even. In interviews

60 Paras. 50-55 of the Concordat.

some senior officials in the Ministry of Justice have acknowledged that their knowledge of the judges and judicial issues is not what it used to be, and this might sometimes place them at a disadvantage. As successive functions have transferred out of the Lord Chancellor's Department/Ministry of Justice, the 100 or more officials who supported the Lord Chancellor on judicial matters in 2005 have shrunk to just 15 or so in 2012 (the largest loss being the 90 staff who worked on judicial appointments, who went to the JAC). It is no surprise that the Ministry has lost some of its intelligence and expertise.

But informational power also includes the power to project information and ideas, to shape the thinking of others, and influence public debate. Here the Executive once again is dominant. Although judges give more speeches and lectures than they used to, and they now have a Judicial Communications Office, it is tiny by comparison with the much larger publicity machine available to the government. The Executive largely sets the terms of public debate about the judicial system and the criminal justice system.

11. Conclusion

This chapter has charted the greater separation of powers and functions flowing from the Constitutional Reform Act 2005, and evaluated the nature of the new partnership between the Executive and the Judiciary. Despite the greater formal separation, the partnership relies on close working between the two branches of government. In some areas (the Courts Service, judicial appointments, complaints and discipline) there is joint responsibility, with a mutual veto. But in other areas where one side or the other is formally in the lead, there is consultation and co-ordination before most important decisions are made.

But the situation is still evolving. Ken Clarke (Lord Chancellor 2010-12) was less interested in judicial matters as Lord Chancellor than Jack Straw (2007-10), and his officials found it hard to interest him in judicial appointments, discipline, postings and promotion. Chris Grayling, the new Lord Chancellor appointed in 2012, may be less interested still, having no background in the law or the legal profession. The direction of travel has been and continues to be all one way, with the Executive showing less and less interest. The risk to the judiciary, as the Executive also shrinks its capacity, is that the Executive becomes less capable of showing an intelligent interest, and its occasional interventions become clumsy and ill informed.

The Judiciary have become more powerful. They have acquired greater constitutional autonomy; they now have more resources under their control, in the Judicial Office; they have developed more informational power vis-a-vis the Executive. But much of this is soft power. In terms of hard power, and in particular the capacity to set the agenda on legal and judicial policy, and to change the law and the legal framework, the Executive is still dominant.

Finally, does the new system strengthen or weaken judicial independence, and judicial accountability? Formally judicial independence has been strengthened, through the multiple statutory duties laid on the Lord Chancellor and all ministers and those involved in the administration of justice to uphold it; and through the multiple independent bodies (HMCTS, JAC, OJC, JACO) which help in part to safeguard it. The judiciary still bemoan the passing of the old Lord Chancellor; but they would not wish any of these independent bodies to be abolished. As for judicial accountability, that also remains strong, not least because the Lord Chancellor still has to agree all important decisions about the financing, management and direction of the justice system. The one aspect of judicial accountability which has weakened is that the Lord Chief Justice no longer gives an adequate account of his leadership of the judiciary through his occasional reviews. But that is easily remedied, through making the reviews annual, and more systematic.

III – Independence of Regulatory Agencies, Supervisory and Enforcement Authorities

The Different Levels of Protection of National Supervisors' Independence in the European Landscape

*Annetje Ottow**

1. Restricting the Principle of Autonomy

EU law is based on the principle of material norms being anchored in European law and on their transposition being based on the national legal order. The effect of European law on the national legal order is felt via national rules of law. This applies both with respect to national institutional structures and national procedural rules and is referred to in European law as the principle of *institutional and procedural autonomy* of the Member States.[1] Looking, however, at various European rules adopted in recent years, it seems there are now a number of exceptions to this principle. Although the European Court of Justice (ECJ) consistently emphasises that the respect EU law has for the institutional structure of the Member States, secondary European legislation (in the form of regulations and directives) contains more and more stipulations that undermine this autonomy and significantly curtail the freedom available to the member states at a national level.[2]

* Prof. dr. A.T. Ottow is Professor public economic law at the European Institute, Utrecht University, the Netherlands and member of the board of the telecommunications authority in the Netherlands (OPTA) until 1 April 2013. This Article is a revision of A.T. Ottow & S. Lavrijssen, Het Europese recht als hoeder van de onafhankelijkheid van nationale toezichthouders, *Tijdschrift voor Toezicht* 2011, No. 3, p. 34-50 and based on the speeches given by the author at the Centre For Media Pluralism and Media Freedom of the European University Institute, Fiesole, November 12, 2011 and the International Conference on Judicial and Quasi-Judicial independence, University of Groningen, Groningen, May 25, 2012.

1 J.H. Jans *et al.*, *Europeanisation of Public law*, Europa Law Publishing, Groningen, 2007, p. 40-42.

2 For a discussion of the European influence on the principle of legality via ECJ case law and various European Directives, *see* S. Lavrijssen & A.T. Ottow, The Legality of Independent Regulatory Authorities, *in* L.F.M. Besselink, F. Pennings & S. Prechal (eds.), *The Eclipse of the Legality Principle in the European Union*, Kluwer International, The Hague, 2010, pp. 73-96.

2. National Supervisors' Independence: the Rationale

The move towards curtailing national autonomy is particularly evident where various sectors – including telecommunications,[3] energy, the media and, more recently, the railways – are regulated.[4] These fields are interesting from the perspective of independence as it is specifically in these sectors that European law has had a substantial influence on the requirements set in respect of national supervisors' independence. This is because national and local governments have traditionally played an important role, as shareholders in enterprises operating in these sectors. In many cases, state-owned entities, often operating as monopolies, were felt to be the most appropriate means of providing services of general interest to the public. Over time, however, technological developments and ideas on competition led to many of these traditional monopolies being dismantled and privatised. An important issue then was to prevent unfair competition from the state and to ensure that the state's involvement in the sector was placed at arm's length. This resulted in various supervisors being established to oversee the liberalisation process and these bodies required the ability to operate independently of the state.

The European legislator included various requirements for independence in the liberalisation directives adopted for the infrastructure sectors. These requirements have become increasingly stringent; whereas they originally focused only on the need for supervisors to be independent of *market parties*,[5] they have since been extended to include independence from the *political arena*.[6]

Independence from market parties
It was deemed necessary for the supervisors to be independent of market parties in order to ensure that all the interests at stake in the various markets and in potential conflict situations would be given proper consideration and without

3 A.T. Ottow, *Telecommunicatietoezicht. De invloed van het Europese en Nederlandse bestuurs(process) recht* ('Supervising telecommunications – The influence of European and Dutch administrative (procedural) law'), Sdu Uitgevers, The Hague, 2006.

4 *See* A.T. Ottow, Europeanization of the Supervision of Competitive Markets, *European Public Law*, Vol. 18, 2012, No. 1, p. 191-221.

5 In *France v. Commission*, ECJ 19 March 1991, case C-202/88, *ECR* 1991, I-1223, the ECJ derived the principle of independence from the EC (now EU) Treaty. See also ECJ 27 October 1993, *Decoster*, case C-69/91, *ECR* 1993, I-5335. The principle of independence was subsequently developed in more detail in various European Directives. *See* A.T. Ottow, Onafhankelijkheid van toezichthouders. Hof van Justitie EU 9 maart 2010, Commissie/Duitsland, zaak C-515/07, *Tijdschrift voor Toezicht*, 2010, No. 3, pp. 78-86, A.T. Ottow & S.A.C.M. Lavrijssen, Het Europese recht als hoeder van de onafhankelijkheid van nationale toezichthouders, *Tijdschrift voor Toezicht*, 2011, No. 3, p. 34-50 and S. Lavrijssen & A.T. Ottow, Independent supervisory authorities: a fragile concept, *Legal issues of Economic integration* Vol. 39, 2012, No. 4, p. 419-446.

6 For these two aspects of independence *see* Ottow 2010 *supra*; Lavrijssen & Ottow 2012 *supra*, p. 427-430; T. Tridimas, Community Agencies, Competition Law and ESCB Initiatives on Securities Clearing and Settlement, *in* P. Eeckhout & T. Tridimas, *Yearbook of European Law 2009*, Vol. 28, 2009, Oxford University Press, Oxford, 2009, p. 216-307 and T. Prosser, *The regulatory enterprise. Government, regulation and legitimacy*, Oxford University Press, Oxford, 2010, p. 226-235.

interference by states, many of which still held stakes in market parties in these sectors. No conflicts of interest were permitted. Not only were supervisors required to be legally separate from and functionally independent of market parties, but there also had to be a genuine structural separation between the regulatory (and supervisory) tasks and a Member State's shareholding in a market party.[7] These provisions did not, however, extend to stipulating how supervisors should be incorporated into the constitutional order of a Member State. It remained unclear, therefore, as to whether a supervisor could be a body falling under ministerial responsibility in a Member State or even be part of a ministry.[8]

Independence from the political arena

Over time, the European Commission indicated that political interference, too, should be excluded as this represented an obstacle to an objective assessment by supervisors. Politics driven by short-term interests can create regulatory uncertainty and is often driven by political or other specific interests, rather than being based on a balanced analysis by experts. The requirement for independence from the political arena is, however, more controversial in that it results in direct interference in the institutional, democratic systems of the Member States.

Despite the sensitivity of this issue, the European legislator has since further tightened the requirements for independence, as well as imposing far-reaching obligations on Member States in the new telecommunications and energy directives so as to ensure supervisory independence from the political world. Staff at the supervisory authority are not permitted to "seek or take direct instructions from any government or other public or private entity when carrying out the regulatory tasks".[9] In order to safeguard supervisors' independence, Member States must ensure that the authority "can take autonomous decisions, independently from any political body, (...) with autonomy in the implementation of the allocated budget, and adequate human and financial resources to carry out its duties".[10] These changes mean the new directives go significantly further in terms of the degree of independence required as they now also include independence at a political and institutional level.

---

7 Article 3(2), Framework Directive (Directive 2002/21/EC, *OJEC*, L108/33).

8 For a more recent case, *see* ECJ 6 March 2008, *Comisión del Mercado de las Telecomunicaciones v. Administración del Estado*, case C-82/07, at <www.curia.europa.eu>. The ECJ found in this case that the Framework Directive did not require the assignment of the national numbering resources and the management of the national numbering plans to be allocated to separate regulatory authorities.

9 *See* Article 35(4)(b)(ii) of Directive 2009/72/EC of the European Parliament and of the Council of 13 July 2009 concerning common rules for the internal market in electricity and repealing Directive 2003/54/EC (*OJEC 2009*, L 211/55). See also Article 3(3)(a) of Directive 2009/140/EC of the European Parliament and of the Council of 25 November 2009 amending Directives 2002/21/EC on a common regulatory framework for electronic communications networks and services, 2002/19/EC on access to, and interconnection of, electronic communications networks and associated facilities, and 2002/20/EC on the authorisation of electronic communications networks and services (*OJEC* 2009, L 337/37).

10 Article 35(5)(a) Directive 2009/72/EC.

Complete independence

The ECJ seemingly followed the same line of increasing independence in the significant judgment reached in March 2010, in which it ruled that the authorities responsible for monitoring the processing of personal data (pursuant to Article 28(1) Directive 95/46/EC)[11] were expected to perform their tasks 'with complete independence'.[12] The ECJ concluded from this that the supervisory authority should be able to fulfil its obligations objectively and impartially; in other words, without being exposed to any *direct* or *indirect* influence. The Court rejected Germany's claim that this broad interpretation represented an infringement of the principle of democracy in Europe. The Court found that a broad interpretation of the term 'complete independence' did not violate the principle of democracy as the legislator is permitted to define the powers available to the supervisor and can also require it to report on its activities to parliament. Similarly, parliament or the government may appoint the board members of the supervisory authority. This judgement is recently confirmed in the case of October 16th, 2012 *Commission vs Austria.*[13]

These judgments clearly constitute interference in the institutional autonomy of a Member State, as the ECJ concludes that any form of influence – whether direct or indirect – is prohibited. This case should, however, be viewed in the context of the relevant directive and the need to protect personal data. The question remains as to whether these far-reaching requirements will also apply in other situations, such as in the regulation of network sectors and the media sector.[14] The more recent directives in these sectors have not yet imposed such far-reaching restrictions. It was expected that the same high level of protection seen in the data protection regulation, would be implemented in the media regulation. This would have been relatively straightforward from the perspective of protecting media pluralism and the freedom of expression and free speech. Also these fundamental rights (such as in the case of privacy protection) should be safeguarded against direct or indirect influence of the state by sufficient independence requirements. However, for the media sector, there has been no such high level of protection of independence explicitly laid down in the media directives.[15]

---

11 Directive 95/46/EC of the European Parliament and of the Council of 24 October 1995 on the protection of individuals with regard to the processing of personal data and on the free movement of such data (*OJEC* 1995, L 281/31.

12 ECJ 9 March 2010, *Commission v. Federal Republic of Germany*, case C-518/07, annotated in *Tijdschrift voor Toezicht*; Ottow 2010 *supra*.

13 ECJ October 16, 2012, *Commission v. Austria*, case C-614/10, not yet published.

14 See the annotation with regard to the judgment in A.T. Ottow & M. Aelen, Commission v. Federal Republic of Germany, *European Human Rights Cases*, Vol. 11, 2010, No. 6, pp. 679-688.

15 *See* the report for the media sector: Hans Bredow Institute for Media Research/Interdisciplinary Centre for Law & ICT (ICRI), KU Leuven/Center for Media and Communication Studies (CMCS), Central European University/Cullen International/Perspective Associates (eds.), *INDIREG. Indicators for independence and efficient functioning of audio-visual media services regulatory bodies for the purpose of enforcing the rules in the AVMS Directive* (Study conducted on behalf of the European Commission), February 2011.

3. Central Question

What effect do these requirements actually have on national market authorities in practice? This is the central question in this paper. Five published cases are used here to illustrate the impact of these provisions on national practices.[16] All these examples relate to the regulated sectors; in other words, to the areas where the influence of the state has traditionally been felt.[17] The liberalisation of these markets that has resulted from European rules and regulations makes these fields particularly interesting from a perspective of supervisory independence. As these examples show, national governments in various Member States have sought to establish the extent of their boundaries and to use their influence to exert pressure on the independent supervisors. These cases serve to emphasise how important the various European requirements are with respect to independence. These cases concern the independence of *national* authorities only.[18] The independence of European agencies are not dealt with here. Another caveat must be made. This article deals with the *de jure* independence (*legal* requirements). The *de facto* independence is not considered in this article.[19]

4. Case 1: Dutch Gas Case

This particular case involved a policy rule issued by the Dutch Minister of Economic Affairs instructing the Board of the Netherlands Competition Authority (NMa) on how to deal with the rates charged by the state-owned company GTS (Gas Transport Services BV). The Office of Energy Regulation, which is the body responsible for enforcing sector-specific regulation, is part of the Netherlands Competition Authority. The Dutch Gas Act of 2000[20] gives the Competition Authority statutory powers to set gas transport rates. The party bringing the action, EnergieNed (the Dutch Association of Energy Producers), claimed that this policy rule should not be regarded as a general policy rule, but instead as an individual instruction to the Board with respect to the transport rates charged by GTS, given that the policy rule set such specific parameters that the Board had virtually no scope to include considerations of its own.

---

16 Other cases can be found in the implementation overviews of the Commission, although not many details can be derived from the published information. *See e.g.* Commission staff working paper. Situation in the different sectors accompanying the Report from the Commission: 28th annual report on monitoring the application of EU law (2010)', COM(2011) 588 final, SEC(2011) 1094 final and Electronic Communications – Revised Regulatory Framework Infringement procedures opened for non-communication of transposition measures.

17 *See* for more sectors: Hanretty *et al.*, *Independence, Accountability and perceived Quality of Regulators* (Report Study 15), Centre on Regulation in Europe (CERRE), 2012.

18 For the independence of European authorities *see* Lavrijssen & Ottow 2012 *supra*.

19 Gilardi & Magetti use the term *de facto* independence for their effective autonomy in the day-to-day practice: F. Giraldi & M. Magetti, The independence of regulatory authorities, *in* D. Levi-Faur (ed.), *Handbook of Regulation*, Edward Elgar, Cheltenham, 2012, p. 204.

20 Article 12f Gaswet.(Dutch Gas Act).

Dutch requirements
EnergieNed claimed that the minister had contravened Article 5 of the Dutch Competition Act by essentially issuing instructions to the Board of the Competition Authority in an individual case, rather than limiting herself to general policy rules. As a result, EnergieNed claimed, the minister had exceeded her authority by wholly taking over the Board's powers to set rates, whereas Article 5d of the Dutch Competition Act only authorised the minister to issue *general* policy rules. Indeed, in 2001, when the Competition Authority was transformed into an autonomous administrative authority, it was stated that independence is required to ensure specific expertise. The minister cannot give instructions in individual cases. The legislator had deemed it important for there to be no scope for political interference in individual decisions taken by the Board of the Competition Authority. The state believed in this case, however, that there was no question of an *individual* policy rule and that the instructions were purely of a *general* nature.

The Dutch Trade and Industry Appeals Tribunal (CBb) disagreed with the state's view and ruled the decision taken by the Board in respect of this 'general' policy rule to be invalid. The Trade and Industry Appeals Tribunal believed, therefore, that the instructions constituted individual instructions, and that would be incompatible with the Dutch Competition Act.

European requirements
Article 25(1) of the European Gas Directive applying at the time (Directive 2003/55/EC) stated the following with respect to national regulatory authorities' independence:

> 1. Member States shall designate one or more competent bodies with the function of regulatory authorities. These authorities shall be wholly independent of the interests of the gas industry.[21]

The Board of the Netherlands Competition Authority is a designated regulatory authority and therefore needs to be able to operate independently. EnergieNed claimed that the minister, as the shareholder of GTS, was not authorised to adopt the specific policy rule as it resulted in the Board – in other words, the regulatory authority – no longer being able to set the rates charged by GTS on the basis of cost. By issuing an individual instruction (in the form of a policy rule) the minister violated the Board's independence and denied it the opportunity to adopt an independent position. Being able to issue individual instructions in this way would also have contravened Article 25(1) of the Gas Directive in that it allowed the state's role as a shareholder to become blurred with the tasks of the supervisor (in other words, the regulatory authority).

21 Directive 2003/55/EC of the European Parliament and of the Council of 26 June 2003 concerning common rules for the internal market in natural gas and repealing Directive 98/30/EC, *OJEU* 2003, L 176/57.

The examination conducted by the Dutch Trade and Industry Appeals Tribunal was based directly on the Dutch Competition Act and no account was taken of the Gas Directive. Nevertheless, the message conveyed was clear: there was a conflict of interests, with the minister having issued an individual instruction in respect of the rates charged by GTS, an entity with the Dutch state as its sole shareholder. Even if Article 5d of the Competition Act had not contained such a prohibition, the Tribunal would nevertheless have had to declare the policy rule invalid on the grounds that it contravened the Gas Directive. The Board of the Netherlands Competition Authority, as the regulatory authority designated responsible for implementing the provisions of the Gas Directive, has to be able to perform these tasks independently of any interest in a market party. And the policy rule issued constituted an obstacle in this respect.

The parliamentary history of the review of the Dutch Competition Act shows that, as well as the requirement for independence from *market parties*, there is also a prohibition on *political* interference. The Competition Act goes further in this respect than the old Gas Directive. The requirement for independence from political influence has since also been incorporated into the recast Gas Directive,[22] which contains more stringent requirements, in Article 39(4) and (5), with respect to national regulatory authorities' independence. These requirements cover aspects such as the performance of regulatory tasks 'independently from any political body', the funding of the regulatory authority and the appointment and periods in office of board members.

These requirements for independence had to be transposed into national legislation by 3rd March 2011. According to the minister, the provisions of the European directive would not result in any substantial changes in the case of the Netherlands,[23] although it will need to be stated in the Electricity Act (*Elektriciteitswet*) and the Gas Act (*Gaswet*) that 'Our minister will refrain from issuing instructions relating to an individual case'.[24]

The minister believes that Article 21 of the Dutch Framework Act on Autonomous Administrative Authorities (*Kaderwet zelfstandige bestuursorganen*) continues to allow the minister the right to determine the range of interests to be taken into

22 Directive 2009/73/EC of the European Parliament and of the Council of 13 July 2009 concerning common rules for the internal market in natural gas and repealing Directive 2003/55/EC, *OJEU* 2009, L 211/94. See also Article 35(4) and (5) Directive 2009/72/EC of the European Parliament and of the Council of 13 July 2009 concerning common rules for the internal market in electricity and repealing Directive 2003/54/EC, *OJEU 2009*, L 211/55.

23 Amendment of the Electricity Act 1998 and the Gas Act, *Parliamentary Papers II* 2010-2011, 32 814, No. 3, p. 5 ff. Since the Framework Act on Autonomous Administrative Authorities (*Kaderwet zelfstandige bestuursorganen*) came into force, the minister's power to adopt policy rules relating to the exercising of powers assigned to the Netherlands Competition Authority has been included in this Framework Act rather than in the Competition Act.

24 *See* Articles I C and II B of the Amendment to the Electricity Act 1998 and the Gas Act, *Parliamentary Papers* 2010/11, 32 814, No. 2 (Bill).

account by the Netherlands Competition Authority when performing its tasks. It would appear that the minister is authorised to issue general policy rules, provided certain limits are respected. The text of the new energy directives can be read in such a way that policy rules are not allowed to extend to the regulatory tasks of the national supervisor. The minister does not wish, however, to impose such a restriction *ex ante* on the right to issue policy rules. Policy rules may in any event relate to the parameters of government policy in the energy market within which the national regulatory authority ('NRA') has to operate.[25]

This is also confirmed in a European Commission staff working paper:[26]

> The Electricity and Gas Directives do not deprive the government of the possibility of establishing and issuing its national energy policy. This means that, depending on the national constitution, it could be the government's competency to determine the policy framework within which the NRA must operate, e.g. concerning security of supply, renewables or energy efficiency targets. *However, general energy policy guidelines issued by the government must not encroach on the NRA's independence and autonomy.*'[27]

Although general policy rules are, therefore, permitted within certain limits, the question of whether the Competition Authority's discretionary powers are being too severely restricted, thus leaving it too little freedom to take decisions in individual cases, needs to be decided on a case-by-case basis. The above working paper also states that the requirements should apply to the *entire* staff and management and not only to board members:

> 'The new legislation also prohibits the NRA's staff and the persons responsible for its management from seeking or taking direct instructions from any government or other public or private entity. This provision aims to tackle the situation where someone working for the NRA is seeking or taking direct instructions. According to the Commission's services, this provision also implies that it is forbidden for anyone to give such instructions. An instruction in this context is any action calling for compliance and/or trying to improperly influence an NRA decision and thus includes the use of pressure of any kind on NRA's staff or on the persons responsible for its management. In the view of the Commission's services this requires Member States to provide for dissuasive civil, administrative and/or criminal sanctions in case of violation of the provisions on independence as well as for any attempts by public and private entities to give an instruction or to improperly influence an NRA decision.'[28]

---

25 See also the opinion of the Dutch Council of State in this respect, *Parliamentary Papers II* 2010/11, 32 814, No. 4, pp. 7-8.

26 Commission staff working paper, Interpretative note on Directive 2009/72/EC concerning common rules for the internal market in electricity and Directive 2009/73/EC concerning common rules for the internal market in natural gas, The Regulatory Authorities, Brussels, 22 January 2010.

27 Commission staff working paper, p. 7 (emphasis added).

28 Commission staff working paper, p. 7.

It follows from these new provisions of the recast Gas Directive (and the corresponding provisions in the Electricity Directive) that it is not only the Board of the Netherlands Competition Authority that has to comply with the requirements for independence but also the other staff at the Office of Energy Regulation. This is a sensitive issue in the Dutch context since only the Board of the Competition Authority constitutes an independent administrative authority (a so called 'small' independent authority) and not the entire Competition Authority. The bill implementing the energy directives consequently states that "The Board of the Competition Authority and the staff available to the Board will not demand or receive instructions relating to an individual case."[29] The Competition Authority's staff regulations will therefore have to take account of these new requirements as all staff involved with implementing the Gas or Electricity Directives will have to be able to act independently.

This Dutch case illustrates the importance of independence requirements for autonomous decisions by a national regulatory authority – in this case, the Office of Energy Regulation (and the Board) of the Netherlands Competition Authority. The new energy directives set stringent standards for this independence and the way in which it is implemented in day-to-day practice. The Dutch Trade and Industry Appeals Tribunal rightly found the general policy rule in the GTS case to constitute an individual instruction and subjected it to stringent review. The Dutch legal framework itself provided sufficient scope for this. If, however, this had not been the case, the Tribunal would have had to declare the policy rule and/or the decision by the Competition Authority to be invalid on the grounds that it contravened the then applicable Gas Directive.

5. Case 2: German Telecommunications Case

Rather than a 'general' policy rule this case involved statutory provisions with which the German legislator issued an instruction to the German telecommunications supervisor on how to deal with specific rules and regulations. In these new legislative provisions the German legislator specified how the term 'new markets' should be defined, how the principle of non-regulation in these new markets should apply, and imposed more restrictive conditions on the German telecommunications supervisor than provided for in the European Telecommunications Directives. In addition, it imposed a specific objective of regulation on the German supervisor instead of the various objectives set in the European Directives. These statutory provisions significantly curtailed the discretionary powers the telecom supervisor normally enjoys. According to the German government, this legislation simply provided more precise clarification of the European rules. Germany claimed that the Telecommunications Directives allowed sufficient freedom to

29 See Articles I C and II B of the Amendment to the Electricity Act 1998 and the Gas Act, *Parliamentary Papers* 2010/11, 32 814, No. 2 (Bill).

national legislators to define abstract concepts. The European Commission, however, disagreed and submitted the case to the ECJ for consideration.

In the recent judgment *Commission v. Federal Republic of Germany* the ECJ gave a number of important findings in support of national supervisors' independence. The Court imposed limits on the extent to which national legislators could seek to influence these supervisors and stated that European law had assigned responsibility for supervising the telecom sector to an independent supervisor, which should have broad discretionary powers. The national legislator was not permitted, therefore, to exclude certain markets from regulation in advance or to specify *ex ante* that only certain objectives should be taken into account. The Court's findings included the following:

> 54 Pursuant to Article 3(2) and (3) of the Framework Directive and recital 11 in its preamble, *in accordance with the principle of the separation of regulatory and operational functions*, Member States must guarantee the independence of the national regulatory authority or authorities with a view to ensuring the impartiality and transparency of their decisions. (...)
> 61 In carrying out those regulatory functions, the NRAs have a broad discretion in order to be able to determine the need to regulate a market according to each situation on a case-by-case basis[30] (...)
> 74 It should be added that, in any event, (...) the Framework Directive *confers on the NRA, and not on the national legislature, the task of determining the need for regulation of the markets.*
> 78 Therefore, by laying down a legal provision, according to which, as a general rule, the regulation of new markets by the NRA is excluded, Paragraph 9a of the TKG [German Telecommunications Act] encroaches on the wide powers conferred on the NRA under the Community regulatory framework, preventing it from adopting regulatory measures appropriate to each particular case. (...) the German legislature cannot alter a decision of the Community legislature and cannot, as a general rule, exempt new markets from regulation.
> 79 It follows that Paragraph 9a(1) of the TKG, by establishing a principle of non-regulation of new markets, is not compatible with Article 16 of the Framework Directive. (...)
> 83 However, it must be held that the limitation of the German NRA's discretion as a result of Paragraph 9a(1) of the TKG necessarily affects the NRA's ability to define the market' (emphasis by author).[31]

In this case the German legislator had sought to circumvent the supervision provided by its own independent national regulatory authority by including certain instructions already in the applicable telecommunications legislation. This

30 The ECJ in this respect referred to the judgment of 24 April 2008 in *Arcor*, C-55/06, *ECR I-2931, paras. 153 - 156.*

31 ECJ 3 December 2009, *Commission v. Federal Republic of Germany*, case C-424/07 (emphasis added).

significantly reduced the discretion available to the telecommunications supervisor. The ECJ saw through this attempt and declared it to be in contravention of the applicable European Telecommunications Directives. As the Court stated, the European legislator has conferred on the independent national regulatory authorities, and not on the national legislature, the task of determining the need for regulation of the markets. If, by laying down a legal provision in national legislation, the German legislator was to be able to prevent the national regulatory authority from adopting the regulatory measures that the authority considered appropriate, the national regulatory authority would be subjected to *political* influence that would restrict its powers and also constitute a threat to its independence.

The judgment in this case represents a significant curtailment of national autonomy as it means that national legislators are not free to disregard the system of independent supervision provided for in the European directives and to assign these powers to themselves. It can be concluded from this case that the ECJ regards the importance of independent supervision as a basic principle and will therefore closely examine any intervention by national legislators.

6. Case 3: Dutch Television Case

The above German case is of importance for a case – the Dutch television case – currently attracting attention in the Netherlands.

Influence of the Dutch House of Representatives
The central issue in this case concerns the extent to which cable companies should be required to allow their competitors to access their networks. The issue of cable networks has been politically very sensitive in the Netherlands for many years. Although OPTA, the Dutch Independent Post and Telecommunications Authority, had earlier decided to require access to the cable networks to be granted,[32] its decisions were subsequently overturned by the Trade and Industry Appeals Tribunal[33] and in 2011 OPTA was forced to review its decision. Shortly before OPTA was due to announce its new decision, the Dutch House of Representatives adopted two amendments[34] in which the obligation to grant access was laid down in law (in the Dutch Media Act (*Mediawet*) and the Dutch Telecommunications

32 OPTA's decisions of 17 March 2006, 21 December 2007 and 5 March 2009, <www.opta.nl>. The first and third of these decisions were overturned by the Dutch Trade and Industry Appeals Tribunal. The new decision that OPTA was consequently forced to take in 2011 resulted in a draft opinion on regulation of the television market being published on 23 June 2011, submitted for consultation and finally adopted at December 20th, 2011, see: Trade and Industry Appeals Tribunal 5 November 2012 *Tele 2 et al. v. OPTA, LJN*: BY2135, para. 2.2.

33 Trade and Industry Appeals Tribunal 24 July 2007, *Casema et al. v. OPTA, LJN*: BB0186; Trade and Industry Appeals Tribunal 17 December 2008, *UPC et al. v. OPTA, LJN*: BG7099, and Trade and Industry Appeals Tribunal 18 August 2010, *Delta et al. v. OPTA, LJN*: BN4243.

34 *Parliamentary Papers II* 2010/11, 32 549, No. 28 and 2010/11, 32 549, No. 18.

Act (*Telecommunicatiewet*)).[35] These amendments require large cable companies to cooperate in the resale of their standard packages. In this way the Netherlands has circumvented the discretionary powers available to OPTA under the European framework that allow it first to delineate the market and then to decide which measures are necessary and proportional. This Dutch case is very similar, therefore, to the German telecommunications case discussed above.

OPTA and the minister's views

OPTA's draft opinion on the market, in which it stated that the television market was by now sufficiently competitive and not in need of more regulation, was published in the very same week as the amendment.[36] As the opinion stated, it was not appropriate – in OPTA's view – to impose an obligation to allow access to the television network. In a letter of 23rd June 2011 sent to the Dutch House of Representatives concerning the amendments that had been adopted the Minister of Economic Affairs, Agriculture and Innovation stated that:

> This amendment deviates, however, from a principle that I consider very important and that is also established in European law, being *the requirement for an independent regulatory authority to decide on whether and how competition in markets should be regulated, with all the safeguards that this entails.* In my view this basic principle is of great importance in giving market parties the assurance that regulation will be applied professionally and consistently. This is also the reason why we have designated OPTA as the authority responsible for regulating the cable market. OPTA bases its opinions on in-depth market analyses and its decisions are subject to judicial review. My predecessors and I have emphasised this point, with reference to the legal risks involved. I will arrange for this issue to be discussed with the administrations of the European Commission, specifically with regard to the legal viability of this aspect of the Bill.[37]

As the legislative amendment allows the Dutch legislator and not, as required by the European telecommunications framework, the national independent regulatory authority (in this case, OPTA) to decide whether to impose a specific obligation (in this case the obligation to allow access to the network), the Commission initiated an infringement procedure against the Netherlands.[38] The Commission alleges that the new legislation consequently contravenes the provisions of the European Telecommunications Directives.[39]

35 This was achieved via an amendment to the Media Act in the form of the addition of Article 6.14 and an amendment to the Telecommunications Act in the form of the addition of Article 6a.21.a.

36 OPTA's draft opinion on its analysis of the television market of 23 June 2011, <www.opta.nl>. This draft decision is confirmed in the final decision of OPTA of December 20, 2011, <www.opta.nl>. This decision of OPTA is uphold by the CBb in its judgement of 5 November 2012, *Tele 2 et al. v. OPTA*, *LJN*: BY2135, <www.rechtspraak.nl>.

37 Emphasis added.

38 Case number 2012/4144, Brussels 24.10.2012, C(2012) 7394 final.

39 Specifically Articles 7(a) and 16 of Directive 2009/140/EC.

7. Case 4: French Government Commissioner of Autonomous Administrative Authorities

The issue of the appointment of government commissioners at various autonomous administrative authorities in France (*Autorités Administratives Indépendantes, 'AAI'*) has recently garnered considerable attention. This attention was directly triggered by an amendment to the French telecommunications legislation that affected the telecom regulator ARCEP (*Autorité de Régulation des Communications Électroniques et des Postes*). The amendment, which was approved by the *Assemblée Nationale,*[40] allowed the government to appoint an official at ARCEP. Many people saw this as compromising the telecom regulator's independence. Under the amendment, the government official would be responsible for announcing details of the government's analyses of the postal and electronic communications markets to ARCEP. In addition, the official would be authorised to include any question relating to this field on the agenda, while a request for investigation of such a question could not be refused. The government official was not permitted, however, to attend consultations of the telecoms regulator. The brief explanatory notes to the amendment stated that it was based on a recent parliamentary report on the French AAI, in which the appointment of a government official at each AAI was recommended.[41]

This amendment is certainly questionable from a European perspective. Indeed a European Commission telecommunications spokesperson indicated that the Commission would examine the amendment to see whether it was compatible with European legislation:

> La Commission Européenne va examiner "de très près" un projet français visant à nommer un commissaire du gouvernement au sein de l'Autorité de régulation des communications électroniques et des postes (Arcep), car elle veut s'assurer de l'indépendance de cet organisme, a indiqué jeudi un porte-parole.[42]

Catherine Trautmann, a member of the European Parliament, described herself as *absolument ahurie et scandalisée* (absolutely stunned and shocked) by the amendment.[43] Éric Besson, the initiator of the amendment, defended the move by stating that he was seeking to reinforce the dialogue between the regulatory authority and the government and to increase the effectiveness of the work. He also stated that

40 The amendment was approved during the night of 13 January by six votes to five: Les députés valident la création du commissaire du gouvernement à l'Arcep, *Le Monde* 14 January 2011, <www.lemonde.fr>.

41 Assemblée Nationale, *Rapport d'information fait au nom du comité d'évaluation et de contrôle des politiques publiques sur les autorités administratives indépendantes*, Vol. I – Report, No. 2925, filed on 28 October 2010, pp. 101-102.

42 Bruxelles veillera à 'l'indépendance et l'impartialité' de l'Arcep, *Le Monde* 13 January 2011, <www.lemonde.fr>.

43 Guerric Poncet, Amendement – Le gouvernement va limiter l'indépendance du gendarme des télécoms, *Le Point* 13 January 2011, <www.lepoint.fr>.

the appointment of a government official at a regulatory authority was nothing new as such an official had already been appointed at other important regulatory authorities such as the French Authority for the Financial Markets (*Autorité des marchés financiers*), the Competition Authority (*Autorité de la concurrence*) and the Energy Regulation Committee (*Commission de Régulation de l'Energie*).[44]

The appointment of a government official to such a position was clearly very much at odds with the requirement for independence stipulated in the telecom and energy directives. Although this official would not have had any formal powers and would not have been permitted to attend board meetings, his presence would obviously have put indirect (and maybe even direct) pressure on the activities of the independent regulatory authority. Appointing such an official in order to increase effectiveness was also unnecessary as there are other means of achieving this, and these other means respect the need for independence. Following a warning by European Commissioner Kroes that she would initiate infringement proceedings if this amendment was adopted, the French Senate voted against the amendment and the idea of appointing this new government commissioner (at least in the case of ARCEP) has now been abandoned.[45] In view of the strict requirements imposed, as discussed above, in the European energy directives, the government commissioner at the French energy regulator should also be removed from office.

8. Case 5: Hungarian Media Case

In December 2010 the Hungarian parliament passed a law, which came into force on January 1st 2011, which severely tightens indirect government control of the media.[46] This legislation also changes the supervisory regime of the country's media. It creates a new Media Council, elected by Parliament, and whose chairman is directly appointed by the Prime Minister for a nine year mandate. Since the current (right-wing) party is in power and has a vast majority in Parliament, no representative of the opposition will sit on the Media Council for at least nine years. This new organisation is supposed to emerge as the modernised head of media supervision in the country, including both analogue and electronic media. The scope of the new legislation is large, as it is including every kind of media (press, television, internet media as well as online media).

44 See footnote 35.

45 <www.senat.fr/amendements/commissions/2010-2011/225/jeu_complet.html>.

46 Act CLXXXV of 2010 on media services and mass media, *Magyar Közlöny* (Official Journal) 31 December 2010, Act LXXXII of 2010 on the amendment of certain acts on media and telecommunications, *Magyar Közlöny* (Official Journal) 10 August 2010 and Act CIV of 2010 on the freedom of the press and the fundamental rules on media content, *Magyar Közlöny* (Official Journal) 9 November 2010.

Commissioner Kroes called[47] the new legislation 'unsatisfactory' and urged Hungary to bring the new act in conformity with European legislation, more specifically with the Audiovisual Media Services Directive.[48] It was announced by the Hungarian State that proposals were made to change the new legislation and bring it in conformity with EU law.[49] However, there was no mention of the original compliant by the Commission about the composition of the new members of the Media Council.[50]

What does EU law require with respect to the independence of media regulators? The only requirements for independence and efficient functioning of national regulatory bodies in the audiovisual media sector are found in Article 30 of chapter XI (Cooperation between regulatory bodies of the Member States) of the Media Service Directive. This article provides:

> Member States shall take appropriate measures to provide each other and the Commission with the information necessary for the application of the provisions of this Directive, in particular Articles 2, 3 and 4 hereof, in particular through their competent independent regulatory bodies.

The scope and impact of this provision is further explained in two specific recitals of the directive:

> (94) In accordance with the duties imposed on Member States by the Treaty on the Functioning of the European Union, they are responsible for the effective implementation of this Directive. They are free to choose the appropriate instruments according to their legal traditions and established structures, and, in particular, the form of their competent independent regulatory bodies, in order to be able to carry out their work in implementing this Directive impartially and transparently. More specifically, the instruments chosen by Member States should contribute to the promotion of media pluralism.
>
> (95) Close cooperation between competent regulatory bodies of the Member States and the Commission is necessary to ensure the correct application of this Directive. Similarly close cooperation between Member States and between their regula-

47 N. Kroes, State of play of Commission's examination of Hungarian Media Law, *Extraordinary meeting of the European Parliament's Civil Liberties, Justice and Home Affairs Committee Strasbourg*, 17 January 2011, SPEECH/11/22: "the Media Law does not appear at first sight to be satisfactory".

48 Directive 2010/13/EU of the European Parliament and of the Council of 10 March 2010 on the coordination of certain provisions laid down by law, regulation or administrative action in Member States concerning the provision of audio-visual media services, O.J. 2010, L 95/1, hereafter and the Media Service Directive.

49 Act XIX of 2011 on the modification of Act CIV of 2010 and Act CLXXXV of 2010 *Magyar Közlöny* (Official Journal) 22 March 2011. See also: <http://europa.eu/rapid/press-release_MEMO-11-89_en.htm>.

50 Financial Times February 16, 2011.

> tory bodies is particularly important with regard to the impact which broadcasters established in one Member State might have on another Member State. Where licensing procedures are provided for in national law and if more than one Member State is concerned, it is desirable that contacts between the respective bodies take place before such licenses are granted. This cooperation should cover all fields coordinated by this Directive.

The current text of Art. 30 Media Services Directive reflects a difficult compromise between the different visions of the European Parliament, the Commission and the Council. Recital 94 and Article 30 do not impose a formal legal obligation on Member States to create an independent supervisor where these do not yet exist.[51] However, if a new supervisory body is created, this authority should be independent. But what does that mean? The Media Services Directive does not provide – contrary to the communications and energy directives – specific legal requirements.

It is questionable whether the Media Services Directive provides sufficient safeguards to intervene in the Hungarian case with regard to the independence of the new Media Council. Nonetheless, the Commission has started an infringement procedure.[52] As media pluralism and the freedom of expression must be considered fundamental rights, it is at the very least remarkable that the media directive does not provide stricter provisions and safeguards to ensure the 'depolitisation' of media regulation and independent supervision. Lessons have to be learned from other sectors, such as the communications sector, to amend the legal requirements of the Media Service Directive in that respect.

9. Conclusion: Three Levels of Protection

As the examples discussed in this paper demonstrate, the independence of national supervisors is fragile and can come under pressure, not only from market parties, but also from the legislator and the political sphere and administration. Experience in various Member States prompted the European Commission to issue proposals designed to reinforce the independence of the national supervisors in various sectors. These more stringent requirements have since been incorporated into various European directives and not only provide for independence vis-à-vis market parties, but also vis-à-vis the political arena. To date, the ECJ has recognised the importance of and actively sought to protect the indepen-

51 *See* the Preliminary report by Hans Bredow Institute *et al.*, Indicators for independence and efficient functioning of audiovisual media services regulatory bodies for the purpose of enforcing rules in the AVMS Directive, SMART 2009/001, January 2011, p. 323.

52 1 September 2011, IP/11/1002. See also IP/11/1173 and report *Hungarian media laws in Europe. An assessment of the consistency of Hungary's media laws with European practices and norms*, CMCS, center for Media and Communications Studies, Budapest, 2012, <https://cmcs.ceu.hu/news/2012-01-05/new-study-hungarian-media-laws-in-europe-an-assessment-of-the-consistency-of-hungary>.

dence of national supervisors in its case law. The approach adopted by the Court is expected to continue in the future. Overlooking the European landscape of the above-mentioned regulated areas, three levels of protection can be distinguished. First, there is the area of data protection, where the European legislator and court have recognised the importance of independence and have secured a *high* level of protection of independence. A middle category is the energy and communications area, with legal requirements, which qualify as a *medium* level of protection of independence. Finally, there are sectors, such as the media sector, where so far the level of protection is *low*.

What lessons can we learn from the discussed cases? There will certainly be a tendency for governments, particularly in areas in which they have interests at stake, to seek a degree of involvement. There are various ways in which this involvement manifests itself. From a European perspective, however, any involvement by a government in individual cases in markets in which the state is also a market party is forbidden. Although general instructions (policy rules) may be issued to independent supervisors, the question of whether these instructions go too far in addressing concrete situations, will always be assessed critically. Political influence, even if the state is not a market party, is not allowed in the telecommunications and gas sectors on which the European directives have imposed far-reaching requirements. The legislator is not permitted to curtail the activities of the supervisors in these sectors either via legislation or policy rules in individual cases, but the legislator and the minister may define a general policy framework supervisors have to take into account in matters of general interest, such as security of supply and sustainability. The independent supervisors need, however, to have sufficient discretion within this framework to be able to take autonomous decisions in individual cases, based on the provisions of European law. A balance will have to be found between policy considerations from the legislator and ministries on the one hand and sufficient discretion for the independent authority on the other hand. Absolute independence is not realistic and can conflict with the democratic principle of the Member States.

Regulatory Enforcement in the Netherlands: Struggling with Independence

*Heinrich Winter**

1. Introduction

In this chapter, the issue of independence of regulators will be addressed. Three questions are answered. First, what is the degree of independence of the politico-administrative system of inspections and authorities in the Netherlands? Second, the question of what degree of independence is needed is discussed. Third, an answer is given to the question of how this desired degree of independence can be accomplished.

The second paragraph starts by pointing out the motives for a discussion on this issue now. In the third paragraph the concept of independence is addressed. What is independence in relation to inspectorates and authorities? What are the constraints and incentives? In this paragraph the first question is answered. The second question is addressed in the fourth paragraph, where the official line of thought in the Netherlands will be described. Different scholars focus on the desirability of more independence of inspectorates and authorities. Paragraph 5 focusses on different ways to safeguard independence. Then, of course, ministerial responsibility is discussed as well as organising inspectorates and authorities at a certain distance of the departmental structure. Finally, some conclusions will be drawn and the discussion will be put into perspective (paragraph 6).

2. The Debate on (In)dependency: Three Motives

There are at least three motives for the urgency of a discussion on independence of regulatory enforcement in the 21st century. The first one can be labeled as the public discussion on inspectorates and authorities. The second motive makes a reference to the political and administrative interferences with regulatory enforcement. The third motive focuses on the incentives from European law.

* Prof. dr. H.B. Winter is Professor of regulatory compliance at the department of administrative law and public administration of the Faculty of Law, University of Groningen, the Netherlands. He is also director of Pro Facto, a research and consultancy firm, active in the fields of public law and public administration.

2.1 *The Public Debate on Regulatory Enforcement*

Over the past few years a fierce public debate is been raging in the Netherlands concerning the merits of regulatory enforcement in general and about the use and nuisance of inspectorates and authorities in particular. Fuel for the discussions was provided by an important government document, the second memo on regulatory enforcement from October 2005 ('Kaderstellende visie op toezicht', *Parliamentary Papers II* 2005/06, 27 831, nr. 15). The title of this document is significant as it translates as 'Less burden, more effect'. In my opinion this title symbolises the current situation of regulatory enforcement in the Netherlands. Inspectorates and authorities have to deal with different constraints and incentives. *Less burden* indicates that regulatory enforcement is supposed to function on a more limited scale. The regulated should be bothered less. In this respect, we encountered the rather surprising concept of an 'inspection holiday' in the previous Dutch government's coalition agreement (Rutte I, 2010 – 2012). This meant that civilians, businesses and organisations that behave according to the law, will be trusted based on their previous performance and will be inspected in a lighter way than would usually be the case. In itself this of course is not a particularly controversial concept, but it leads to many potential misunderstanding and misinterpretations, which is understandable as it implies that inspectorates and authorities interfer too much with businesses and private citizens.

At the same time *more effect* should be brought about according to this vision memo. This means that if the inspector acts, it should be effective. Societal outcomes of inspections need to be clearly recognisable and substantiated.

Both starting points are useful, one could argue, but in practice the combination leads to paralysing effects. In short: the inspector can do no good. He is always to blame. If there is an incident, he did not anticipate the risks and failed to take measures. If there is no incident, then the inspector will be accused of creating a burden of supervision, he is evaluated as being too expensive and the conclusion could be that we can do without him. There are currently several inspectorates are involved in such ambivalent discussions. The Dutch Healthcare Inspectorate for instance, is an example of an inspectorate that attracts a great deal of public attention. It seems everyone disagrees with the organisation, from hospital management, patient organisations, consumer protection programmes on Dutch television, Dutch parliament and the National ombudsman. The debate focuses on the intensity of the activities of the Healthcare Inspectorate: some argue it is too reluctant to impose sanctions and fails to address the real problems, others argue that the inspectorate interferes far too much.

The public focus on inspectorates and authorities leads to insecurity surrounding purpose and function in regulatory organisations. It results in budget cuts and reorganisation and in the Dutch parliament passing a resolution aiming to build one nationwide inspection in a big and comprehensive merger. Indeed, there was such a resolution a few years ago, initiated by parliamentarian Aptroot, unscrupulously aiming to form one inspectorate. We have seen deep budget cuts on inspectorates over the last few years and we also witness different inspectorates recently reorganising and merging. The argument for the independence of inspectorates and authorities find relevance in its function as a shield against these kinds of interventions.

2.2 *The Political and Administrative Domain*

The second incentive sparking public debate about regulatory enforcement and independence can be found in the way enforcement is executed within the politico-administrative domain. Research on inspections and authorities tells us that interventions from politicians and administrators often results in preventing inspectorates and authorities from acting as they want to. Research in the field of local environmental enforcement suggests that aldermen and deputies are frequently reluctant to impose sanctions that can put regional employment or other public interests at risk.[1] These concerns are raised by managers of firms complaining that the penalties civil servants threaten to impose and by counselors lobbying for (their own) agricultural interests. Businesses in this process threaten to leave the municipality or the province if the enforcement action is carried out. This lack of independence is one of the triggers that led to Biezeveld and Stoové coming up with their proposal of establishing an independent environmental authority.[2]

2.3 *European Regulation and Jurisprudence*

Third, the discussion on regulatory independence is relevant because of European regulation and jurisprudence by the European Court of Justice. An important milestone seems to be the EU Court's verdict of March, 9th, 2010, *Commission v Germany*, concerning the independence of the privacy authority in the German Länder, who are subjected to a certain degree of administrative control.[3] The verdict addresses the interpretation of the term 'full independence' mentioned in the Privacy Directive. The EU Court of Justice is of the opinion that this term should be interpreted in a very strict sense which means that the privacy authority should be fully independent from state administration. Full independence thus can be compared with the independence of the judiciary. Other European Directives, for instance concerning energy or telecoms, are not as radical as the Privacy Directive but also in these fields independent enforcement seems not to be subjected to direct instruction from the government or by other public or private entities. This

1 N. Struiksma, J. de Ridder & H.B. Winter, *De effectiviteit van bestuurlijke en strafrechtelijke milieuhandhaving* (WODC-reeks Onderzoek en beleid, nr. 253), Boom Juridische uitgevers Den Haag, 2007 en J. de Ridder, N. Struiksma & M.J. Schol, *Grip op milieuzaken. Evaluatie van de strafrechtelijke milieuhandhaving*, Rijksuniversiteit Groningen, Groningen, 2009.

2 G.A. Biezeveld & M.C. Stoové, Naar een Nederlandse Omgevingsautoriteit. Een pleidooi voor onafhankelijk milieutoezicht, *Tijdschrift voor Toezicht* 2011, No. 3, p. 9-33.

3 ECJ 9 March 2010, C-518/07, Commission *v.* Germany. See also: A.T. Ottow, Onafhankelijkheid van toezichthouders, ECJ 9 maart 2010, *European Cie. v. Germany*, zaak C-515/07, *Tijdschrift voor Toezicht* 2010, No. 3, p. 78-86.

is illustrated by the Dutch case concerning a policy regulation by the Dutch Minister of Economic Affairs addressed to the board of the Dutch Competition Authority on how to determine the rates for gas transportation. The Dutch court argued that the Minister lacked authority to issue such a policy regulation, as it interfered with the independent judgment of the board of the Competition Authority.[4]

3. Independence and the State of the Art in the Netherlands

What are the constraints to and the incentives for independence and what does independence really mean? To start with this last question, regarding regulatory enforcement independence has a twofold meaning. First, there is (in)dependence in the relationship to the regulated field or sector. A sufficient degree of independence means that inspectorates are able to gather information on the behaviour of the regulated with little interference. Also, inspectorates should be free to come up with an analysis of this information and finally with the intervention they think is appropriate. When deciding upon interventions, independence usually is more endangered by more unobtrusive threats, like agency capture.

The other interpretation of independence of regulatory enforcement focuses on the relationship between the inspectorate on the one hand and politico-administrative leadership on the other. The most radical position would be that an inspectorate should be free to gather information it judged appropriate, and intervene when necessary, autonomous from the opinions of politicians and administrators.

3.1 Independence and the Regulated

First a few remarks on independence versus the regulated. In many evaluations of the financial crisis the world experienced following the bankruptcy of Lehman Brothers, we frequently saw reference made to the interdependence of the banking system and the supervisors. The relationship was tackled in terms of 'regulatory capture', did the financial inspectorates operate at a required distance from the regulated? There seems to be much evidence of close ties between the regulated and the regulators. We see a small world of bankers and inspectors, where job rotation between the sectors is predominant and where professionals meet in different kind of gatherings. The mixture of financial institutions and supervisors made it very difficult for the regulators to intervene or even to clearly distinguish what exactly was going on. This was true worldwide, and certainly in the Netherlands where the analysis of DSB's bankruptcy in 2009 by the commission-Scheltema[5] and the analysis of the crisis in the Dutch financial sector by parliamentarian

4 CBb 29 juni 2010, LJN: BM9470 (Gaszaak).

5 Rapport van de commissie van Onderzoek DSB Bank, Den Haag, 23 juni 2010. <www.nuzakelijk.nl/algemeen/2280594/rapport-commissie-scheltema.html> (last consulted on 29 March 2013).

commission-De Wit[6] came to similar conclusions. The financial supervisors maintained an old boys network with the financial institutions they were supposed to supervise. A remarkable story comes from the report by the commission-Scheltema on DSB where we witness a reverse case of capture. Auditors of the Dutch Central Bank had what they thought was a tough talk with bankers of DSB, pointing out that things had to change drastically within the bank. The DSB bank management interpreted this same encounter as a pleasant conversation about the state of affairs, resulting in the bank of course not reacting to the sharp criticism from the central bankers. The usual way of handling things, the close ties between central bankers and insurance companies and banks on which the central bankers relied, did not work at all in this case because DSB was a newcomer in the financial market, an outsider headed by a general manager who worked his way up from an insurance salesman to a banker with an official banking permission. DSB did not understand the usual way of handling things between supervisors and bankers, representatives of the central bank also did not understand that customs in the financial sector had changed rapidly, so they did not anticipate the radical change in relationship.

There seems to be more sensitivity for this aspect of the functioning of inspectorates and authorities than used to be the case. In the past for instance, one and the same inspector of the Dutch Inspectorate of Education could supervise schools in a certain district during his whole career, without ever changing his working area. Most inspectorates and authorities nowadays have the risk of 'capture', and there being too close a relationship between the regulator and the regulated, much more in mind.

Of course independence from the field is an absolute pre-condition for effective inspections. Inspectors inevitably must rely on cooperation by the regulated. Such cooperation is not self-evident. In this respect, in May 2012, a significant incident attracted attention. A newspaper article reported the secretary of Justice's withdrawal of a protocol composed several years ago by the ministry of Justice. The protocol was directed to civil servants working in institutions for juvenile delinquents.[7] The intention of the protocol was to brief the staff not to be too honest or too negative to the visiting inspectors. The personnel ought to stress what was going well and which measures for improvement had already been taken. Apparently, cooperation is no automatism, as we all know.

6 Tijdelijke commissie onderzoek financieel stelsel, *Verloren krediet*, *Parliamentary Papers* II 2009/10, 31 980, No. 4 and *Verloren krediet II – de balans opgemaakt*, Parliamentary Papers II 2011/12, 31 980, No. 61.

7 <www.telegraaf.nl/binnenland/12208602/__Teeven_trekt_handleiding_in__.html>, *Telegraaf* 25 mei 2012, Teeven trekt handleiding bezoek inspectie in (last consulted on 16 October 2012).

3.2 *Independence and the Minister*

The focus of this chapter is on the relationship between inspectorates and authorities and the minister. These relationships are shaped in different ways depending on the jurisdiction where inspectorates and authorities operate, from a large degree of independence and autonomy to close relationships where elaborate interference by the ministers is possible. Close relationships exist for instance in the areas of health care, education, food safety and work safety. We can illustrate this by taking the Healthcare Inspectorate as an example. This inspectorate can be seen as the extended arm of the minister, some people argue. The close links to the minister could endanger the independence of the inspectorate. This can be substantiated by taking a closer look at the position of the Inspector-General, the CEO of the Healthcare Inspectorate. His office is partly in the ministry, in the surroundings of the staff of the minister. Moreover, he is part of the management team of the ministry of Healthcare, Welfare and Sports. As a consequence he holds responsibility for management decisions affecting the health care sector in the Netherlands, the sector he has to supervise.

In general, there seems to be a strong tendency to pull the management of inspectorates towards the ministries, as Mertens earlier described.[8] This is also the case with the ministry of Education and the ministry of Agriculture, Economics and Innovation, the Inspector-General of the Inspectorate of Education and the Inspector-General of the Food Authority as they are all part of the management team of the ministry. On the one hand, this is understandable. As an expert, the inspector can advise the minister on the policy to be issued, more specifically on questions of enforcement relevant for policy development. The question is whether it is sensible that inspectors are so closely linked to policymakers. Do they harm their independent position by doing so?

In contrast with inspectorates such as the Healthcare Inspectorate, the inspectorate of Education and the Food Authority, who seem to be closely linked to the departmental structure and to the minister, also through ministerial responsibility, the independence of several other authorities in the Netherlands is arranged for more formally. This for instance holds true for the Dutch Competition Authority, the Privacy Authority and for the two supervisors of the financial system. The choice for this independent position is made on the basis of several arguments. In the first place there is the European perspective. Several European directives and regulations require authorities to be structured as independent from interference from the minister. This is true for the Privacy Authority, for the Competition Authority and also for the Authority regulating the energy markets. In paragraph 4 we will take a closer look.

8 Ferdinand Mertens, *Inspecteren. Toezicht door inspecties*, Sdu, Den Haag, 2011, p. 119-139.

4. The Official Policy on Independence and the Degree of Independence Needed

What is the official line of thought on independence of inspectorates? Seen from the perspective of the previously mentioned *Kaderstellende visie* of October 2005, regulatory enforcement should be selective, determined, cooperative, transparent and professional. And it also should be independent. These are the six principles of good enforcement. Following this document, 'independence' means that inspectors function within the reach of ministerial responsibility. The minister has the authority to give general and particular instructions to the inspector and the inspectorate. This authority can be derived from article 44 of the Dutch Constitution, unless the authority is limited by the law. The formal position of an inspectorate is thus more or less independent, following the wishes of the legislator in specific cases of certain authorities and inspectorates. I will make a few remarks on this issue later on.

The material independence of inspections is expressed in the way in which they fill in their role within the borders of ministerial responsibility. According to the *Kaderstellende visie,* society must be able to trust the independent judgment of inspectors. Inspectors need to independently gather information, come to conclusions and formulate interventions. In other words, independence is part of the vision in this policy document, although not in the sense of a search for autonomy of inspectorates but more in a search for safeguards that can empower the inspector to gather information, come to conclusions and intervene.

At the same time, the *Kaderstellende visie* struggles with this issue. To cite: "The inspector plays his own role by determining the enforcement goals, the methods used and the capacity invested". "The inspector formulates independent on the basis of his own professionalism his own independent judgment". But at the same time it says: "The inspector plays his own role by determining the moment and the severity of a possible intervention; the minister is responsible".

From a legal perspective, things are quite clear. Following article 44 of the Dutch Constitution, an inspectorate or authority functions under the umbrella of ministerial responsibility, which means the minister can give general and specific instructions to the organisation under his responsibility. This responsibility however, can be restricted, so it is not always the minister who is responsible. Following European legislation, for instance, it is sometimes required to set up and organise an inspectorate or authority at arm's length from a minister. The independent administrative organisations (*zelfstandige bestuursorganen*) are organisations that play a role in the processes of national government but that themselves are not government departments or part of one, and that accordingly operate to a greater or lesser extent at arm's length from ministers Independent administrative organisations, in particular those for service delivery and policy execution used to be very popular organisations but recent years have seen their popularity in the Netherlands diminish. Recently, we have not seen many new independent administrative organisations emerging. The discussion on fading government control and fragmentation of government, as this phenomenon is labeled, seems to lead to a repositioning of these types of (quasi-) independent government organisations.

Even if an inspectorate or an authority is organised in a semi-autonomous way still the question remains of whether this correctly conforms to European legislation and jurisprudence. Recent jurisprudence seems to show that there is reason to doubt this. For all of these autonomous government organisations in the past one legal framework has been developed. This framework act for independent government organisations (*Kaderwet zelfstandige bestuursorganen*) contains provisions that have possible consequences for the material independence of these organisations. For instance: Article 12 of this framework says that the minister appoints, suspends and discharges the members of the independent government organisation. Article 21, first paragraph, makes it possible for the minister to issue policy rules for these organisations' activities and Article 22, first paragraph, gives the minister the authority to annul their decisions. Discussing these authorities and with a reference to the decision by the European Court of Justice from March 9th 2010, mentioned above, Ottow asks herself if the relationship between the Dutch Privacy Authority and the minister fulfils the obligations of the Privacy Directive and answers to the requirement of full independence.[9] Her conclusion is that the privacy law (*Wet bescherming persoonsgegevens*) institutionalising the Privacy Authority in the Netherlands, needs to be changed.

The authority to determine policy rules that follow from Article 21 of the framework for independent government organisations raises the question as to the character of these policy rules. Perhaps this authority fits the independence of these authorities if their character is a general one. When the policy rules tend to get rather specific, one doubts whether that still would be the case. In a dispute regarding a policy rule, issued by the minister of Economic Affairs, to the energy chamber of the Dutch Competition Authority the Trade and Industry Appeals Tribunal (*College van Beroep voor het bedrijfsleven*) judged that a certain policy rule did not contain general rules, but specific rules and as such was unlawful.[10]

It is mostly European legislation that makes a radical choice for non-departmental organisations an inevitable one, for instance in the case of the Privacy Authority or with market authorities. Although perhaps that is not the only situation where formal independence is needed. I refer again to empirical data on environmental enforcement and interference from local government authorities who withhold inspectors to issue enforcement measures they deem necessary. The advisory committee-Mans named after its chairman, thought this was one of the reasons

9 A.T. Ottow & S.A.C.M. Lavrijssen, Het Europese recht als hoeder van de onafhankelijkheid van nationale toezichthouders, *Tijdschrift voor Toezicht*, 2001, No. 3, p. 34-50.

10 CBb 29 juni 2010, LJN: BM9470 (Gaszaak).

to plead for regional environmental enforcement agencies.[11] As already mentioned, Biezeveld and Stoové believe we should go beyond that and establish an independent Dutch Environmental Authority, an environmental agency, organised as an independent administrative organisation.

That more inspectorates will become formally independent is not very probable. On the contrary, the merging of several market authorities (NMa, OPTA en CA) into one larger new authority comes with a different organisational structure, which perhaps also diminishes the independence of the organisation, backs this up. In the context of the above – in short – described jurisprudence and the broader discussion on independence of inspectorates and authorities, the organisational change of these market authorities could become very interesting.

5. How to Safeguard Independence?

How to accomplish independence, is the third question to be answered in this contribution. The clearest way to safeguard independence is to set up and organise inspectorates and authorities as independent administrative organisations. Already above, it was concluded that at this time this is unlikely to be adopted. The task of establishing a certain degree of independence from the minister, when the inspectorate is not set up as a formally independent organisation, proves to be a challenging one. Which safeguards should apply in a situation of full ministerial responsibility where the inspectorate wishes to create material independence for its actions? Perhaps there are easier ways of realising independence. Since July 2002, the work of the Inspectorate for Education is based on a law.[12] This law states that the minister has no authority to give instructions to the inspectorate about the way the inspectorate judges educational quality.[13] The parliamentary history of this article is interesting. Parliamentarians amended the law against the background of a discussion on independence of the education inspectorate. In the law a distinction is made between the gathering of information and the judgment. On this basis there is the exclusive domain of the inspectorate on the one hand and the intervention for which the minister should act on the other. In this sense, the ministerial responsibility for education inspections is made clear. Most other inspectorates lack such a legal basis for their activities, or, if they have such a basis it is much less precise. A few years ago several ministries were working on legislation concerning other inspectorates, but these proposals were never presented. The suggestion of working on a legislative framework for inspections that can offer minimal safeguards for material independence, while at the same time ministerial responsibility stays intact, could be very fruitful in this respect.[14]

11 Commissie-Mans, *De tijd is rijp*, Den Haag 2008.

12 Wet op het Onderwijstoezicht, *Staatsblad* 202, 387.

13 Article 8, third paragraph.

14 Ph. Eijlander, De ministeriële verantwoordelijkheid voor inspecties en inspectieoordelen. Naar een wettelijke basis voor onafhankelijk toezicht?, *RegelMaat*, 2003, No. 3, p. 94-99.

6. Conclusions: Independence in Perspective

Even with formal independence as is the case with several inspectorates and authorities in the Netherlands, independence must be put into perspective. Can we imagine an inspectorate being independent when the Inspector-General is a member of the management team of the ministry? Aside from this, it is true that independence is not an absolute value. Independence towards civilians, businesses and institutions is important, but at the same time there is dependency high and low. Inspectors need information from and the cooperation of the regulated. Independence from politicians is important too but at the same time independent market authorities need budgets and the means to organise themselves. On this issue, we should talk about a continuum, upon which variation is possible. Sometimes more independence is needed, sometimes we are satisfied with an optimum position.

Independence, thus, is not an absolute quantity. Depending on the characteristics of the task, the (European) legislation and the jurisprudence, either more or less independence is wanted. Autonomous government organisations could be an appropriate way for organising independence from the minister in certain fields of government activity. But even in these cases, as we have seen, it sometimes is questionable whether the status of autonomous government organisations fulfils all the requirements of European legislation. Some scholars of constitutional law in the Netherlands argue the re-installment of total political control. They seem to choose the wrong fight. From the other side: total independence as such does not exist either. It is always the material, factual situation that is decisive.

A Call for Independent Environmental Law Enforcement

*Gustaaf Biezeveld**

1. Introduction

Thirty years ago Dutch society was shocked by the first serious environmental crime that came to light.[1] In 1982 police investigators discovered that over a ten year period a couple of companies belonging to Uniser Holding had emitted a great amount of dangerous substances into Dutch rivers. The companies involved had gone bankrupt leaving behind seriously polluted plants as well as tanks, cellars, and ships full of chemical waste. In reaction to the so-called Uniser Case the Dutch Cabinet of Ministers asked an independent commission to analyse the causes of these crimes and recommend what should be done to prevent such environmental crimes. This commission concluded that fragmented operating governmental bodies and services involved had strongly contributed to the failure of the competent authorities in this case. I cite: "Public servants' thinking and acting proves to be characterised to a great extent by orientation on their own formal responsibility. There proves to be little inclination to call in the help of other public services and get jointly a concrete result".[2] To change this situation, the commission recommended that from then on the social problem should be the starting point instead of fragmented public competences and services. Therefore the organisation of the government should match effective regulation of industrial activities.

The Uniser Commission's report prompted the Dutch Minister of Environment to take action in order to encourage the competent authorities involved and their services to give more attention to environmental supervision and to promote cooperation among them.[3] Since then environmental supervision has been an item on the political agenda. A great deal of effort has been made and much money

* Prof. dr. G.A. Biezeveld retired in 2012 as Professor of environmental law at the Faculty of Law, University of Groningen, the Netherlands and as environmental public prosecutor in the Netherlands.

1 Report of the Uniser Commission (1983), *Rapport van de onderzoekscommissie naar de bestuurlijke aspecten van de uitvoering van de milieu- en andere relevante wetgeving bij Drisolco BV, EMK, Uniser e.a.*, see: *Parliamentary Papers II* 1982/83, 17 600, chapter XI, No. 104.

2 Report Uniser Commission 1983 *supra*, p. 87.

3 Report of the Commission Mans (2008), *De tijd is rijp*, The Hague, 2008 (Annex to the letter from the Minister for Housing, Spatial Planning and the Environment on 10 July 2008, *Parliamentary Papers II* 2007/08, 22 343, No. 201).

has been spent building up law enforcement capacity and expertise, in both the administrative and the criminal sector. Looking back it can be concluded that the Uniser Case was a wake up call for environmental law enforcement in the Netherlands.

However, in 2008 another independent commission reported to the Dutch Ministers of Environment and Justice that there was still a lot to do to improve the effectiveness of environmental supervision and guarantee a level playing field for the companies involved. So even after three decades both the organisational and the practical side of environmental supervision still require political attention and effort. How could this have happened?

In the first part of my contribution I give you an overview of the institutional features of environmental supervision in the Netherlands as well as the shortcomings acknowledged by the Cabinet of Ministers, the Parliament and the competent authorities involved. When I refer to environmental supervision I use this term in a broad sense. It covers three subsequent actions:

(1) research by inspections or otherwise in order to determine if an action or situation or good meets the requirements, (2) to assess the results and (3) to intervene, if necessary.

In the second part my focus will be on a potential major cause of the shortcomings. I conclude with a short survey of the possibilities and implications of restructuring environmental supervision in accordance with the present standards of supervision on economic actors and activities. Although my contribution mainly deals with the Dutch situation I pay attention to the European context as well.

2. Features of Environmental Supervision in the Netherlands

In my view environmental regulation is mainly a specific kind of economic regulation. The main objects of environmental regulation cover a great variety of economic activities. The scale on which these activities take place varies from local to global. Therefore the scale on which environmental violations can be committed varies as well. This does require from the environmental supervision system that it covers the whole range of economic activities and matches with the various scales on which violations of environmental regulation may happen. However, it also requires from supervisory authorities that they can and will guarantee a level playing field for the companies involved.

Although environmental regulation of economic activities originates to a great extent from the European Union or its predecessor, the Member States are autonomous as far as the organisation of supervision is concerned.[4] This is in contrast with the situation in other domains of European economic regulation.[5]

In the Netherlands no distribution of the parts has been made between the administrative and the criminal environmental law enforcement sector. Both the administrative and the criminal law enforcement system apply to the whole range of environmental regulations. This implies that with almost every violation of environmental law both an administrative authority and the environmental prosecutor are competent to enforce. Both environmental law enforcement systems differ fundamentally on the institutional side. All environmental prosecutors are part of one organisation that is practically independent although it operates under the political responsibility of the Minister of Security and Justice. However, all supervisory authorities are political organs that are not exclusively focused on their responsibility for environmental supervision. In total there are roughly 450 competent administrative authorities, spread over three levels of government: local, regional, and national. Most of these authorities are assisted by inspectors belonging to their own organisation. The others are assisted by joint inspection services, working for a number of municipalities.

Although the supervisory authorities at the provincial and municipal level behave as autonomous organs that are only accountable to the representative body at its own level of government, in constitutional terms they are not fully autonomous. For their actions the Minister of Environment is accountable to the Parliament as well, based on the concept that environmental management is essentially a responsibility of the State and competences in this field that have been entrusted to governmental organs at a lower level of government should be exercised in accordance with the public interest.

From the beginning institutional fragmentation of environmental supervision has been a complicating factor for co-operation between the various supervisory authorities as well as their inspectors. Their natural tendency to behave autonomously has been strengthened by potential frictions between their supervisory task and other political tasks and responsibilities. So it is not surprising that there have been many environmental scandals over the past few decades, such as the TCR-affair,[6] and the Probo Koala case,[7] and many other complaints by non governmental organisations and companies expressing concern regarding the lack of effectiveness and a level playing field. The independent commission that reported

---

4 R.H. Lauwaars & C.W.A. Timmermans, *Europees recht in kort bestek*, W.E.J. Tjeenk Willink, Deventer, 1999.

5 See the contribution of Annetje T. Ottow in this volume.

6 R.J.J. Eshuis & E.A.I.M. van den Berg, *Dossier TCR. Tien jaar schone schijn*, WODC, The Hague, 1996.

7 Report of the Commission Hulshof (2006), *Rapport van bevindingen naar aanleiding van het onderzoek rond aankomst, verblijf en vertrek van de Probo Koala in juli 2006 te Amsterdam*, <www.amsterdam.nl>.

in 2008 to the Ministers of Environment and Justice came to the same conclusion.[8] It recommended defragmentation by forming 25 regional supervision services on behalf of the supervisory authorities at the provincial and local level of government. This network should create better conditions for environmental supervision as well as a level playing field for companies. Therefore, it should have a proper legal base. In the view of this commission there was no need to reshuffle or reduce the number of supervisory authorities.

Both the former and present Cabinet of Ministers agreed with this recommendation but preferred voluntary development of regional services by means of a bottom up process over legislation. This preference was prompted by strong opposition from municipalities against new legal obligations.

It is expected that from the summer of 2013 in 28 regions at least a part of the environmental supervision tasks of provinces and municipalities will be executed by joint services. Yet it is still uncertain whether the regional services will result in better environmental supervision in co-operation with the Public Prosecutor's Office and the police. Apart from shrinking budgets for environmental supervision a significant lack of enthusiasm among the majority of supervisory authorities involved might become an obstacle for fully fledged and robust organisations with enough professional inspectors. At the very least it is disquieting there has been no discussion in most regions until now on questions such as:
- what conditions should be fulfilled for more effective environmental supervision and better guarantees for a level playing field for companies? and;
- what does the formation of joint services imply for the role and position of supervisory authorities?

Is this an indication that both the independent commission and the Cabinet of Ministers may have overlooked the political status of supervisory authorities as a major cause of the shortcomings of environmental supervision? In my view it is. To clarify this I must explain something about the Dutch and European standards for supervision of economic actors and activities.

3. Standards for Economic Supervision

In 2001 the Dutch Cabinet of Ministers published a white paper with standards for supervision on economic or social organisations by governmental bodies at the national level of government.[9] Its key message was that it ought to be ensured to subjects of supervision as well as to citizens, responsible ministers and the

8 Report Commission Mans 2008 *supra*; *cf.* A.B. Blomberg, Verplichte regionale omgevingsdiensten: een institutionele herziening van de uitvoering en handhaving van het omgevingsrecht, *Tijdschrift Omgevingsrecht*, 2008, No. 4, p. 125-135.

9 *Parliamentary Papers II* 2000/01, 27 831, No. 1 (Framing vision on supervision 2001).

Parliament that supervision will be *independent, transparent,* and *professional* as much as possible. This implies that:

a. the supervisor must be enabled to research the facts and make up his mind without being influenced by the subject of supervision involved or the responsible minister;
b. the supervisor's objective judgement should be made public as much as possible, so that both the Parliament and the society can take note of it; and
c. a professional process of judging by the supervisor is required.

Therefore the supervisor's organisation should be built in such a way that these standards for supervision can be guaranteed. At least this implies that within the government structure supervision is positioned as a recognisable entity, separate from policymaking and licensing.

The white paper gives no reason to assume that these standards do not apply to supervision exercised by provinces and municipalities under the responsibility of a minister. Therefore this Dutch government document provides strong arguments for the thesis that supervision of the observance of environmental law ought to be organised and exercised in a independent, transparent, and professional manner.

These Dutch standards for supervision coincide to a great extent with the European requirements on supervision of economic actors, as pointed out by prof. Ottow in her contribution to this book.

When we look at the public authorities that are competent concerning environmental supervision, it becomes clear that these standards have not been applied to supervision on the observance of European and Dutch environmental law. Neither in the European Union nor in the Netherlands has any legal action been taken to guarantee independence of environmental supervision of economic actors and activities. This is particularly remarkable because according both the EC-Treaty and the Treaty on the Functioning of the European Union, European environmental regulations and directives must be compatible with the objectives of the internal market. In my view there is no good reason why supervision regarding environmental regulations and directives is treated as different to supervision regarding other kinds of economic European law.

An explanation for the different approach taken by the European legislator might be that generally speaking negotiations regarding a new environmental regulation or directive are focussed more on the intended environmental protection levels and the accompanying costs for companies than on guarantees for a level playing field in the supervision phase.

The conclusion of this short survey is clear: there is no legal obligation for independent environmental supervision. At the same time we have not found good reasons why the standard of independence should not apply to environmental supervision. On the contrary. Therefore it seems worthwhile exploring whether there might be a connection between the structural shortcomings of environmental supervision in the Netherlands and the political position of supervisory authorities.

4. Environmental Supervision in Practice

As I mentioned before, since the Uniser Case a number of other serious environmental cases have come to light.[10] Most of these cases were analysed by an independent research team. Each of them concluded that the supervisory authorities involved had let other interests – mostly economic or financial interests – prevail over the interest of human health or environmental quality. This outcome is not surprising in a situation where the supervisory authority is a political organ with a great variety of tasks and responsibilities on behalf of the public interest. In such circumstances each supervisory authority has no choice: it is always trying to balance various and often conflicting interests, mostly by compromise. Given the political importance of economic interests and employment it proves almost inevitable that these interests outweigh the interests served by environmental supervision. So it is understandable that for most politicians the supervision portfolio is not an attractive one. Environmental offenses quite often place supervisory authorities in a difficult dilemma.

Their political position not only influences their performance as supervisor and their own decision making but it also influences the supervision culture within the government body involved as well as the attitude of inspectors towards economic actors that do not comply with environmental provisions. Most inspectors prefer a soft approach to companies above a strict one, even in contacts with evidently calculating economic actors. So in my view environmental supervision in the Netherlands can be characterised as highly politicised. Thanks to this the effectiveness of environmental supervision, as well as the willingness of economic actors to comply with environmental provisions, has been seriously affected. Under such circumstances the protection of human health and the environment as well as a level playing field can never be guaranteed.

In my opinion it is not fair to blame the supervisory authorities for this. It is the legislator who made the wrong choice by charging political organs with environmental supervision of economic actors and activities. This choice has been taken for granted over many, many years. This explains why until recently no one publicly linked the shortcomings of environmental supervision in the Netherlands with the political position of the supervisory authorities in this field. Although I worked for many years as an environmental prosecutor, my eyes were only quite recently opened when I was informed about the European legislation and jurisprudence on independent supervision on economic actors and activities. I then

10 G.A. Biezeveld & M.C. Stoové, Naar een Nederlandse Omgevingsautoriteit. Een pleidooi voor onafhankelijk milieutoezicht, *Tijdschrift voor Toezicht*, 2011, No. 3, p. 9-10.

realised that the lack of independent supervisory authorities had been overlooked as a major cause of the shortcomings of environmental supervision in the Netherlands. It explains why for over thirty years the efforts made by successive Cabinets of Ministers to improve environmental supervision has failed.[11] This insight has also helped me to understand the formation of regional supervision services as a process with great difficulty due to the fear that many supervisory authorities at the local level of government have of losing their control over inspectors and inspections. Although many authorities are not particularly happy with this task, as long as they bear the political responsibility for both economic development and environmental supervision most of them are inclined to defend their power to balance the various interests in individual cases. Therefore I foresee that many supervisory authorities will not be ready to voluntarily transfer their competence to impose sanctions on economic actors to the head of the regional service and make that a non-political supervisory authority. I fear that if I am right, the formation of regional services will not lead to effective environmental supervision and a level playing field.

I have done no research into the situation in other Member States of the EU without independent environmental supervision. Yet I assume that there are no significant differences from the Dutch situation. This implies that there are no guarantees for effective law enforcement of European environmental regulations and directives as well as a level playing field which is a prerequisite for the internal market. From this point of view the European level is the right level to agree on the necessity of independent environmental supervision by declaring the standards for supervision on economic actors and activities applicable for this field as well. However, in my view there are also good reasons for the Dutch legislator to review his choice for political supervisory authorities, in anticipation of future European legislation. Therefore, I conclude by presenting my ideas for a possible solution for the Dutch situation.

5. Towards Independent Environmental Supervision in the Netherlands

In a democratic constitutional state governing politicians must be accountable to the Parliament or a comparable representative body at a lower level of government for supervision of the compliance of legal provisions. This accountability regards at least the conditions and means for supervision as well as the effectiveness and efficiency of the supervision in practice. For failing supervision in general or in individual cases the responsible politicians can be held accountable as well. However, this does not imply that they should have the power to intervene in individual cases as this would be incompatible with the concept of independent supervision.

Therefore the first question to be answered is: who should be accountable for environmental supervision? In my view in the Dutch context the best option

11 Biezeveld & Stoové 2011 *supra*.

would be the Ministers of Environment and Nature management. This is in line with the present system based on the concept that environmental management is essentially a responsibility of the state. Moreover, given the various scales on which economic actors operate and economic activities take place, it is wise to organise responsibility and accountability for supervision at the highest level of government.

As mentioned before, the environmental supervision system should cover the whole range of economic activities and have the ability to respond to the various scales on which environmental violations may happen. In my view only a nationwide organisation can meet these requirements.[12] Therefore I would prefer an organisation comparable to the organisation of the Public Prosecutors Service that is headed by an, in principle, independent board and consists of a combination of national and regional units. Incidentally, the organisation for the police, which until 2013 consisted of 26 autonomous police forces, is being changed into a national police force and will also consist of a combination of national and regional units.

In my view the board of the ideal national environmental supervision organisation that should become the new competent authority for environmental supervision, should take over all the powers on environmental supervision that now belongs to approximately 450 political competent authorities. This will provide better conditions for both effective supervision as well as a level playing field.

The inspectors, lawyers and staff that now work partly at the national level, partly at the provincial and local level should become officials of the new organisation. This will provide better conditions for professionalism, co-operation, the gathering and exchange of information and similar responses in comparable situations.

What does this imply for the on going formation of regional supervision services? Should this process be considered out of date by new insights? Certainly not. In my opinion the implementation of the decision to build a network of regional supervision services can serve as a first, important step towards a national environmental supervision organisation. When these regional services operate, further steps can be made by harmonising procedures and IT-systems, by pooling expertise and by integrating management and information activities. In addition to this the legislator should make a provisional regulation on the transfer of the power to impose sanctions from the present supervisory authorities to the heads of the regional services. This would be a first step towards independent supervision.

12 Compare the reform of the Dutch police that came into force in January 2013. The previous organisation that consisted of 25 autonomous regional police forces and a national police force proved to be inadequate for the abatement of crime that exceeded the regional scale. Therefore the legislator decided to form a national police.

To be successful and efficient within a period of four to six years such a process of organic development should be furthered and directed by the national government.

Still one difficult question remains: will all supervisory authorities be ready to transfer their powers to the heads of the regional services? To be honest, I am not sure. So in my view European rules on independent environmental supervision are indispensable. The implementation of the Seventh Environment Action Programme of the European Union provides an excellent opportunity to present a view on this.[13]

6. Closing Remarks

In this contribution I have shown that independent environmental supervision is not primarily a political or public management concept. In the Netherlands we have experienced that independence is a prerequisite for both effective supervision and a level playing field. The economic and social costs of a lack of independent environmental supervision are enormous. Hopefully the Dutch and the European legislator will acknowledge this soon and take adequate action.

13 Proposal for a decision of the European parliament and of the Council on a General Union Environment Action Programme to 2020, *Living well, within the limits of our planet*, Brussels, 29 November 2012, COM(2012) 710 final, 2012/0337 (COD), priority objective 4: To maximise the benefits of EU environment legislation, p. 23-26.

IV – Independence of Advisory and Complaint Committees and Final Dispute Resolution by Administrative Courts

Advisory Objection Procedures in the Netherlands: A Case Study on their Usefulness in Dutch Competition Law

Jan Jans and Annalies Outhuijse

1. Introduction

Article 7:1 of the Netherlands General Administrative Law Act (GALA) states one of the principles of judicial protection in Dutch administrative law: before you can appeal against a decision of an administrative authority to an administrative court, you must first lodge an objection with the administrative authority that adopted the decision.[1] Consequently, there is no access to the courts until the administrative authority has reviewed its decision, and this also applies to fines imposed by the Netherlands Competition Authority (*NMa*). The value of this procedure has regularly been questioned in the past; one of its most notorious critics is a leading Dutch competition lawyer, Mark Biesheuvel, who expressed his dissatisfaction with the objection procedure in the Dutch legal journal *Nederlands Juristenblad* more than 15 years ago. To quote:

> Generally, the procedure involves a time-consuming and wholly unnecessary ritual filing past public servants who have dug themselves into entrenched positions (...) (...) in practice, the procedure regularly amounts to a legal restraining order which wrongly denies individuals access to the courts for long periods of time, sometimes years.[2]

On 1 January 2013, the Netherlands Competition Authority is merging with the Independent Post and Telecommunications Authority of the Netherlands (*OPTA*) and the Netherlands Consumer Authority (*CA*). The new organisation is to be known as the Consumer and Market Authority (*ACM*). To enable the *ACM* to operate effectively and efficiently, a bill is currently being prepared which will

* Prof. dr. J.H. Jans is Professor of Administrative Law at the University of Groningen, the Netherlands, and Vice Chair of the Advisory Commission on Competition Act Objections (*Adviescommissie bezwaarschriften Mededingingswet*), but this article is written in a purely personal capacity. A. Outhuijse is a student at the Law Department of the University of Groningen. The article has been written within the context of the faculty research programme *Public Trust & Public Law*.

1 Art. 7:1.1 GALA: "A person who has the right to appeal a decision to an administrative court, must first lodge an objection, unless: [there follows a list of decisions in relation to which this does not apply]".

2 M. Biesheuvel, Weg met bezwaarschriftenprocedure, *Nederlands Juristenblad*, 1996, p. 930.

streamline the procedures and enforcement instruments available to the *ACM*.[3] One of the proposed changes concerns abolishing the objection phase for decisions imposing fines.

The aim of the present article is to discuss the reasons for this proposed change. We will be concentrating on sanctions under the Netherlands Competition Act (*Mw*) and the role played by the Advisory Commission on Competition Act Objections (*Adviescommissie bezwaarschriften Mededingingswet* (*AbM*)). As not all readers will be equally familiar with the objection procedure in Dutch law we shall first discuss it briefly.

2. The Objection Procedure in the GALA[4]

2.1 *General*

As noted above, under the GALA, an interested party can only contest an administrative decision before a court if he has previously lodged an 'objection' with the administrative authority that took the decision in the first place. This means the administrative authority is required carry out a 'full review' of the decision being contested. By contrast with a judicial appeal, the administrative authority must consider not only the lawfulness of the contested decision, but also policy aspects. Moreover, the review must be carried out with regard to the situation, both in fact and in law, applying at the time of the review, in other words *ex nunc*: in principle this means taking changed policies, changed legal rules, and also changed circumstances into consideration. The objection procedure is thus both about legal protection and extended administrative decision-making.

Under Article 7:2 GALA, before giving a decision on the objection, the administrative authority must give interested parties the opportunity to be heard. For this, it has two options. First, under Article 7:5 GALA, it may conduct a hearing itself, as the OPTA does. Alternatively it can appoint an external advisory committee under Article 7:13 GALA, as the competition and consumer authorities (*NMa* and *CA*) do. Under article 7:13 GALA, an advisory committee must consist of a chair and at least two members, and the chair must not be a member of the administrative authority or work under its responsibility. The chair should not have had any previous involvement in the matter. Although not a requirement, in most cases all members of an advisory committee are independent, as is the case for the competition authority. It is entirely up to the administrative authority whether or not to appoint an advisory committee.

3 *Wetsvoorstel stroomlijning markttoezicht ACM*, at <www.internetconsultatie.nl/materielewetacm>.

4 *See generally*: H.B. Winter, *De Awb-bezwaarschriftprocedure: een praktische handleiding*, Kluwer, Deventer, 2003; L.M. Koenraad, K.H. Sanders, *Besluiten op bezwaar*, Kluwer, Deventer, 2006; *Handreiking bezwaarschriftprocedure Algemene wet bestuursrecht*, Ministerie van Justitie, The Hague, 2004.

It is clear from the legislative history of the GALA that the original purpose of the objection procedure – offering an easily accessible, informal procedure – was to avoid large numbers of appeals to the administrative courts.[5] During the objection procedure, the administrative authority would have the opportunity to repair obvious and simple errors by either taking a new decision or giving better reasons for the original decision, so that disputes between individuals and the administration could be resolved more effectively and the number of judicial appeals reduced. In addition, the objection procedure would serve to ensure that cases that do come before the courts are more clearly defined and better presented. This was supposed to reduce the length of judicial procedures significantly.

2.2 *Pros and cons of external advisory committees in objection procedures*

The administrative authority is free to decide whether or not to appoint an external committee to hear objections. The literature mentions a number of advantages of appointing an external committee.[6] In the first place, an external committee acts as 'a fresh pair of eyes'. If the aim of the objection procedure is to be able to correct errors as simply as possible, this can best be achieved if the reassessment is carried out by an external, independent body bringing a new perspective to the situation.

A second advantage is that an external committee is preferable from the point of view of procedural justice.[7] An external committee is independent and has no axe to grind, and, because an advisory committee is itself also deemed to be an 'administrative authority',[8] its members must perform their duties impartially, as required by Article 2:4 GALA. It may be supposed that the person or persons lodging an objection and any other interested parties will be more willing to accept the decision on the objection if it is based on the advice of an external committee than if it was handled entirely by the administrative authority itself.

A third advantage can be described as the 'mediator function' of an advisory committee. In accordance with the intention of the GALA objection procedure, the advisory committee must seek to find a solution for the dispute.

Finally, it has been noted as an advantage that an external committee brings expertise into the organisation. This is particularly relevant where the 'administrative authority' is only a relatively small entity, such as a committee in one of the smaller municipalities.

5 PG Awb I, p. 279; available at: <www.pgawb.nl>.
6 *See* footnote 4.
7 See in general on procedural justice: N. Luhmann, *Legitimation durch Verfahren* (6th ed.), Suhrkamp, Frankfurt am Main, 2001 (1969); John Rawls, *A Theory of Justice*, Harvard University Press, Cambridge Massachusetts, 1971.
8 Administrative Jurisdiction Division of the Council of State 19 March 2003, AB 2003/301 with note by Peters.

Obviously, there are also disadvantages to appointing an external advisory committee. Objections take longer to deal with, are more expensive and, as will be explained below, the committee may not carry out a full review.

Generally, external members of an advisory committee take on the job in addition to other work and so are not available on a full-time basis. This means that the organisation cannot dispose of their time freely, and this may result in longer objection procedures. Another possible disadvantage is the cost. Members of an external advisory committee generally receive a fee for preparing and attending meetings and drafting recommendations. This inevitably leads to higher costs compared to procedures where there is no external advisory committee. Finally, the procedure involves a full review of the decision, which means an evaluation both of the lawfulness and the merits of the decision. Although an external advisory committee is also required to carry out a full review, such committees often fail to review the merits of a decision.[9] This is because committees of this kind often feel uncomfortable commenting on what they regard as the policy and/or decision-making discretion of the administrative authority, and thus generally confine their recommendations to factors concerning the lawfulness of the decision.

2.3 *Relationship between Advisory Committee and Responsible Authority*

After the hearing, the advisory committee reports to the administrative authority. It advises the authority how to deal with the objection and makes a proposal for the decision to be made on the objection. Under Article 7:13.6 GALA, the recommendation must be given in writing and include a record of the hearing. The administrative authority must consider the review on the basis of the committee's recommendation. As an advisory committee is deemed to be an 'adviser' for the purposes of the GALA, the administrative authority must satisfy itself that the advisory committee prepared its recommendation with due care, both as regards the way it performed its duties and the content of the recommendation (Art. 3:9 GALA). The administrative authority must read the recommendation with a critical eye, as it retains primary responsibility for the decision on the objection. It must always form its own judgment on the objection and must decide what the right decision is in law. Only when the administrative authority has satisfied itself that the examination was carried out with due care and is not defective may it base its decision on the committee's recommendation. If the decision is based on the committee's report, interested parties must be informed of the recommendations (Art. 3:49 GALA).

The committee's recommendations are not binding and the administrative authority is not required to adopt them. However, if an administrative authority

9 See on this concerning review at the municipal level: A. Schwarz, *De adviescommissie in bezwaar: inrichting van de bezwaarprocedure bij gemeenten* (PhD. Groningen), The Hague, 2010, p. 273 et seq.

chooses to involve an advisory committee in dealing with an objection, it cannot simply ignore the committee's recommendations. Under Art. 7:13.7 GALA, it is then obliged not only to state the reasons for its decision on the objection, but also for its departure from the recommendation, and it must enclose the recommendation with its decision.

3. The Advisory Committee on Competition Act Objections

3.1 General

According to Art. 5 of the decree establishing the Advisory Committee on Competition Act Objections (*AbM*),[10] the Advisory Committee is responsible for advising the Netherlands Competition Authority on objections against sanctions (fines and orders subject to a financial penalty) the authority has imposed under Article 62(1) of the Netherlands Competition Act. Currently, the Committee consists of 15 members (lawyers and economists). Six of these have a primarily academic background, seven a judicial, and two are in public service. Its members are independent and have no ties with the Competition Authority.[11] All its members have special experience or expertise in the field of administrative law, European law (specifically competition law), and/or the economy.

The Committee is responsible for hearing interested parties under Art. 7:2 GALA, and this means both the companies concerned and the Competition Authority. Generally, objections are heard by a subcommittee of three or five members. The members involved in handling a case decide the Committee's recommendation by majority vote. If there is an even number of members involved in a case, the subcommittee's chair has a casting vote in the event of a tie. Like other external committees, the Advisory Committee on Competition Act Objections reports to the administrative authority (in this case the Competition Authority) in writing. Here too, the Competition Authority is not bound by the Committee's recommendations and it will be shown below that the Competition Authority relatively often departs from the Committee's recommendations. As explained above, this means that it must give reasons not only for its decision but also for its departure from the Committee's recommendations, and must enclose the report with its decision.

3.2 Relationship to Direct Appeals Act

As noted above, the bill currently before Parliament aims to abolish the objection procedure in relation to sanctions imposed by the new Netherlands Consumer

10 Besluit tot instelling Adviescommissie bezwaarschriften Mededingingswet, *Stcrt.* (Government Gazette) 1998, nr. 146, p. 3.

11 Under Art. 6 of the decree, they must ensure they do not "deal with any case they have in any way been involved in". This obligation also follows from Art. 2:4 GALA. Members of the Committee regularly declare themselves unavailable on this ground when the cases are being allocated.

Authority. It is, however, important to add that it is already possible under current legislation to bypass the objection procedure. Under the *Wet rechtstreeks beroep* (Direct Appeals Act), which entered into force on 1 September 2004, Art. 7:1a was inserted in the GALA, by which a person lodging an objection may, in derogation from Art. 7:1, request the administrative authority to consent to direct appeal to the administrative courts. Under the third paragraph of Art 7:1a, the administrative authority may consent to the request if the case lends itself to such a procedure, but must refuse the request if another objection has been lodged against the decision which does not contain a similar request (second paragraph). It is Competition Authority policy to consent to such requests as a rule. At the time the provision entered into force, the Advisory Committee on Competition Act Objections believed – no doubt encouraged by the many lawyers at hearings moaning about the pointlessness of the whole objection procedure – that this would result in a substantial reduction in the number of objections. Nothing could have been further from the truth.

From the evaluation of the Direct Appeals Act, it emerged more generally that only sporadic use was made of the possibility of bypassing the objection procedure.[12] This reticence was due not to ignorance, but was often a deliberate choice. Attorneys regarded skipping the objection procedure as a missed opportunity. From the evaluation of the Act, it also emerged that where an independent committee advised during the objection procedure, the procedure was more likely to be regarded as a success.

We would add that the Competition Authority regularly departs from the recommendations of the Advisory Committee, particularly where the Committee recommends declaring an objection well founded in whole or in part.[13] Our hypothesis is that the parties believe they have more chance of a successful appeal to the administrative courts if they have the backing of an 'expert report' from the Advisory Committee. From this perspective, the objection procedure affords an additional opportunity for objectors to be 'proved right', albeit only in a favorable report from the Advisory Committee. The worst that can happen is that the Committee will recommend declaring the objection unfounded. In other words, given that *reformatio in peius* is not allowed, objectors stand only to gain from the objection procedure. Add to this the fact that objections and appeals have suspensory effect on a decision imposing a sanction (Art. 63 Competition Act) and it is clear why the objection procedure is so popular in relation to Competition Authority decisions and why so little use is made of the possibility of appealing directly to the administrative courts, avoiding the objection procedure.

12 B.M.J. van der Meulen, M.E.G. Litjens & A.A. Freriks, *Prorogatie in de Awb, Invoeringsevaluatie rechtstreeks beroep*, WODC, The Hague, 2005.

13 See below.

3.3 *The Advisory Committee as a 'Zero Tier' Administrative Court*

If we look at the practice of the Advisory Committee, there are several points worth mentioning. These are above all based on the experience of the first author as a long-standing member of the Committee. The first is that the Advisory Committee objection procedure is very similar to a first instance appeal before the administrative courts. Its approach is what could be termed 'semi judicial'. After the written objection and the grounds upon which it is based have been received, an 'instruction note' is written, generally by the secretary, for the subcommittee charged with the hearing. An instruction note basically sets out the points that need to be decided and generally takes the form of a draft recommendation. It is, of course, intended only for internal use within the Advisory Committee. Before the hearing is held, the Competition Authority responds within the 10 days referred to in Art. 7:4.1 GALA by sending the parties and the Advisory Committee a written explanatory note. The explanatory note generally addresses the grounds put forward for the objection and is often the central document in the discussion at the hearing. The hearing itself is also similar to a hearing before an administrative court: the objector explains his case, the authority responds, the Committee questions the parties, and the objector may be given the opportunity to reply. This format is reinforced by the fact that the 'individual' in the proceedings is almost always a professional organisation represented by highly qualified lawyers and other legal professionals. The Competition Authority is generally represented by at least a lawyer from its legal department, sometimes supplemented by economic expertise from within the organisation. In other words, the debate at the hearing is a professional one between subject material experts.

It will be clear from the above that, as a rule, the objection procedure is supposed to facilitate a full *ex nunc* review of the original decision. However, in proceedings before the Advisory Committee there is no question of a full review in the sense originally intended by the legislature. In the first place, this has to do with the type of decisions that are subject to the advisory opinion of the Committee. Generally only two questions are in fact relevant: can the authority prove the facts alleged, and do they constitute an infringement of the provisions of the Competition Act? The Committee is, as it were, virtually compelled to carry out an *ex tunc* review. Moreover, given the size of the dossiers, a full integral review of the complex of facts is not really possible. The Committee does not feel it has to repeat the examination of the facts all over again and generally confines itself to deciding whether the authority has proved the facts alleged to the Committee's satisfaction and, bearing in mind the authority's duty of care and/or to give reasons for its decisions, if the Committee is not convinced it will recommend reviewing the case further in this respect. Though Art. 9 of the decree establishing the Advisory Committee does give it the power to hear witnesses and experts even where Art. 7:8 GALA does not apply (i.e. other than at the request of interested parties), this power has never been used as far as we are aware. The main reason for this, in our view, is that an independent investigation of the facts by the Advisory Committee would result in too big a delay in decision-making. Moreover, it is felt that correctly establishing the facts is above all a matter for the administration. Nor do the purely policy aspects of decisions imposing sanctions really qualify for full review by the Advisory Committee. Though the statutory power to make decisions imposing fines is a discretionary power,[14] this discretion is significantly hedged in by policy rules (e.g. guidelines for fines, leniency reductions etc.) which the Competition Authority is obliged to apply under Art. 4:84 GALA except in 'special circumstances'. Once it has been established that the guidelines for fines are generally adequate for determining the size of the fine, the Advisory Committee is no longer in a position to question the appropriateness of the policy rules in any specific case. Its recommendations are therefore confined, as a rule, to whether or not the administrative authority has applied the guidelines correctly and whether or not there is, in the particular case and having regard for the proportionality principle, a 'special circumstance' which would justify a departure from the policy rules. Essentially, in our opinion, this differs little from way the first-instance administrative courts operate. In short: the objection procedure before the Advisory Committee is very similar to the procedure before a first-instance administrative court, both in terms of procedure and of what is reviewed.

4. The Reasons Given in the Bill for Abolishing the Objection Procedure in Relation to *ACM* Decisions Imposing Fines

Against the background of the above, more general comments, we shall now discuss the reasons given in the bill for abolishing the objection procedure in relation to *ACM* decisions imposing fines.[15] The most important reason given is 'that the benefits of the objection procedure in general do not apply to objections to *ACM* decisions imposing fines'. Apparently, decisions of the *ACM* imposing sanctions are of such a specific and special type that the usual benefits of an objection procedure do not apply.

The proposal also notes 'that abolishing the objection procedure is expected to have a positive effect on the time taken to process cases, so that the *ACM* will be able to keep within the reasonable time required by Article 6 of the European Convention on Human Rights in more cases'. The explanatory memorandum notes that both parties and non-parties benefit from obtaining the earliest possible clarity and legal certainty concerning the interpretation of a rule by the administrative courts.

Finally, the explanatory memorandum mentions as an 'important' advantage that scrapping the objection procedure will lead to a reduction in costs both for trade and industry and for the *ACM* itself. Let us consider these arguments more closely.

14 See Articles 56 et seq. Competition Act.
15 Explanatory memorandum, point 2.3.2 at pp. 14-15.

4.1 *Objection Procedure Does not Operate as 'Sieve' in Relation to ACM Decisions*

One of the most important advantages of the objection procedure is said to be the way it may act as a 'sieve', offering a way of resolving disputes without the intervention of an administrative court. However, according to the explanatory memorandum, it emerges from figures from the Competition Authority, the Telecommunications Authority and the Consumer Authority for the period 1 July 2009 to 1 July 2011 that this effect is relatively small for decisions imposing fines: 71% of infringers who lodge an objection against a Competition Authority decision end up making an appeal, for the Telecommunications Authority the figure is 91%, and for the Consumer Authority 67%. In our view, this shows that the objection procedure does in fact work for ACM decisions, but to a lesser extent than by comparison with decisions in other areas.[16] A possible explanation, at least as regards Competition Act related decisions, may be that the Competition Authority relatively often departs from the Advisory Committee's recommendations. This point will be discussed in more detail below. Also worth noting is that the effect is even less notable in relation to decisions of the Telecommunications Authority. One possible explanation could be that the Telecommunications Authority does not work with an external advisory committee at all, whereas both the other authorities do. If this hypothesis is correct, it is quite possible that appeals to the courts against decisions of the competition and consumer authorities imposing fines could rise by approximately 20% when the bypass procedure is abolished. In other words, even though the effect is relatively small, it does exist and particularly where use is made of an external advisory committee.

The supposedly special nature of decisions imposing sanctions in competition cases is also demonstrated by the way the Competition Authority treats recommendations of the Advisory Committee. A recommendation is, after all, exactly that: a recommendation, and can thus be departed from. From research currently being carried out at Groningen University into municipal objection procedures, it emerges that municipal authorities depart from advisory committees' recommendations in fewer than 2% of cases.[17] From an analysis of 34 normal Competition Authority cases in the period 1999 to 2009,[18] it emerged that the authority departed, to a greater or lesser extent, from the recommendation of the Advisory Committee in 50% of the cases. In only nine of the 17 cases in which the Authority followed the recommendation did it to do this without any reservation at all. In the other eight cases, it gave different and/or additional reasons for its decision

16 An effect (also referred to as a 'filter' effect) of more than 90% is certainly no exception. *See particularly* K.H. Sanders, *De heroverweging getoetst. Een onderzoek naar de functies van bezwaarschriftprocedures* (PhD Groningen), Kluwer, Deventer, 1998; J.G. van Erp & C.M. Klein Haarhuis, *De filterwerking van buitengerechtelijke procedures. Een verkennend onderzoek* (WODC Cahiers 2006-06), The Hague, 2006.

17 Further information on this study can be obtained from Ms. Rink herself at: e.m.rink@rug.nl.

18 The list was made available to us by the Competition Authority. These were all the 'normal' cases that were handled in that period. Cases involving a sanction imposed via the 'accelerated procedure' (the construction industry fraud) were kept out of the study.

on the objection. Notably, it followed the recommendation in all cases where the Advisory Committee advised declaring the objection unfounded. In other words: the Competition Authority only departed from the recommendation when the Advisory Committee advised that all or part of the objection should be declared well founded. These data provide sufficient basis, in our view, for the hypothesis that the relatively limited effect of the objection procedure as a sieve in relation to decisions imposing sanctions under the Competition Act can to some extent be explained by the fact that the Competition Authority departs from its Advisory Committee's recommendations relatively frequently.

We have, incidentally, also taken a look, albeit a cursory look, at how the administrative courts – both at first instance (Rotterdam district court) and on appeal (Trade and Industry Appeals Tribunal, *CBb*) – view the differences in opinion between the Advisory Committee and the Competition Authority. From our very provisional analysis, it emerges that the district court took the side of the Competition Authority in approximately 60% of cases, while sharing the view of the Advisory Committee in 35%, whereas on appeal the tribunal took the side of the Advisory Committee in 60% of cases and that of the Competition Authority in 20%. These figures afford some basis for the hypothesis that the Competition Authority may well adopt too rigid a position during objection procedures. Further research is, however, necessary on this point.

From our analysis, it also emerges that in 50% of cases the differences of opinion between the Competition Authority and the Advisory Committee concerned factual and evidentiary issues, and the classification of facts in the light of statutory concepts (was X present at meeting Y?; what is the relevant market?; does action X constitute a noticeable restriction of competition? etc.). In 25% of cases the difference of opinion concerned the proportionality of the fines imposed: have the guidelines been correctly applied (was the infringement minor or serious?; has the appropriate multiplication factor been applied?); is the case a 'special case' within the meaning of Art. 4:84 GALA? In only 10% of cases was the difference purely on a matter of law (what is the correct interpretation of Art. 34 Competition Act?). During the passage of the Direct Appeals Act through Parliament it was noted that direct appeal to the administrative courts is particularly valuable 'in cases where the dispute is in any case no longer capable of resolution during the objection phase',[19] for example 'in cases where there is a fundamental difference of opinion on a question of law, in which it is clear from the start that the parties want the opinion of a court'.[20] In our study, as will be clear from the above, we did not come across many cases of the type: 'fundamental differences of opinion on points of law'. Most objections could be summarized as: 'I did not do it; if I did, it was not wrong; and if it was, the fine is too high.'

19 Memorandum further to the report, *Parliamentary Papers II*, 27 563, p. 6.
20 Memorandum further to the report, *Parliamentary Papers II*, 27 563, p. 2.

4.2 *No Dossier Building in ACM Cases?*

Another benefit of the objection procedure generally also proves less prominent in relation to decisions of the Competition Authority, the Telecommunications Authority and the Consumer Authority, again according to the explanatory memorandum. In general, objection procedures ensure that, where a dispute is nevertheless brought before the administrative courts, the court receives a more clearly defined and better presented case (dossier building). According to the explanatory memorandum this is less the case in relation to fines imposed by the three authorities referred to above. To quote: "The practice at the Competition Authority, the Telecommunications Authority and the Consumer Authority shows, however, that, as a rule, infringers do not present new grounds in the objection procedure compared to the views expressed under Art. 5:50 in conjunction with Art. 5:53 GALA. Infringers have had more than sufficient opportunity to present their views in the pre objection procedure. Moreover, after the parties have been offered the opportunity to present their views in writing, it is customary for the three authorities to organise a hearing at which the parties have the opportunity to explain their views orally. All the arguments of infringers are thus generally already known before the objection procedure."

Although some degree of repetition cannot be denied, it must be said that the objection procedure is in fact the first opportunity for parties to present their objections to the *size* of the fine imposed. The views expressed concern the inspector's report (Art. 59 Competition Act in conjunction with Art. 5:48.1 GALA). Such reports generally contain information about the procedure and the nature of the evidence, an extensive review of the facts and circumstances of the case (organisation, anti-competitive behaviour, agreements, market sharing etc.), a legal determination of these facts (decision, concerted practice, abuse etc.) and an assessment in the light of the relevant statutory provisions (Art. 6 Competition Act, Art. 101 TFEU, etc.), and the allocation of blame among the parties. The report does not contain a draft decision or other information about the fine to be imposed. Indeed, the administrative authority is not obliged to give this information except where specific statutory requirements apply.

Questions of law will therefore land fairly and squarely on the plate of the first instance courts, unless there is some form of 'compensation' in the sense of adjusting the primary decision-making phase. The Dutch competition law association (*Vereniging voor Mededingingsrecht*) has observed: "that the ACM will design the procedure following the report phase in such a way that the parties concerned will be able to express their views on all formal and substantive matters in the decision to be taken. For this, the decision will have to be fully open to inspection. The parties concerned should, for example, be able to comment on the fine and its basis; it should also be possible to hear witnesses at Competition Authority hearings".

In our view, the explanatory memorandum does not give a wholly accurate description of the function of 'dossier building'. It is indeed, particularly as regards decisions of the Competition Authority and the Telecommunications Authority where parties are generally represented by highly qualified legal practitioners, not surprising that the grounds for appeal submitted to the courts do not differ greatly from the views expressed and the grounds for objection. It is also true that there is a danger of repetition in the three phases of an administrative appeal (expression of views, grounds for objection and grounds for appeal). Nevertheless, as far as dossier building is concerned, it is also important that the often numerous grounds for objection are reduced to a few crucial ones (objections of 100 plus pages, with a recent high of 460 pages are no exception at the Competition Authority). It would be better to describe this as the 'reduction function' of the objection procedure. In other words, a large dossier (in exceptional cases 1 m^3 of paper) is regularly reduced to several manageable points of dispute in the objection phase. If this phase goes, then so does this simplification and the first instance courts will be faced with the full burgeoning dossier.

4.3 Length of Objection Procedure

Under Art. 7:10.1 GALA, the administrative authority must give its decision within six weeks from the day after the day on which the time limit for filing an objection has expired, or within 12 weeks if a committee has been established as referred to in Art. 7:13. Art. 7:10.3 provides that the administrative authority may postpone the decision for not more than six weeks. These time limits are almost never met in objections against Competition Authority decisions imposing a sanction. From data made available to us by the Competition Authority, it emerges that the average period from the time the objection is received until the recommendation is given is 8.9 months. This picture is to some extent distorted by the fact that in most cases a pro forma objection is lodged first, and the grounds for objection are then filled in after a time limit set by the authority, sometimes much later. The time the Competition Authority then needs to take a decision on the objection varies from case to case, most cases being concluded within five months of receipt of the recommendation, but more than 12 months (with a high of more than two years)[21] is no exception.

It is clear from the decisions of the trade and industry appeals tribunal that it is impossible to determine in the abstract what a reasonable time is for procedures under Art. 6 of the Competition Act (and the same applies to Art. 101 TFEU), "but that this must in each case be assessed in the light of the circumstances of the specific case. Account must be taken of the complexity both in fact and in law of the case and the conduct of both the company concerned and the administrative authority, and it is also relevant what is at stake for the company concerned."[22] The

---

21 See, for example, District Court Rotterdam 4 March 2008, LJN: BC8958: objection lodged on 14 January 2004, *AbM* report of 29 September 2004, followed by the decision on the objection, dated 9 November 2006.

22 *See e.g.* Trade and Industry Appeals Tribunal 3 July 2008, *AB* 2009/305 with note by I. Sewandono, LJN: BD6629; Trade and Industry Appeals Tribunal 7 July 2010, *AB* 2010/235 with note by

diversity and the fact that these proceedings are not very repetitive mean "that it cannot be assumed as a general rule that a reasonable time has been exceeded if the court has not given its decision within two years after the start of the time limit." In two recent decisions dating from August 2012 – relating to fines in connection with fraud in the construction industry – the tribunal arrived at the conclusion that the reasonable time should be set at three and a half years, of which two years could be attributed to administrative decision-making and review in respect of an objection and eighteen months to the first instance judicial proceedings.[23]

Although it cannot be denied that the length of the review in objection proceedings is much greater than the standard period allowed by the GALA, it cannot be said, based on the information made available to us and the published case law, that the duration of the objection procedure has caused great difficulties in relation to Art. 6 ECHR.

4.4 *Lower Cost: No Demand for Low Threshold Procedure*

According to the explanatory memorandum, creation of a low threshold procedure is also less important in relation to *ACM* decisions imposing fines. To be sure, an objection procedure is cheaper and thus more accessible than an appeal to an administrative court. Clearly, abolishing the objection procedure would result in doing away with the direct costs accompanying the procedure, namely:

- Costs of the advisory committee (fee and secretariat);[24]
- Organization of hearing (report, logistics costs, possible translation fees);
- Competition Authority costs (preparation, hearing, assessment of recommendation, drafting decision on the objection);
- Cost of legal practitioners of objectors and possible other interested parties.

It must, of course, first be noted that the initial costs concerning the preparation of the case, which are currently incurred during the objection procedure, both by the Competition Authority and interested parties, will shift to the judicial procedure. Interested parties' costs for drafting an objection will now be made when the appeal is made to the court. Nor will this be very different for the administrative authority. Little is thus to be expected in the way of benefit or cost saving. Above, we have argued that if the objection procedure were abolished, this should be coupled with 'compensation' in the primary decision-making phase. Obviously this

---

R. Stijnen, LJN: BN0540. Recently confirmed in Trade and Industry Appeals Tribunal 28 August 2012, case numbers AWB 09/982 and AWB 09/983.

23 Trade and Industry Appeals Tribunal 28 August 2012, case numbers AWB 09/982 and AWB 09/983. In the earlier decision of 3 July 2008 (see previous footnote), a period of 2 years and 6 months was regarded as reasonable for the administrative phase, given the complex nature of the case.

24 When asked, the Competition Authority informed us that there were no public data which would make it possible to work out the cost of the objection phase, for example the total cost of the Advisory Committee.

would entail new costs, both for the administrative authority and for interested parties.

The cost saving anticipated by the government does not therefore appear to be very substantial and will have to be set off against expected higher judicial costs. We have argued above that more appeals will be made to the courts, particularly where competition and consumer authority decisions imposing fines are concerned, and we also expect, certainly in relation to competition decisions, that the work will become more complex for first instance administrative courts, because the 'reduction function' of the objection procedure will have disappeared. In other words, abolishing the objection procedure will mean a shift in costs from the administrative authorities to the courts.

5. Conclusion

It is not our intention in this article to express a preference about the proposed abolition of the objection procedure in relation to *ACM* decisions imposing sanctions as entertained in the bill to streamline the procedures and enforcement instruments available to the *ACM*. Our aim is to give a more complete and accurate picture of the pros and cons than the bill does.

The arguments for abolishing the objection procedure can be summarised as follows: it is true that some of the general aims of the legislature in creating a mandatory objection procedure in the GALA feature less prominently in relation to *ACM* decisions imposing sanctions. Access to an informal, low threshold, cheap review procedure to repair manifest errors of the administration is simply less important in relation to these decisions. If we confine ourselves to competition decisions:

- the decisions are made by a professional, competent organisation and address professional market parties which call in the assistance of qualified legal professionals, generally also during the preparation of the primary decision;
- the decisions are made after a thorough preprocedure, including a hearing at which interested parties can express their views on the report on which the decision-making is based. To a certain extent the exchange of arguments in the objection procedure can be regarded as repetitious. However, if the objection procedure is abolished in relation to these decisions, it will in our view be necessary to reinforce the primary decision-making phase and give interested parties the opportunity to present their views further to a draft decision which includes the size of the proposed fine. If no such changes are made in 'compensation', abolition of the objection procedure will imply a loss of legal protection for companies that are fined;
- the objection procedure in competition cases is highly formalised and judicialised. There is hardly any question of an informal exchange of opinion between the 'individual' and the 'administration' (mediator function);

- the review of competition decisions during the objection procedure leaves little room for a genuine, integral review and is essentially no more than a lawfulness test.

Another advantage of abolishing the objection procedure would on the face of it seem to be a significant time gain, even if the limits set by Art. 6 ECHR do not pose a real problem here.

One of the advantages of appointing an external advisory committee – that expertise is brought in that is lacking within the organisation – is hardly relevant in relation to competition decision-making. However 'expert' the members of the Advisory Committee may be, it cannot be said that they bring expertise into the decision-making process that is lacking at the Competition Authority.

The disadvantages of abolishing the objection procedure can be summarized as follows. Though the objection procedure only operates as a sieve to a limited extent compared to decision-making at the local and regional levels, it cannot be denied that this effect does exist and particularly in relation to the Competition Authority and the Consumer Authority, organisations where the procedure is farmed out to external advisory committees. As regards the limited effect in relation to competition decisions imposing a sanction, this can to some extent be explained by the way the Competition Authority so conspicuously ignores the Advisory Committee's recommendations. We would expect that the effect would be greatly enhanced if the Competition Authority were to follow the recommendations more often. It seems as if the authority, once it has adopted a particular position, is reluctant to review a contested decision on substantive grounds. Abolishing the objection procedure, in particularly in relation to competition and consumer authority decisions where an external advisory committee is involved, must be expected to have a negative impact on the legitimacy of the decision-making process in the eyes of interested parties. It would be well to remember: "that justice should not only be done, but should [...] be seen to be done".[25]

If the objection procedure is abolished, it is also to be expected that the first instance administrative courts will face a significantly increased caseload. Not only because the number of appeals against decisions imposing sanctions will increase, but also because the courts will more often be faced with dossiers that have not yet been reduced to the main points at issue. Certain grounds for appeal (for example concerning the size of the fine) are only independently reviewed for the first time by the first instance courts. In other words, the administrative courts will have to deal with more cases, and each case will take longer to deal with properly, which may in turn give rise to difficulties in relation to Art. 6 ECHR.

It is indeed debatable whether abolishing the objection procedure will result in a substantial cost saving, or whether the costs will not simply be shifted from an administrative authority (*ACM*) to the judiciary. In our view, the cost benefit for

25 *R v Sussex Justices, Ex parte McCarthy* [1924] 1 KB 256, 259.

the parties concerned must also be examined more closely. If the costs of objecting were truly a factor of importance, it would have been reasonable to expect much more use to have been made of Art. 7:1a GALA (application to bypass objection procedure) in the past. Apparently, the companies concerned feel no great need to bypass the objection procedure.

Finally, it is perhaps worth returning to the parliamentary handling of the Direct Appeals Act. After the Act had been debated in the Senate of the Dutch Parliament, the justice minister wanted to clarify one or two points and stressed that direct appeal had to remain the exception:[26]

> Only in very special cases, in which the objection procedure must be regarded as a needless delay in the resolution of the dispute, should it be possible to do without it. Two examples were mentioned in the Parliamentary discussion:
> - cases (...) "in which all concerned have already exchanged arguments during the preparation of the decision so exhaustively that it is already certain that an objection procedure will have no added value";
> - cases in which there is no difference of opinion whatever concerning the determination and interpretation of the factual constellation, but parties need a judicial decision on a point of law to end their dispute.

How special *are ACM* decisions imposing sanctions in actual fact? And are they so special that departure from the general regime under the GALA is justified? We eagerly await the opinion of the legislature.

26 *Parliamentary Papers I*, 27 563, F.

Advisory Committees on Damage Compensation in Zoning and Infrastructural Planning: A Quest for Independence

*Dick Lubach**

1. Introduction

This contribution concerns advisory committees on damage compensation in zoning and infrastructural planning.[1] Only recently have they been regulated in a formal act despite having existed in practice for over 20 years. Based on my experience with several damage compensation committees over the years I will make some observations within the framework of this conference. Although there are mainly two reasons for establishing such committees: independence and competence, I will focus on the first aspect. I will defend the position that, although neither the legislator nor the jurisprudence is convincingly clear in this respect, independence is needed and that in practise this independence is not always guaranteed and sometimes threatened. To develop a convincing argument for this position the reason for independence has to be discussed and the practice of these committees has to be evaluated. To be able to do this properly a short description of the development of the pertinent regulation in Dutch law is useful.

2. Development of Damage Compensation in Spatial Planning Law and the Position of Advisory Committees.

Aside from some rare early examples, the theory and practise of compensation for damages caused by *per se* lawful decisions in the field of physical planning developed in the second half of the 20th century. The predecessor to the current Spatial Planning Act 2008[2] is the Spatial Planning Act 1962.[3] The latter contained, for the first time, a provision for damage compensation (*planschade*). However, there was no legal obligation based on the act to install an advisory committee in the decision-making process.

---

* Prof. dr. D.A. Lubach is Professor of construction law at the University of Groningen, the Netherlands, and Of Counsel for Damsté Advocaten en Notarissen in Enschede. He is chairman of several municipal advisory committees on damage compensation. He is also member of the Decision-making committee (DMC) of the Schadeschap Schiphol.

1 *Planschade- en nadeelcompensatiecommissies.*

2 Wro: Wet ruimtelijke ordening, *Stb.* (Law Gazette) 2006, 566

3 WRO: Wet op de Ruimtelijke Ordening, *Stb.* (Law Gazette) 1962, 286.

These advisory committees were first introduced in several municipal by-laws and later the administrative courts held that advisory committees had to be consulted in order to comply with the demand of an accurate way of decision-making.

This resulted in specific legal provisions issued in 2008. The Spatial Planning Act 2008 provides the legal basis for national, provincial and municipal orders.[4] These orders contain among others rules for establishing of advisors or advisory committees. Municipalities are bound by the (national) Spatial Planning Order[5] where rules are given for the content of provincial and municipal orders. These are mainly procedural provisions. Most importantly, rules shall be given based on the *competence and independence* of the advisor.[6] An example of these rules can be found in the relevant Municipal Order of the city of Groningen:[7]

> A (subsidiary) member of the committee does not work under the responsibility of the municipal council or the board of mayor and aldermen.
> A counseling member of the committee shall not be involved in the project for which damage compensation is asked.[8]

Another example can be found in the Order on the Damage Compensation Council (*Schadeschap*) Schiphol Airport.[9]

3. Why an External Advice?

From the examples mentioned above we can say that at least[10] two reasons play a role: competence and independence. Apparently the legislator thought it necessary to call upon external advice to deal with a presumed lack of expertise and/or independence. However, a lack of expertise does not as such bring about the need for external advice. It is possible to provide the necessary expertise from within

4 Art 6.7 Spatial Planning Act 2008.

5 Art 6.1.3.3 Besluit ruimtelijke ordening (Bro), *Stb.* (Law Gazette) 2008, 145.

6 Art. 6.1.13 section 2 sub a Spatial Planning Order 2008.

7 Art. 5 sub 4 Procedureverordening voor de advisering tegemoetkoming in planschade, Gemeenteblad Groningen 2009, 144.

8 Art. 6.2 provides for a possibility to challenge the nomination of one or more members of the committee.

9 *Stcrt.* (Government Gazette) 2012, 8910. In art.7 the following provisions are given in order to assure competence and independence of the advisory committees: the advisory committee gives advice to the Decision-making Committee (DMC, the *Besliscommissie* is the competent administrative authority). The advisory committee is nominated by the DMC. The advisory committee consists of three independent experts. There is a list of experts (not composed by the DMC) from which they have to be chosen. The nomination of experts can be challenged.

10 Yet another reason for external advice might be to put policy aspects at a distance. The policy aspects mainly have been dealt with in the decision-making process of the decision that causes the pretended damage. In deciding on the damage compensation claim these aspect do not play a role. At least they should not. Therefore that reason as such does not play a role here and is therefore not dealt with.

the public authority itself. Of course there can be all sorts of good reasons for this to not be feasible, especially in smaller organisations. Since the focus in this contribution is on the aspect of independence we will not elaborate on this issue.

The issue of independence is to be dealt with in a more specific way. First of all, we have to know what is meant by 'independent'. The example of the Groningen[11] order shows that the meaning is twofold:

- An independent counselor does not work under the responsibility of the decision-making public authority;
- An independent counselor is not involved in the project at stake.

This clarifies how 'independence' can be organised. Namely, by putting the counselor at a distance from the subject and object of the decision-making. This aspect of distance is in my opinion important. That is, at least in the type of decision-making discussed in this paper. I will elaborate on that later.

The Groningen order does not however, make clear why we need 'independence'. That is as such rather obvious because – as we have already seen – it has to comply with the rules of the Spatial Planning Order.[12] Nevertheless, it seems appropriate to elaborate on that question.

The notion of independence is related to unbiased decision-making and made without prejudice. That this is important under the rule of law is almost self-evident.[13] Less evident is that external advice is needed to guarantee such of behaviour from a decision-making authority.

De Graaf and Marseille take the position that there is a need for independent external advice only if it is not possible to provide a nonbiased civil servant.[14] And they cannot think of a good reason to prefer external advice when it comes to the issue independence.[15] In that respect they state rather straightforwardly:

> *Regardless the position of the expert opinion – intern or extern – it has to deal with and to focus only on the common interest. And as their definition of independent decision-making is: decision-making in the common interest without the influence of other (individual) interests, every advice -intern or extern-has to be independent. Hence the demand for independence does not ask for external advice.* (translation by author)

This reasoning seems at first conclusive but it does not answer the question at stake here. How can the development described in paragraph 2 be explained? The

11 *See* footnote 8.

12 *See* footnote 6.

13 As shows art. 2:4 General Administrative Law Act (GALA).

14 K.J. de Graaf & A.T. Marseille, Over onafhankelijk en deskundig voorbereide overheidsbesluiten, in: Bart Krans et. al.(eds.), *De deskundige in het recht*, Zutphen 2011, p. 21.

15 Id.

answer given by De Graaf and Marseille[16] that it is a matter of 'tradition and coincidence' is not satisfactory. To find a more conclusive explanation we have to look into the nature of decision-making when it comes to damage compensation claims resulting from changes in zoning and infrastructure.

4. The Nature of Decision-Making on Damage Compensation Claims and the Need for Independence

First of all we have to keep in mind that in the case of damage compensation as dealt with in art 6.1 Wro[17] we do not discuss the lawfulness of the decision that causes the damage for which compensation is requested. The decision to change a zoning plan for example as such requires balancing the different interests at stake.[18] And although financial aspects play a role in finding the appropriate balance,[19] the decision to change a zoning plan is not unlawful because damage compensation ex art 6.1 Wro has not (or not yet) been given. Nor is it mandatory to challenge the decision that causes the alleged damage, to be entitled to damage compensation. In short, in cases dealt with under art 6.1 Wro concern compensation for damages caused by a *per se* lawful decision.[20]

That a decision to change a zoning plan is lawful means that the inherent balance of different interests is correct, not only in the sense that it complies with the law, but also that it is the most appropriate way of serving the common interest.

Serving the common interest is the core business of a public authority, in fact it is the only thing it has to do. In cases such as changing zoning plans it is sometimes rather complicated and difficult to find the proper balance that best serves the common interest. Almost every decision in this field is apt to be challenged. Once a decision has been made and has been held as lawful by a court the decision-making authority is satisfied that the decision has come a long way.

Worthy of discussion is whether the decision-making authority being in that 'state of mind' is able to decide on damage compensation claims completely on its own and still be truly 'independent'.[21] Unlike in a situation where it is confronted with a judgment where what it has done is unlawful and damage compensation is an almost 'logical' consequence, a change of mind is required. The lawful decision has to be checked on a, from the claimants point of view, drop in the desirability

---

16 Id, p. 33

17 *See* footnote 3.

18 *See also* footnote 11.

19 A zoning plan has to have a sufficient economic base; its realisation has to be financially feasible.

20 Damage in this sense is referred to in Dutch as 'nadeel' and is distinguished from damage caused by an unlawful act, which is called 'schade'. In this paper 'damage compensation' has to be translated from 'nadeelcompensatie' and not in the more common terminology 'schadevergoeding'.

21 'Independent' in the sense of De Graaf & Marseille 2011 *supra*.

of the area and potential harmful effects on his privacy, view etc. all resulting in a possible decrease in the value of his property.

It is clear that in these cases an opinion from an independent and completely separate actor can be useful in order to come to the right decision; although the decision has to be made by the public authority itself. And from the claimant's point of view, they tend to mistrust the appeal decision that comes from the same authority that may have ignored their demand to adapt the zoning plan in the first place.

My experiences over the years show that claimants appreciate members of the advisory committee *not* being civil servants and *not* working under the responsibility of the public authority that has made the harmful decision. The very fact that the advisory committee is not seen as a part of the public authority contributes to the acceptance of a decision that is made in accordance with the given external advice.

However, the position of the external advisory committee should not be mistaken. The committee does not represent the claimant's interest. Although at a distance from the public authority he does not defend the claimant's interests. Nor does he defend the interests of the public authority of course. I do not follow De Graaf and Marseille in the cases discussed here, where they state that a close connection between the advisory committee and the public authority is desirable as it shows that the advisor is capable of giving advice 'in the spirit of the common interest, served by the public authority'.[22]

This does not mean that an external advisor does not have to acknowledge the public authority's obligation to serve the common interest and that its advice has to contribute to reaching that goal. But at least in the cases we are discussing here its position is not the same as the position of the public authority itself.

In my opinion there is a relevant distinction here. A distinction originating from private law could be helpful in this context. In the theory of the legal nature of binding advice a distinction is made between 'pure' and 'impure' binding advice. The first category is advice that is meant to establish a missing element in a legal relationship. Often such advices are asked to provide (expert) information to be able to make an initial decision. The latter is actually a form of litigation.[23] Indeed, also in administrative law the first category is present. For example, expert advice is involved with establishing the degree of disability someone has which prevents them from working entitling them to a disability benefit. Indeed in these situations it is not obvious that distance to the decision maker is required. The

22 Id, p. 33.

23 I do not discuss here the question whether or not advices in administrative law can be seen as binding advices in private law. See A.H. Santing-Wubs, Bindend advies en deskundigenbericht, in: Bart Krans et al. (eds.), *De deskundige in het recht*, Zutphen, 2011, p. 85.

reason for the advice is the lack of expertise on the part of the decision maker. In these situations that expertise can be provided for internally and there is little reason to avoid having a close relationship between advisor and decision maker.

The questions of damage compensation are however of a different nature. As explained earlier they relate to a decision already made that is later judged as lawful. The question of whether or not somebody is entitled to damage compensation has therefore more the character of litigation. And advice in this field resembles in my opinion an 'impure' binding advice, although the advice for the public authority on damage compensation is not binding.

Following this opinion the advice plays an important role in litigation. And in that sense, the appreciation of the independent nature of the committee should not come as a surprise. In these situations it is undesirable that the advisory committee has a (too) close relationship with the public authority. This being so, it might provide an explanation for the described development,[24] leading to the legal obligation to obtain external advice from an external advisory committee, whose independence has to be guaranteed.

5. Practices Menacing the Independency of the Advisory Committee (?)

Jurisprudence rarely rewards complaints regarding to a lack of independence[25] of an advisory committee. In the cases discussed here the explanation for that attitude given by De Graaf and Marseille is unsatisfactory. They state that the court's rather lenient attitude towards an advisory committee's supposed bias be explained by the fact that a close connection between advisor and public authority is an indication of the capability of giving advice 'in the spirit of the common interest, served by the public authority'. That reasoning only applies to the first category of advice as indicated earlier. In those cases the court can judge that a lack of independence is not problematic and therefore dismiss the complaint even in cases where there is indeed a close connection between advisor and public authority.[26]

In the cases at stake here however, the lack of independence can indeed harm the credibility of the committee and the acceptance of the decision in accordance with the advice. Therefore, it has to be seen if there are circumstances that threaten the independence of the advisory committee. Or at least contribute to the idea with the claimant that the committee is not independent.

24 *See* par. 2.
25 *See* De Graaf & Marseille 2011 *supra*, p. 31.
26 *See* footnote 23.

In this respect the following issues prompt discussion:
a. The set-up of the committee and the way their decisions are (pre) structured;
b. The position of the committee towards the claimant on one hand and towards the public authority on the other;
c. The role of the committee in the phases of review and appeal;
d. The role of the committee in mediation.

Ad a. In general there are two options when it comes to establishing an advisory committee in the field of zoning and infrastructure.[27] The first option is to refer to a professional expert bureau that serves several public authorities all over the country. The second is to establish a local committee that only serves the local authority.[28] I will not discuss here the pros and cons of the two options in general but focus on the question of independence. It is clear that when it comes to the question of independence the two options are different. In the first, the advice is prepared and formulated separately and at a distance from the public authority.[29] In the case of a local committee the administrative support often comes from within the municipality itself. The secretary is often a civil servant that works for the municipality. Although obviously he or she is not a member of the committee it is almost inevitable that there is some influence. The relevant documents are compiled and often initially interpreted by the secretary. He or she – especially a (hopefully) very competent person – usually participate in the discussion. And sometimes the committee has to remind itself that the secretary is not a voting member of the committee. Eventually the text of the advice is edited by the secretary, which gives him or her another potential means of exerting influence. In this respect it is advisable that the committee provides a format that can be used in standard cases. In my own practice I have not seen examples of problems in this respect but both the administrative secretary and the members of the committee have to keep their different positions in mind.

Ad b. Claimants are different. Sometimes they are affluent individuals or enterprises who are represented by a lawyer and the expertise of the claimant is not unlike that of the committee. In those cases the committee tends to keep the contact fairly formal. In local practice however, these claimants are a minority. In most cases the claimants are middle class individuals who do not have much expertise, nor the financial means to gain that expertise from a professional lawyer.[30] In these cases a committee must be aware of their position as an independent body. That means that there is a limit to the extent a committee can be 'user friendly'. In this respect it important that the rather lenient position the committee has taken

27 Theoretically establishing an ad hoc committee is not excluded but they are rare and I will not discuss them here.

28 Almost always a municipality.

29 For instance the bureau SAOZ, a bureau based in Rotterdam which works for a municipality in the northern part of the country.

30 Although since the Spatial Planning Act 2008 came into force the legal demands for justification of the claims are more severe (formerly one phrase: 'Help, your decisions cause damage to me' was sufficient to start up the case). Legal assistance or an evaluation report is not obligatory.

in the past towards claimants who fail to comply with the demands to provide the necessary information is now restricted by the legal obligation for the committee to come forward with their advice and for the public authority to decide within the proper time frame.[31]

Ad c. The legal position of the advisory committee is limited to the phase of the initial decision-making process. Strictly speaking, it does not have a role in the following phases of the procedures for legal protection. The objection procedure that aims at reviewing the initial decision provides its own advisory committee.[32]

In the process of appeal it is the public authority that has to, without advice, defend its decision although in practice this is not as clear cut as it may seem here. The objection procedure is designed as an opportunity to rethink the initial decision in full scope. It is obvious that also merits of the advice given in the initial phase will be reconsidered. It is often the case that in the objection procedure the advisory committee in that procedure contacts the advisory committee of the initial decision to discuss the way they have to deal with the points of view expressed in the initial advice. As such that is not surprising. The committee in the objection procedure is a more general advisory committee that is involved in all kinds of cases on a wide scale of subjects. It does not have the specific expertise of the initial advisory committee.

At the appeal phase the complaints often specifically regard the value that can be attributed to the advice. The question is often whether the public authority could have reasonably made the allegedly unlawful decision following the initial advice. Nor should it come as a surprise that the public authority once more contacts the advisory committee to discuss the arguments brought forward in the court procedure to see if these cause a change of opinion with the committee.

As long as one regards the position of the advisory committee as a 'lengthening piece' of the public authority all this does not pose a problem. But it can easily be understood that the independent position of the advisory committee is at risk. It is the public authority that has the opportunity to contact and discuss with the advisory committee in two subsequent phases of the procedure of legal protection. Obviously that opportunity does not exist for the claimant. He will tend to see the committee as a barely independent counselor to his opponent.

Ad d. There is still another position that the committee can take in the relationship between claimant and public authority. That is the role of mediator. To comply with the call for alternative dispute resolution sometimes the members of the committee are asked (by both parties of course) to take the role of mediators. It cannot be the committee itself taking that position because the law does not

---

31 From 1 October 2009 art. 4:17 GALA provides for financial consequences in the case of a not timely decision.

32 Art 7:13 GALA.

attribute that role to the advisory committee. The members of the committee are asked for their expertise and indeed because of their independence from both parties and 'independence' from their previous position as advisory committee. The role of mediator presupposes a certain distance from the reasoning that is the base of the initial advice leading to the disputed decision. So this role requires independence, it does not threaten it.

6. Summary and Conclusions

Since 2008 specific legislation has called for external advisory committees in the decision-making process concerning compensation for damages resulting from changes in zoning and infrastructural planning. Both expertise and independence can be reasons for the obligatory installment of such committees.[33] Neither the jurisprudence nor the lawmaker is convincingly clear on why exactly the independence of those committees is required. This paper tries to find the reason for advisory committee independence in the litigious nature of the decision on compensation for damages caused by lawful decisions. The idea that the advisory committee can be seen as a 'lengthening piece' of the public authority whose mandate it is to advise 'in the spirit of the common interest' does not take into account that the advice basically is meant to serve the resolution of a dispute.[34]

Once convinced that independence is a value that should not be neglected the existing practice is evaluated. It appears that in particular the local committees are susceptible functioning too close to the public authority. Both the members of the committee themselves as the administrative secretarial support have to keep in mind that they are supposed to take an independent position. The fact that the expertise of the committee is also invoked in the phase of the objection procedure and appeal reinforces the threat to independence. It is clear it is independence that is required if members of the same committee are to play a role as mediator.

33 *See* footnote 7.

34 I am grateful to my colleagues Kars de Graaf and Bert Marseille for the possibility they unknowingly gave me to develop and clarify my rather dormant ideas on this subject by taking the opposite position in their article mentioned in several footnotes above.

Final Dispute Resolution by Dutch Administrative Courts: Slippery Slope and Efficient Remedy

*Kars de Graaf and Albert Marseille**

1. Introduction

Dutch administrative authorities are competent in a number of fields to decide on the legal position of citizens, either in response to an application or *ex officio*. Sometimes the legislator grants discretionary power to a public authority and sometimes the law leaves no room to balance the interests involved. In most cases the decision-making process will lead to a decision that is potentially the subject of judicial review by an administrative court. The classic role of administrative courts is simply to assess the lawfulness of the decision taken. The judgment entails either the statement that the challenged decision is lawful, or the annulment of the challenged decision. If the latter is the case, the public authority will have to decide on the matter again at a later date. At least until that date, there is no final resolution to the dispute.

The courts are independent and impartial with regard to administration in the classical 'separation of powers' sense. The call for final dispute resolution within a reasonable time however calls for effective and efficient administrative adjudication and demands of courts that they direct the plaintiff and the public authority towards a final resolution of their conflict. A simple annulment of the decision by the court is no longer sufficient. Ideally the procedure will end with clarity on the legal position of both parties. This means that it is clear which decision of the public authority applies in the future.[1] If the contested decision is upheld by the court, the decision that applies in the future is of course the contested decision. But what if the contested decision is annulled? The Dutch General Administrative Law Act (GALA) under certain conditions grants administrative courts the power to bring about the final settlement of the dispute even when the contested decision is annulled.

* Dr. K.J. de Graaf is Associate Professor of administrative and environmental law at the University of Groningen, the Netherlands. Prof. dr. A.T. Marseille is Professor in Empirical Studies of Administrative Law at Tilburg University, the Netherlands. They thank Derek Sietses and Jasper Wesselman for their help in preparing this chapter.

1 B.J. Schueler, J.K. Drewes et al., *Definitieve geschilbeslechting door de bestuursrechter*, Boom Juridische uitgevers, The Hague, 2007.

This chapter deals with the question of how much effort administrative courts should invest in final dispute resolution and how the use of the powers to bring about final dispute resolution relates to the classic ideas of independence and impartiality and the relationship between administrative courts and administration. To that end, we discuss recent amendments in the GALA that provide courts with more effective instruments and powers to bring about final dispute resolution and case law that proves courts either too careful or surprisingly careless. This chapter is divided into three parts. First, we will explain what the powers of the courts to bring about the final settlement of the dispute imply. Second, we will examine the extent to which those powers are used. Third, we will show the criteria the courts apply when deciding whether they should use these powers in their quest for the efficient offer of effective remedies. We will indicate the limitations of the courts' powers and show that Dutch case law is in some respects moving towards a 'slippery slope'.

2. The Powers of the Court to Bring about Final Dispute Resolution

When an administrative court in the Netherlands comes to the conclusion that the contested decision of a public authority is unlawful and has to be annulled, it has three instruments to prevent the dispute between the parties from continuing while the citizen waits for a new decision by the public authority. These powers are awarded to the courts in Article 8:72 and Article 8:51a GALA.

First, administrative courts can decide that the legal consequences of the annulled decision shall be allowed to stand (Article 8:72(3)(a) GALA). The court can use that power when it is certain that the defect can be repaired and the content of the repaired decision will be exactly the same as the contested decision.

For example,[2] before appealing to a court against a public authority's decision an objection usually has to be lodged against that decision. Before deciding on that objection, the interested parties have to be given the opportunity to be heard (Article 7:2 (1) GALA). When the public authority fails to meet this obligation and subsequently an appeal is lodged against the decision of the public authority on the objection, one of the grounds of that appeal can be that the public authority violated the law by not hearing the person that lodged the objection. The court will certainly award this ground and as a consequence, it will annul the contested decision. Subsequently, it has to decide whether the legal consequences of the annulled decision will be allowed to stand (Article 8:72(3)(a) GALA). There is a fair chance that the court will apply Article 8:72(3)(a) GALA. When the court concludes that in other respects the decision of the public authority is lawful, it is certain that the public authority will take exactly the same decision again. In that

2 This example was already given by government when the competence of the courts was introduced in the GALA in 1994, see E.J. Daalder, G.R.J. de Groot & J.M.E. Breugel, *De parlementaire geschiedenis van de Algemene wet bestuursrecht. Tweede tranche*, Alphen a/d Rijn 1994, p. 470.

case it is more efficient that the court decides that the legal consequences of the annulled decision will be allowed to stand.

Second, the court can determine that its judgment shall take the place of the annulled decision (Article 8:72(3)(b) GALA). The court can only use that power when it is certain which decision the public authority should take to replace the decision that it annulled. Because it is clear which decision has to be taken instead, the court has the power 'to step into the shoes' of the public authority, and to decide the matter in a lawful manner instead of the public authority. The court has this power because it is deemed to be inefficient for the public authority to take a new decision when it is crystal clear what the content of the decision will be. In such a situation, it is far more efficient for the court to take the decision – by determining that its judgment will take the place of the annulled decision – instead of prescribing that the public authority take a new decision.

For example,[3] when a public authority decides that an objection is unfounded and the court has to give judgment concerning the appeal against that decision, the court can conclude that the objection should have been declared inadmissible. The court will of course annul the public authority's decision. Because there can be no discussion regarding the decision the public authority will have to take after the annulment (the objection will have to be declared inadmissible), the court will decide that its judgment shall take the place of the annulled decision and will decide that the objection is inadmissible.

A third, relatively new power of the court is that it can allow the public authority the opportunity to repair shortcomings or unlawful elements that the court found in the contested decision; in Dutch this procedure is called a *bestuurlijke lus*, an administrative loop. This power is not mentioned in Article 8:72 GALA, but in Article 8:51a GALA. If the court uses this power, it will state in a specific, interim judgment that it has found unlawful elements in the contested decision and that it will annul the decision in its final judgment. Until the final judgment the court will however award the public authority time to try and repair the unlawful elements. The public authority's response to the administrative court of first instance could be that it doesn't agree with the assessment of the court and that there is no need to repair any unlawful element. The public authority could also respond either by offering further information or giving improved reasons for the contested decision or it could take a new decision that will be added to what is subject to judicial review by the court. The court can use the power to allow the public authority an opportunity to repair the decision any time it concludes that the contested decision is unlawful and it argues that allowing the public authority that opportunity could be efficient for reaching a final resolution to the dispute. The court is supposed to use the power in situations where it fears that if it does not take control over the settlement of the dispute, the decision-making process

3 *See* E.J. Daalder, G.R.J. de Groot & J.M.E. Breugel, *De parlementaire geschiedenis van de Algemene wet bestuursrecht. Tweede tranche*, Alphen a/d Rijn 1994, p. 470.

necessary for the new decision by the public authority will take too much time. This power was introduced in 2010 in order to reiterate the notion that administrative courts have a responsibility for final dispute resolution.

The Dutch legislator is keen to support the idea that administrative courts have an important role to play in finding ways to stimulate final dispute resolution. On January 1st 2013 it introduced a new relevant article in that respect. Article 8:41a GALA states that administrative courts will resolve the dispute of the parties where possible.

3. Empirical Data: the Use of the Powers to Bring about Final Dispute Resolution

How often do administrative courts make use of their powers to bring about final dispute resolution? To answer this question, we will compare court activity in 2012 with activity in 2007. The years between 2007 and 2012 ushered in two important developments. In the first place, the administrative courts were provided with additional powers (the administrative loop) to try to bring about the final resolution of the dispute, as we have seen in section 2. In addition, since 2008 the case law of the highest administrative courts indicates that courts are able to use their powers of Article 8:72 GALA in increasingly different situations, as will be explained in section 4.

Ideally, we would have looked at the activities of the courts of first instance. After all, if an administrative judge has to decide whether he will use one of his powers to (attempt to) bring about the final settlement of the dispute, it will most likely be a judge in first instance. Research that concerns their decisions can provide us with valuable insights into the effects of the expanded powers of the administrative courts. However, courts in first instance do not publish all their judgments, so it is somewhat difficult to obtain the necessary information concerning their use of these powers. As a consequence, we turned to the two most important Dutch courts of last resort, the Administrative Jurisdiction Division of the Council of State (Council of State) and the Central Appeals Court for Public Service and Social Security Matters (Central Appeals Court), because they publish all their judgments.[4]

We have analysed a sample of their judgments where they conclude that a decision given by a public authority is unlawful and they therefore have to decide whether it is possible to (attempt to) bring about final dispute resolution, by using their powers of Article 8:72 or Article 8:51a GALA.

4 Council of State: <www.raadvanstate.nl>. Central Appeals Court: <www.rechtspraak.nl>.

Our sample consists of 374 decisions given by these two courts, 200 from the Council of State (101 from 2007, 99 from 2012),[5] 215 from the Central Appeals Court (115 from 2007, 100 from 2012).[6]

We will first focus on the Council of State. We distinguish three different decisions. The first decision that has to be taken when the Council of State concludes that an administrative body's decision must be annulled, is whether it is possible to allow the legal consequences to stand (Article 8:72(3) GALA). If that is not possible, the next decision is whether it is possible to let the courts judgment take the place of the annulled decision (Article 8:72(4) GALA). If that is not possible either, the Council of State has to finally decide whether it will try to bring about the final resolution of the dispute by using the so-called administrative loop (Article 8:51a GALA). In 2007, the administrative courts did not have the power to take this last decision, because Article 8:51a was implemented in 2010.

The first figure shows the results of the two subsequent decisions the Council of State had to take in 2007 when it concludes that a public authority's decision must be annulled.

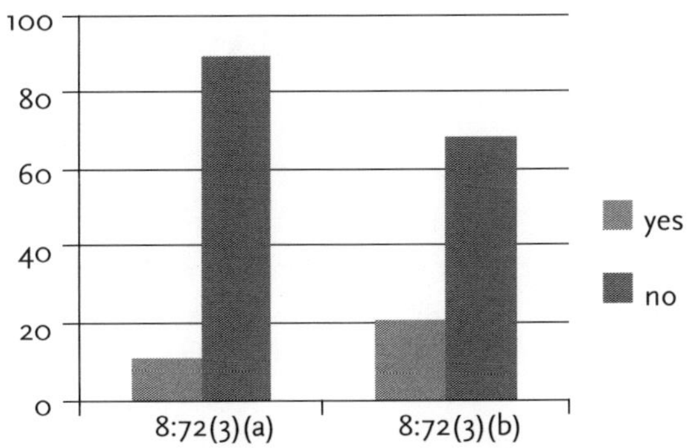

The figure shows that in 11 of 100 cases, the Council of State decided to allow the legal consequences of the annulled decision to stand (the two columns on the left). With regard to the remaining 89 cases, it decided in 21 cases that its judgment should take the place of the annulled decision (the two columns on the right). As a consequence, in 68 of 100 cases in which the contested decision had to be annulled, the Council of State did not succeed in bringing about final dispute resolution.

5 We excluded the procedures concerning immigration.

6 We started our search with decisions published at the end of April, and went subsequently a week ahead and a week back, until we had collected more than 100 decisions from both courts. As a consequence of a more detailed analysis some of them were omitted.

The next figure shows the results of the three subsequent decisions the Council of State had to take in 2012.

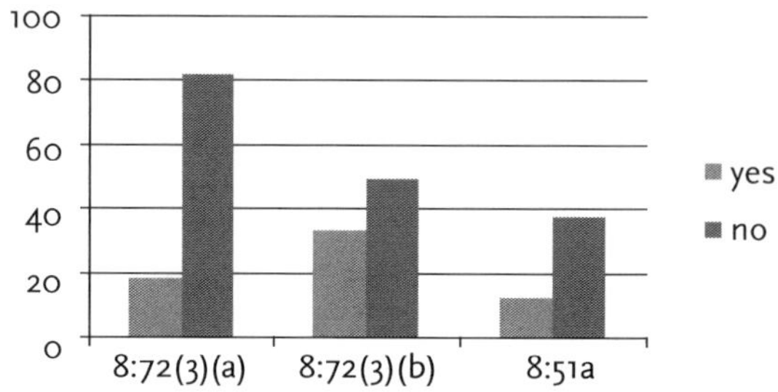

The figure shows that in 18 of the 100 cases, the Council of State decided to allow the legal consequences to stand (the two columns on the left). With regard to the remaining 82 cases (the two columns in the middle), it decided in 33 of them that its judgment shall take the place of the annulled decision. With regard to the remaining 49 cases (the two columns on the right), the Council of State decided to use the administrative loop in 23 cases. As a consequence, in 37 of the 100 cases in which the contested decision had to be annulled, the Council of State was not able to bring about the final settlement of the dispute.

When we compare the 2007 cases with those from 2012, we see an increase in the final settlement of disputes where the Council of State concluded that the contested decision had to be annulled from 32% to 63% of cases. The reason for this increase is not only the introduction of the administrative loop but also an increased use of the two remaining instruments on behalf of the final settlement of the dispute.

If we now switch to the Central Appeals Court, the first figure shows the results of the two subsequent decisions the Central Appeals Court had to take in 2007 when it concluded that an administrative body's decision had to be annulled.

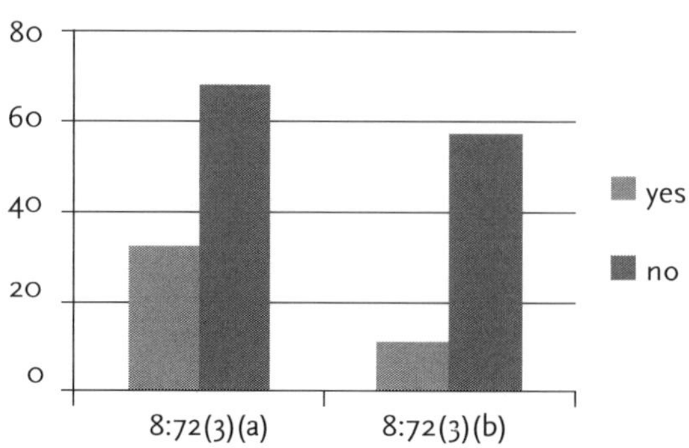

The figure shows that in 32 of 100 cases, the Central Appeals Court decided to allow the legal consequences of the annulled decision to stand (the two columns on the left). With regard to the remaining 68 cases (the two columns on the right), it decided that its judgment should take the place of the annulled decision in 11 cases. As a consequence, in 57 of 100 cases where the contested decision had to be annulled, the Central Appeals Court didn't succeed in bringing about the final settlement of the dispute.

The next figure shows the results of the three subsequent decisions the Central Appeals Court had to take in 2012.

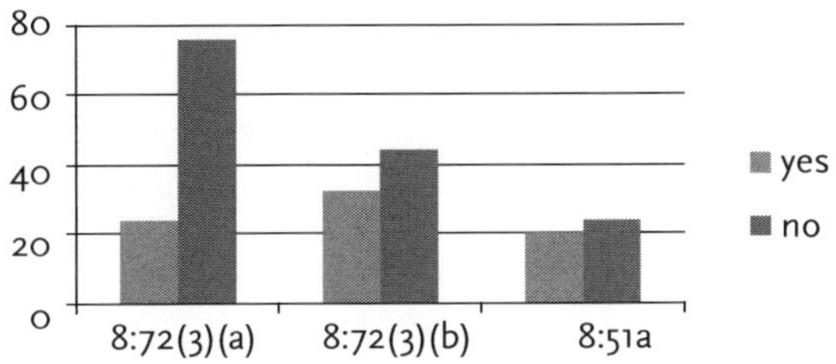

The figure shows that in 24 of 100 cases, the Central Appeals Court decided to allow the legal consequences to stand (the two columns on the left). With regard to the remaining 76 cases (the two columns in the middle), it decided that its judgment should take the place of the annulled decision in 32 cases. With regard to the remaining 44 cases (the two columns on the right), the Central Appeals Court decided to use the administrative loop in 20 cases. As a consequence, only in 24 of 100 cases in which the contested decision had to be annulled, did the Central Appeals Court not succeed in bringing about final dispute resolution, only in 76 did it succeed.

When we compare the figure for 2007 with the one for 2012, we see a significant increase in the number of cases where the Council of State and the Central Appeals Court reach a final settlement for the dispute. The increase is caused partly by the use of the administrative loop but also by an increased use of the powers of Article 8:72 GALA.

When we compare the Council of State with the Central Appeals Court, we observe that the Central Appeals Court used its powers to bring about the final settlement of the dispute in 2007 more frequently than the Council of State did.

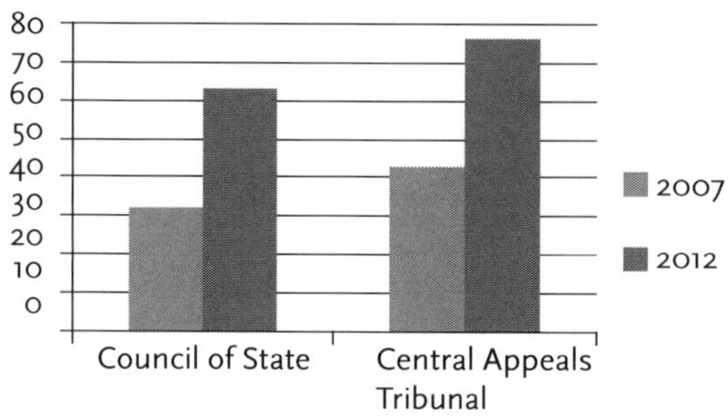

Moreover, the increase of the use of these powers (that can be observed in both courts) is more so by the Central Appeals Court than by the Council of State. The most striking difference between the two courts can be observed when we compare their decision concerning the use of the administrative loop. When they conclude that they cannot use the powers of Article 8:72 GALA (in 2012 at the Council of State in 49% of cases and at the Central Appeals Court in 44% of cases), the Central Appeals Court decides in almost half of the cases to use the administrative loop, the Council of State only in one in five cases.

So we can conclude that these two Dutch administrative courts in last instance increasingly make use of their powers to (attempt to) bring about the final resolution of the dispute but that the extent to which they use their powers differs.

What about the district courts? As earlier indicated, their judgement was not investigated. However, other research in recent years suggests that these courts also make more use of their powers to try to bring about final dispute settlement.[7]

4. The Increased Use Explained and Analysed

The figures presented in section 3 paint a clear picture. The percentage of cases where the courts have tried to bring about final dispute resolution has increased in recent years. Although we should emphasise that this development is a reaction to complaints regarding the functioning of the system of administrative jurisdiction

7 P.A. Willemsen, M.C.J. Busscher, N. Groot, P.M. Langbroek & I.L.A. Langerak, Final dispute settlement in numbers. Report of an examination of final dispute settlement in the Utrecht district court, *Transylvanian Review of Administrative Sciences*, 2009, no. 28E, p. 129-146; A.T. Marseille & R.R. van der Heide, De onderbenutting van de mogelijkheden tot finale beslechting door de bestuursrechter, *JBplus* 2008, No. 2, p. 78-92; B.J. Schueler, J.K. Drewes *et al.*, *Definitieve geschilbeslechting door de bestuursrechter*, Boom Juridische uitgevers, The Hague 2007; K.A. van der Veer & A.T. Marseille, Besluitvorming na een rechterlijke vernietiging: de achilleshiel van het bestuursrecht, *NJB* 2006, p. 2168-2175; P.A. Willemsen *et al*, Definitieve geschilbeslechting becijferd, *JBplus*, 2010/1, p. 32-48.

in the Netherlands, it also raises some questions. The first question in relation to the numbers presented would be: what triggered the increase?

The answer to that question actually seems simple. First, as of 2010 administrative judges have an additional instrument to try to bring about final dispute resolution: the administrative loop. Second, as of 2008 the case law of the highest administrative courts in the Netherlands has contributed to the increase in the percentage of cases where the courts have put effort into bringing about final dispute resolution. The highest courts have emphasised the role of the courts on this issue. Until 2008, their case law indicated that courts could only use the powers mentioned in section 2 in cases where the public authority does not have a choice when it comes to decision-making once the contested decision has been annulled. Usually the case law would indicate that using these powers – either to determine that the legal consequences of the annulled decision shall be allowed to stand (Article 8:72(3) GALA) or to determine that the judgment shall take the place of the annulled decision (Article 8:72(4) GALA) – is allowed only in cases where the outcome of the new decision-making process is evident and crystal clear. The use of the powers was restricted to situations where only one lawful decision (that should be taken by the public authority) remained and that it is just a matter of efficiency to have the court use these powers.[8] However, in its judgment of the 10th of December 2008[9] the Administrative Jurisdiction Division of the Council of State deviated from this existing case law.

The disputed decision concerned the installation of a traffic sign in a small village called Hattem in the Netherlands. The legislator had granted the public authority wide discretion for taking this decision. The Council of State's judgement has two important aspects.

The Council of State found the lodged appeal well-founded and had decided that it would annul the contested decision. It then explicitly considered that 'when a court decides to annul the contested decision, it ought to assess all possibilities of final dispute resolution, such as the use of the powers awarded in Article 8:72 paragraph 3 and 4 of the General Administrative Law Act'. This meant a drastic change in the way courts were to consider their role in bringing about final dispute resolution. This is the first aspect that is of importance for answering the question of the expanded use of the competences. There is however, an even more important reason. The Council of State furthermore explicitly changed the existing boundaries that courts had used until then to assess whether or not they would use the powers mentioned in Article 8:72 GALA. To bring about final dispute resolution, it considered that from now on the use of the discretionary powers was not restricted to situations where only one lawful decision remains to be taken. The reason: efficiency and effectiveness of administrative jurisdiction.

8 See as an example Administrative Jurisdiction Division of the Council of State 28 June 1999, *JB* 1999/196.

9 Administrative Jurisdiction Division of the Council of State 8 December 2008, *JB* 2009/39.

The Council of State also referred to the independence of the administrative court by mentioning the separation of powers. It stated that issues of discretion would remain in the hands of the public authority and that the court would only be facilitating the efficient bringing about of final dispute resolution. Still, this change in the case law is relevant and important.

This judgment and others that were published later,[10] are examples of the new case law on the use of the powers of the court to bring about final dispute resolution. The new Article 8:41a of the GALA, which encourages administrative courts to put more effort into bringing about final dispute resolution, can be considered a sign of support for this new application of the powers of the court. However, the case law has triggered other, more fundamental questions. Should the court be in charge of final dispute resolution between the parties? What should be the exact role of the court in trying to bring about final dispute resolution? How much effort, time and money should courts invest in trying to achieve final dispute resolution? This is to a large extent unclear.

One of the important issues that remains concerns the discretion awarded to the public authority by the legislator. How will courts deal with the existence of discretion for the public authority on the one hand and the obligation to assess the possibilities of final dispute resolution on the other? In what way is it ensured that the courts do not intervene with the powers of the public authority? These questions are important as far as the separation of powers is concerned but also relate to the judicial independence and the impartiality of the courts. Another issue that courts are confronted with is that final dispute resolution often requires further investigation into the relevant facts. However, the courts do not hold the primary responsibility for gathering and establishing the facts that will lead to a lawful decision. It is the public authorities that are best equipped to undertake the investigation and renew the contested decision. These issues suggest that it is not always for administrative courts to bring about final dispute resolution. Public authorities have power and means to do so. The relatively new instrument of course, reflects this idea: the administrative loop (Article 8:51a GALA). The legislator introduced this instrument assuming it would be helpful in bringing about final dispute resolution while guaranteeing the independence of the administrative courts and the separation of powers. The task of the administrative court remains to simply evaluate the legality of a contested decision. The administrative loop does not have any influence on the power of the public authority to decide on the rights and duties of the applicant.

Effective remedy

There are disputes in Dutch administrative law where administrative courts are generally considered suitable for bringing final dispute resolution about.

---

10 See for example Administrative Jurisdiction Division of the Council of State 11 February 2009, *AB* 2009/224.

The General Administrative Law Act explicitly demands a final judgment in cases that concern administrative (punitive) fines. Article 8:72a GALA states: "When a decision to impose an administrative fine is annulled by the court, it shall order that the judgment shall take the place of the annulled decision." The reason for this mandatory use of the power to decide that the judgment will replace the annulled decision is said to lie in Article 6 of the European Convention on Human Rights (ECHR) which demands final dispute resolution within reasonable time in cases concerning criminal charges, such as an administrative fine. Article 6 ECHR furthermore demands full jurisdiction by the court in establishing the facts of the case, in determining the culpability of the offender and in assessing how severe the sanction should be to be appropriate.

In cases of government liability for decisions that were annulled by the court and were thus proven unlawful, the Dutch legislator has recently proposed a special procedure for citizens requesting damages. The essence of this special track is essentially a direct request to the administrative court to award damages contrary to the appeal procedure that is normally lodged against a decision by a public authority.[11] Most authors in the Netherlands argue that nothing should stand in the way of final dispute resolution in these kinds of disputes on (fault) liability of the government. The legislator has therefore devised a special request procedure that has to end with a judgment by the administrative court determining the exact liability of the government.

Slippery slope?

For some disputes it is not clear whether administrative courts should have the obligation to reach final dispute resolution. Strangely enough the Dutch legislator did not propose a special procedure for disputes that involve the no-fault liability of public authorities for lawful decisions. Disputes concerning the no-fault liability of public authorities will have to be brought to court by lodging an appeal against a decision of the public authority concerning its own (no-fault) liability.[12] The administrative court will annul the decision when it is unlawful. The court then has to assess the possibilities for final dispute resolution. Although the administrative court is not obliged to achieve final dispute resolution, most authors trust that courts will in general lead the procedure to a judgment on the exact no-fault liability of the public authority.[13] The court could however, refer the case to the public authority to decide in the matter again. Some authors and case law state that it is up to the public authority to establish the facts and when that duty of care is not properly upheld, the court should refer the case to the public authority. Other authors claim that the issue of awarding damages for no-fault liability is, to a certain extent, at the discretion of the public authority and therefore the courts should not be obliged to determine that the judgment will take the place of

11 See *Parliamentary Papers II* 2010/11, 32 621, nr. 2 (proposed Article 8:88 GALA).

12 See *Parliamentary Papers II* 2010/11, 32 621, nr. 2 (proposed Article 4:126 GALA)

13 See B.J. van Ettekoven & R. Ortlep, Zelf in de zaak voorzien en schadevergoeding, *O&A* 2012, p. 2-18

the annulled decision.[14] Until recently there was no case law clarifying this issue. Only recently has the Administrative Jurisdiction Division of the Council of State seemingly accepted that there is indeed discretion for public authorities in these kind of cases.[15]

The most difficulty we have is with the disputes where it is questionable whether the courts are allowed to use their powers to bring about final dispute resolution. We can explain this by giving two examples of somewhat older court judgments.

'Three strikes and you're out'. These words summed up the main idea in a judgment handed down by the district court in Amsterdam in 1998.[16] It decided in a case where the public authority had not provided proper reasons for refusing a subsidy to a zoo three times in a row. Once the court had annulled the decision refusing the subsidy three times, it then decided that it would grant the subsidy by deciding that its judgment should take the place of the annulled decision. It did so by stating that the public authority would, in a potential future procedure, probably not be able to give proper reasons for another refusal. Although this case could be considered somewhat older and concerns a verdict by a district court, it can serve as an example of what the administrative courts deem appropriate when confronted with a public authority that gives poor reasons for a decision several times. There are other, more recent examples.[17]

'No decision within a reasonable time and you are out'. A second example is provided by the District Court of the Hague that based its (unpublished) judgment on the idea that justice had to be delivered within reasonable time. In this case an appeal was lodged against a decision that concerned the reclaiming of disability benefits. The appeal was well-founded and the court considered that because of the long period it had taken the public authority to reach a decision on reclaiming the disability benefits, the court was allowed to determine that its judgment should take the place of the annulled decision. It furthermore decided that the sum that was reclaimed had to be diminished by 10%.

We think that in both cases the question of whether or not the courts were allowed to use the powers of Article 8:72 GALA is worthy of discussion. Although it was presumably acceptable for the courts to decide that their judgments were to take the place of the annulled decisions, we feel that in general there is only one sound reason to do so and that is the situation where only one lawful decision remains to be taken (by the public authority) and it is therefore a question of efficiency

14 *See* R.J.N. Schlössels, Discretionaire aansprakelijkheidsrecht?, *in* T. Barkhuysen, W. den Ouden & M.K.G. Tjepkema (eds.), *Coulant compenseren? Over overheidsaansprakelijkheid en rechtspolitiek*, Kluwer, Deventer, 2012, p. 36-39; also see M.K.G. Tjepkema, *Nadeelcompensatie op basis van het égalitébeginsel. Een onderzoek naar nationaal, Frans en Europees recht* (diss. Leyden), Kluwer, Deventer, 2010, p. 424.

15 Administrative Jurisdiction Division of the Council of State 5 December 2012, *JB* 2013/11.

16 District Court Amsterdam 16 April 1998, *JB* 1998/153.

17 *See* Central Appeals Court 24 September 2008, *AB* 2009/281.

that the court uses its powers. It is questionable whether this was the case in both disputes.

Against the judgment in the second example the public authority lodged an appeal and the higher court (the Central Appeals Court) decided that the district court had gone beyond its powers.[18] In March 2012 the Administrative Jurisdiction Division of the Council of State seemingly recognised the point that we are trying to make here.[19] It stated that when applying the power to decide that the judgment shall take the place of the annulled decision any administrative court should have come to the conclusion that the public authority would have come to the same decision and that this decision would be lawful. This new way of stating the possibilities to use the power to bring about final dispute resolution comes suspiciously close to the words of the government when introducing the powers: they should only be used when one lawful decision remains to be taken and using the powers is an efficient remedy. And should not be a first step towards a slippery slope.

5. Final Remarks

The emphasis that both society and the legislator put on final dispute resolution leads to a dilemma for administrative courts. The pressure on the courts to bring about final dispute resolution is increasing but they are not allowed to jeopardise the separation of administrative and judicial responsibilities based on the separation of powers doctrine. Interfering in the discretionary powers of the public authority could be a slippery slope. As a consequence, courts should be alert in their efforts to bring about final dispute resolution in administrative disputes and claim powers to do so. In any case in which an administrative court achieves final dispute resolution, it should be because of efficiency reasons and in situations in which either only one lawful decision remains to be taken or it is certain the public authority will take the same decision again, but now carefully prepared and – as a consequence – lawful. Emphasis on final dispute resolution should never be a reason to disregard or change the balance of the separation of powers. The courts' independence from the executive should be respected.

On the other hand one should not forget that in many cases the proceedings in court may be helpful to come to the conclusion that only one lawful decision remains to be taken. The courts have wide discretion in their efforts to reach the point where final dispute resolution by the courts is simply a matter of efficiency. The legislator has recently tried to create an incentive for the courts to try to settle all disputes where possible by implementing Article 8:41a GALA but it remains to be seen what the effects of this provision will be. So far it seems to have more of a symbolic function than creating real drive for the administrative courts to provide final dispute resolution. In addition, there is a growing awareness that

18 Central Appeals Court 7 June 2000, *JB* 2000/229.

19 Administrative Jurisdiction Division of the Council of State 21 March 2012, *AB* 2012/233.

public authorities are, for the most part, better equipped for achieving final dispute resolution than the courts. We should consider their expertise in establishing the facts and their powers in questions of policy. Only when it is more efficient and effective for the court to bring about final dispute resolution, rather than to leave it to the executive, should the courts be considered legitimate in their action and the courts independence from the executive is sufficiently guaranteed.

Previously published in the Governance & Recht series

Volume 1 C.E.C. Jansen, S.A.J. Munneke, F.J. van Ommeren en J.W. Rutgers (red.), *Zorgplichten in publiek- en privaatrecht*, 2011

Volume 2 A.J.J. Kemps en T.J. van der Ploeg (red.), *De toekomst van het toezicht op fondsenwerving voor goede doelen in Nederland*, 2012

Volume 3 P.J. Huisman, *De bevoegdhedenovereenkomst*, 2012

Volume 4 A.P.H. Meijers, *De rechtspersoonlijkheid van geloofsgemeenschappen*, 2012

Volume 5 T.J. van der Ploeg, *Vrijheid, gelijkheid en redelijkheid*, 2013

Volume 6 O.O. Cherednychenko, C.E.C. Jansen, A.R. Neerhof en F.M.J. Verstijlen (red.), *Het publieke van het privaatrecht: hoe regulering van publieke belangen het privaatrecht beïnvloedt*, 2013

Volume 7 H. Bosselaar en G. Vonk (red.), *Bouwplaats lokale verzorgingsstaat. Wetenschappelijke reflecties op de decentralisaties in de sociale zekerheid en zorg*, 2013

Volume 8 S. Comtois and K.J. de Graaf (eds.), *On Judicial and Quasi-Judicial Independence*, 2013

9 789462 360945
13W67575/ T1/ 9789462360945